David Mamet in Conversation

THEATER: Theory/Text/Performance

Enoch Brater, Series Editor

David Mamet
in Conversation

LESLIE KANE, EDITOR

Ann Arbor

THE UNIVERSITY OF MICHIGAN PRESS

2004   2003   2002   2001   4   3   2   1

A CIP catalog record for this book is available from the British Library.

Library of Congress Cataloging-in-Publication Data

David Mamet in conversation / Leslie Kane, editor.
        p.   cm. — (Theater—theory/text/performance)
    Includes bibliographical references and index.
    ISBN 0-472-09764-4 (cloth : alk. paper) —
    ISBN 0-472-06764-8 (pbk. : alk. paper)
        1. Mamet, David—Interviews.   2. Dramatists, American—20th
century—Interviews.   3. Playwriting.   I. Kane, Leslie, 1945–
II. Series.

PS3563.A4345 Z657   2001
812'.54—dc21
    [B]   2001027531

Contents

Acknowledgments

I would like to express my appreciation to those whose assistance was invaluable in preparing this book: LeAnn Fields, Steven Price, Anne Dean, Nicola Scadding, Kevin Heverin, Abbey Potter, Megan Abbott, and Marcia LaBrenz. I am especially indebted to Brian Hubbard, Head of Reference at Westfield State College, who has been unstinting with his time and expertise. In fact, his responsiveness to my endless stream of requests has not only earned my respect but also my gratitude. To the permissions editors and producers, notably Mike Poole, Shelley Hoffman, Annette Miller, and Robyn Goldman, who facilitated the usc of these interviews and responded with graciousness and alacrity, thank you all. Finally, many thanks to the interviewers, whose insightful questions and stimulating conversations with one of America's most compelling contemporary playwrights constitute this book and whose kindness and generosity have made it possible to present a broad range of interviews with David Mamet spanning nearly twenty-five years.

To David Mamet I acknowledge the kindness that he has shown me in this, and other, endeavors. And to Pamela, David, and Stu, my love.

Chronology

1947	November 30, born Chicago.
1963–65	Works as waiter at Second City and backstage at Hull House Theatre, Chicago.
1965–69	Pursues B.A. degree in English Literature at Goddard College, Plainfield, Vermont. During his junior year, studies acting with Sanford Meisner at the Neighborhood Theatre, New York. While at Goddard, completes the first drafts of *Sexual Perversity in Chicago, The Duck Variations,* and *Reunion.* Works as a dancer in Maurice Chevalier extravaganza, *Toutes voiles dehours!!!* staged at the Autostade at Montreal's Expo '67. Writes *Camel* as senior thesis.
1969	Graduates from Goddard and joins theater company at McGill University, Montreal, performing in Pinter's *The Homecoming.* Stage-manages *The Fantasticks.*
1969–70	Works as office manager in a real estate office on North Side of Chicago.
1970	Offered position of acting instructor at Marlboro College, Vermont. *Lakeboat* first produced at Marlboro.
1971	Returns to Goddard College as Artist-in-Residence, where he teaches acting. While at Goddard forms the St. Nicholas Theatre Company with students William H. Macy and Steven Schachter, who perform first versions of *Duck Variations* and *Sexual Perversity in Chicago.*
1972	Returns to Chicago. *Duck Variations* and *Litko* performed at the Body Politic Theatre.
1974	*Sexual Perversity in Chicago,* directed by Stuart Gordon, performed by the Organic Theatre, Chicago. Serves as Artistic Director of the St. Nicholas Theatre Company, whose members include Steven Schachter, William H.

Macy, and Patricia Cox; they perform *Squirrels. Sexual Perversity in Chicago* wins Joseph Jefferson Award.

1975   *American Buffalo* under direction of Gregory Mosher premieres October 23 at the Goodman Theatre's Stage 2, Chicago. *Sexual Perversity in Chicago* opens off-off-Broadway on a double bill with *Duck Variations* at the St. Clement's Theatre, New York. Wins an Obie Award for Best New Play. St. Nicholas opens theater space on Halstead Street, opening season with *American Buffalo,* transferred from Stage 2. *Marranos* staged at the Bernard Horwich Jewish Community Center, Chicago. Writes *Revenge of the Space Pandas* for St. Clement's Theatre. Contributing editor for *Oui* magazine.

1976   *Reunion* staged at St. Nicholas Theatre. *American Buffalo* opens at St. Clement's Theatre, winning an Obie Award and Jefferson Award for its Chicago run. Resigns as Artistic Director of the St. Nicholas Theatre Company.

1977   *American Buffalo* opens on Broadway, winning New York Drama Critics' Circle Award. Yale Cabaret Theatre performs *All Men Are Whores,* directed by Mamet. *A Life in the Theatre* premieres at Goodman Stage 2; enjoys extended run at Théâtre de Lys, New York. *Water Engine* staged by St. Nicholas. *Reunion* opens in double bill with *Dark Pony* at Yale Repertory Theatre. Directs premiere of *Woods* at the St. Nicholas. *The Revenge of the Space Pandas or Binky Rudich* and *The Two-Speed Clock* staged at the St. Nicholas Children's Theatre and Flushing Town Hall, Queens, New York. *Duck Variations* and *Sexual Perversity in Chicago* performed at the Regent Theatre, London.

1978   Joseph Papp produces *The Water Engine* at the New York Shakespeare Festival Public Theater; transfers to Plymouth Theatre (Broadway) with *Mr. Happiness.* Appointed Associate Artistic Director and Writer-in-Residence of the Goodman Theatre by Gregory Mosher, Artistic Director of the Goodman. *American Buffalo* receives European premiere at the National Theatre. Wins Outer Critics Circle John Gassner Award for Distinguished Playwriting. *Prairie du Chien* broadcast on BBC and National Public Radio; *The Water Engine* broadcast on National Public Radio.

1979   The Public Theater stages *The Blue Hour: City Sketches* and *The Woods*. *Lone Canoe, or the Explorer* premieres at the Goodman Theatre. *A Life in the Theatre* broadcast on PBS Television and premieres in London at the Open Space Theatre.

1980   Revised version of *Lakeboat* performed by Milwaukee Repertory Theatre. Revival of *American Buffalo* staged at Long Wharf Theatre, New Haven.

1981   Mamet writes first screenplay for Bob Rafelson's film adaptation of James M. Cain's *The Postman Always Rings Twice*. Begins work on *The Verdict*. *Dark Pony* and *Reunion* staged in London.

1982   *Lakeboat* staged at the Long Wharf Theatre and Goodman Theatre. *Edmond* premieres at Goodman Theatre and opens in New York. Wins Obie for *Edmond*. Earns an Academy Award Nomination for Best Adapted Screenplay for *The Verdict*.

1983   Adaptation of Pierre Laville's *Red River* produced at the Goodman Theatre. Goodman Studio stages *The Disappearance of the Jews* in a triple bill with Elaine May's *Hotline* and Shel Silverstein's *Gorilla*. *Glengarry Glen Ross* premieres at the National Theatre, London. Wins the Society of West End Theatres' Award (SWET) for Best New Play and an Olivier Award.

1984   American premiere of *Glengarry Glen Ross* staged at Goodman Theatre; transfers to Broadway, where it runs for 378 performances. *Glengarry Glen Ross* wins Pulitzer Prize, the Drama Critics' Award for Best American Play 1984, a Joseph Dintenfass Award, and four Tony nominations, including Best Play and Best Director. Mamet and Mosher found the New Theatre Company (NTC). *The Frog Prince* opens at the Milwaukee Repertory Theatre; the Ensemble Studio Theatre mounts *Vermont Sketches*.

1985   New Theatre Company opens season with Mamet's adaptation of *The Cherry Orchard*. NTC moves to Brian Street Theater, where it mounts *The Shawl* and a one-act play, *The Spanish Prisoner*. *Goldberg Street* and *Cross Patch* broadcast on WNUR Radio, Northwestern

University. *Prairie du Chien* premieres with *The Shawl* at the Mitzi Newhouse Theater, Lincoln Center, New York, under direction of Gregory Mosher. *Edmond* receives European premiere at Newcastle Playhouse, a coproduction of the Royal Court Theatre. Founds Atlantic Theater Company with William H. Macy.

1986   Wins Academy Institute Award in Literature. Adaptation of *Vint* mounted at the Ensemble Studio Theatre. *Prairie du Chien* and *The Shawl* staged at Royal Court Theatre, Upstairs.

1987   Writes screenplay for *The Untouchables*. Writes and directs *House of Games,* selected to close New York Film Festival. *House of Games* earns a Golden Globe Nomination for Best Screenplay.

1988   Adaptation of Chekhov's *Uncle Vanya* staged at the American Repertory Theatre. *Speed-the-Plow* opens on Broadway at the Royale Theatre. Writes (with Shel Silverstein) and directs *Things Change,* which opens London Film Festival. Directs *Sketches of War* at Colonial Theatre, Boston. Earns a Writers Guild Award Nomination for Best Screenplay Based on Material from Another Medium for *The Untouchables*.

1989   *Speed-the-Plow* staged at the National Theatre, where play-in-progress, *Bobby Gould in Hell,* receives a reading, later opening at the Mitzi Newhouse Theatre, New York. *The Water Engine* receives British premiere at the Hampstead Theatre. United Kingdom tour of *A Life in the Theatre* followed by West End run at Theatre Royal, Haymarket. Writes screenplay for Neil Jordan's film, *We're No Angels*.

1990   Adaptation of Chekhov's *Three Sisters* is performed by the Atlantic Theater Company at the Festival Theatre, Philadelphia. Mamet's version of *Uncle Vanya,* staged at Harrogate Theatre and at the Goodman Theatre, is filmed by BBC in association with WNET, New York. Completes screenplays *Hoffa, The Deer Slayer, High and Low,* and *Ace in the Hole*.

1991   Writes and directs *Homicide*.

1992   *Oleanna* premieres at the American Repertory Theatre, reopening at the Orpheum Theatre, New York. Mamet writes screenplay for *Glengarry Glen Ross*.

1993	*Squirrels* receives British premiere at King's Head Theatre, Islington. *A Life in the Theatre* filmed for American television network TNT. *Oleanna,* directed by Harold Pinter, staged at the Royal Court Theatre, London; later transfers to Duke of York's Theatre.
1994	Writes and directs film version of *Oleanna. The Cryptogram* directed by Gregory Mosher premieres at Ambassadors Theatre, London. Sam Mendes directs a revival of *Glengarry Glen Ross* at the Donmar Playhouse. *Ricky Jay and His 52 Assistants* performed at the Promenade Theatre, New York. Andre Gregory's film, *Vanya on 42nd Street,* based on Mamet's adaptation of *Uncle Vanya,* opens.
1995	*The Cryptogram,* directed by Mamet, receives American premiere at the C. Walsh Theatre, Boston, and the Westside Theatre Upstairs, New York. *An Interview,* one of three one-acts comprising *Death Defying Acts* (includes Woody Allen's *Central Park West* and Elaine May's *Hotline*), staged at the Variety Arts Theatre, New York. Directed his adaptation of J. B. Priestley's *Dangerous Corner* at the Atlantic Theater Company, New York, following earlier premiere at the Burlington City Arts Festival, Burlington, Vermont. *Ricky Jay and His 52 Assistants* televised on HBO.
1996	Revival of *Edmond* opens at the Atlantic Theater Company. The Ensemble Studio Theatre stages five one-acts and monologues, including *No One Will Be Immune* and *Joseph Dintenfass* (New York premiere) in celebration of its twenty-fifth anniversary and long collaboration with Mamet. Filmed version of *American Buffalo,* from a Mamet screenplay, opens the Boston Film Festival. Cowrote lyrics for *Randy Newman's Faust.*
1997	*The Old Neighborhood* premieres at the American Repertory Theatre, Cambridge, Massachusetts, followed by a run on Broadway at the Booth Theatre. *Wag the Dog,* from a screenplay by Hilary Henkin and David Mamet, nominated for a Golden Globe Award for Best Motion Picture, Best Screenplay, and Best Actor, also earns nominations for an Academy Award for Best Writing Based on Material from Another Medium and Best Screenplay by the Writers Guild of America. Writes

and directs *The Spanish Prisoner,* which opens the Toronto Film Festival. Original screenplay, *The Bookworm,* filmed as *The Edge.*

1998   The British premiere of *Lakeboat* is staged at the Lyric Studio, Hammersmith, London. *The Old Neighborhood* has British premiere at the Royal Court Theatre Downstairs at the Duke of York's. *Jade Mountain* opens at the New York Ensemble Theatre's Marathon of One-Acts 1998. John Frankenheimer's film *Ronin* produced, from a screenplay by Mamet. Directs adaptation of Terence Rattigan's *The Winslow Boy,* which films in England. Coproduces his screenplay *Lansky,* broadcast on HBO. Completes screenplay for a remake of *Dr. Jekyl / Mr. Hyde.*

1999   *Boston Marriage,* directed by Mamet, premieres at American Repertory Theatre. Directs *State and Main,* from original screenplay; writes screenplay for *The Cincinnati Kid. Lakeboat,* directed by Joe Mantegna, is produced.

Introduction

Leslie Kane

Acknowledged as one of the leading playwrights of the English-speaking world, David Mamet is among the most prolific and provocative writers. Yet in a career that spans more than twenty-five years he has granted relatively few interviews, the majority of which have been brief and the writer laconic. Increasingly in recent years, particularly on the occasion of a new play, film, or publication, Mamet has reluctantly engaged in more substantive interviews with critics and the press.

However, even in the most concise of Mamet's conversations, in which he typically spins exquisitely ornate tautologies to avoid a subject (most often relating to his work and personal life), the playwright affords us insights into his life in the theater, his personal aspirations, and the evolution of his craft, revealing a writer "lethally clever . . . in repose," to borrow Michael VerMeulen's phrase, and often as comic and complex offstage as on. *David Mamet in Conversation* renders a portrait of the artist as a young man and then as a reflective writer who in his middle years shows no signs of resting on his estimable laurels. In fact, Mamet continues to challenge himself to work in new genres and to venture into more personal terrain, creating trenchant new works each year. The interviews in this book complicate and intensify one's understanding of the sensibility behind Mamet's plays, films, and prose.

His resistance to the interview mode notwithstanding, Mamet in conversation reveals himself to be an erudite and engaging thinker who reads voraciously, a serious artist who speaks passionately and thoughtfully on a broad range of subjects: his return to Judaism, writing for Hollywood, the seduction of fame, the decay of culture, the search for truth and the merchandising of it. Other subjects include the purpose of theater and the responsibility of the playwright, his home in rural Vermont, his love of actors, the problem of embattled virtue, and the challenge of growing older. Repeatedly, he expounds on the subject of moral imperative and the themes of loyalty, legacy, and learning that followers of his work have come to recognize as Mametic.

Moreover, Mamet talks revealingly about dramatic theory, film, acting, and the interrelationship of these media. He discusses the impact of television on his early episodic works, his vast knowledge of movies and their attraction for him, an American mythology of violence, the difficulty of men and women living together, and his abiding interest in the underworld, con artistry, and the picaresque. And, when pressed by interviewers, he speaks about his works, which in the quarter-century that this anthology spans, include such classics of the contemporary stage as *American Buffalo, Glengarry Glen Ross, Speed-the-Plow, Oleanna,* and *The Cryptogram.* In addition to these plays and others notable for their theatricality and originality, Mamet speaks about screenplays he has penned, such as *The Postman Rings Twice, The Untouchables, Hoffa, The Verdict,* and *Wag the Dog,* and those he has written and directed, among them *House of Games, Homicide, Things Change, The Spanish Prisoner, The Winslow Boy,* and *State and Main.*

Similarly, his remarks to interviewers reveal the influence on Mamet of an eclectic list of writers, artists, philosophers, critics, comics, and directors, including Preston Sturges, Ernest Hemingway, Theodore Dreiser, Frank Capra, Leo Tolstoy, Harold Pinter, Thorstein Veblen, Thornton Wilder, Anton Chekhov, Aristotle, William Makepeace Thackeray, Arthur Miller, Samuel Beckett, Bertolt Brecht, Konstantin Stanislavski, Sergei Eisenstein, Lanford Wilson, Lenny Bruce, and Elaine May. Creeping into discussion in the last decade are Rudyard Kipling, George Orwell, Mark Twain, Henry Fielding, Virginia Woolf, Isaac Luria, and Alfred Hitchcock, references that help set his work in context.

David Mamet has long been interested in role playing, as evidenced by his plays *A Life in the Theatre, Sexual Perversity in Chicago, Lakeboat,* and *The Disappearance of the Jews,* to name a few. Little surprise, then, that his salesmen characters are consummate storytellers and performers whose fecundity, creativity, and assertiveness reflect the playwright's admiration for the virtuosity, imagination, and temerity of working men and women who, in Ricky Roma's words in *Glengarry,* "live on their *wits.*" Yet Mamet, who thrives on his wits, lacks faith in the interview process and approaches it with deep unease—that is, until he settles on a role for himself, typically as instructor or provocateur. Thus, it is not surprising that in his two-person, one-act Kafkaesque play *An Interview,* written in the 1990s (and performed in a triple bill entitled *Death Defying Acts* with plays by Woody Allen and Elaine May), Mamet imagines a mostly one-sided conversation between the panic-stricken Attorney and a Stalinist interrogator identified as the Attendant. Summoned to defend his life, the Attorney reflects a range of emotion—puzzlement, self-assertion, resignation—in his effort to present himself in the best light. Forced into unfamiliar ground and compelled to talk, he is provoked by the Attendant to rethink, retreat, and take cover.

Like the Attendant, those who have interviewed David Mamet and lived to tell the tale have observed, as Polly Ullrich did in 1977, "One doesn't talk with David Mamet. One jockeys for position."[1] Similarly, John Lahr, who has spoken with the writer on several occasions, maintains that "in public conversation . . . Mamet is courtly and wary; his style of discourse is not so much straight talk as Indian wrestling."[2] Yet VerMeulen, a longtime Chicago theater critic who dates his friendship with Mamet to the mid-1970s, when VerMeulen wrote public relations releases for Mamet's St. Nicholas Theatre, probably comes closest when he admits in 1991: "I have almost become used to his speech, which is plastic in the sense of a *plastic medium,* or *plastic explosive.* Lethally clever even in repose, he uses words and syntax like small artillery to convey his ideas, of which there are many, often at the same time. Either that, or he spins elegant impenetrable circumlocutions when he wants to hide. He is the Great Satan as an interview subject: bored by the task but far too expert to be caught out."[3]

In stark contrast to the obscenity-laced speech of many of his characters and his public persona as a macho, poker-playing playwright, Mamet in interview is typically cordial and courteous. He speaks in a low, gentle, frequently comic voice and is "so soft spoken, so fluent" that British journalist Minty Clinch observed, "It's hard to be sure he's kidding."[4] His conversations are sprinkled with show business lore, which he loves, and jokes about Hollywood, which he tells with pitch-perfect timing. His answers, like those of his groundbreaking plays, are terse, pithy, and to the point. Hence, he is rightly perceived by interviewers as formal, ill at ease, blunt, and taciturn, unsettling more than a few interviewers who find themselves having to negotiate what British columnist and novelist Imogen Edwards-Jones characterizes as "stiff silences that follow the dry, deadpan

3

delivery of his answers."[5] He is famously cagey about his work and his personal life and suspicious of both the press and critics, though this has not dissuaded either from beating a path to his door. Instead, Mamet repeatedly seeks refuge in equivocation, as he does when he tells Michael Lerner, "Let me see if I can cunningly deflect your question."[6] And he is known to stop the interviewer literally in his or her tracks, as he does with monosyllabic responses to these Graham Fuller questions:

> FULLER: You're a prolific writer. Does that come out of a happy state of mind, or out of anxiety and restlessness?
> MAMET: Probably both.
> FULLER: Do you have a specific time of day set aside for writing?
> MAMET: I call it "all day."[7]

Or he is just as likely to turn the tables on the interviewer—"Who says that?" he asks, in some of the more contentious exchanges, especially on the subject of his alleged misogyny. In fact, his inability or refusal to answer the questions put to him accounts in large part for his decision in the 1980s to stop granting interviews.

Yet, when he is comfortable with the interviewer, as in interviews with John Lahr, Jeremy Isaacs, Charlie Rose, and the editors of *Playboy*, there are rare surprises, spontaneous bursts of honesty, and wonderful moments in which we glimpse ample evidence of a rapier wit. Such is Mamet's response to Lahr's question about what he might have done with his life if he hadn't found the theater, "I think," quips Mamet, "I would have been a criminal."[8] When asked by Steven Dzielak if success had changed him, he answers, "No, I've always been an asshole and see no reason to change now. But the basic difference is that agents will talk to me now. When I call them about casting I don't get put on hold while they go off to Majorca, as they are wont to do."[9] In speaking with Richard Stayton, Mamet tempers seriousness with jest, "Everything I learned about playwriting I learned from Aristotle. . . . Of course, the most important thing that Aristotle ever said about playwriting was 'Never write anything on spec.'"[10] And, asked by Sylvie Drake if there was any truth to the story that he was "part American Indian," Mamet replies waggishly, "It sounds like something I would make up to test somebody. . . . The high cheekbones. Straight out of Eastern Europe."[11]

The interview mode also illustrates that Mamet is a passionate, talented teacher. He possesses both an encyclopedic knowledge of his craft and the ability to clarify and exemplify his theories and convictions precisely. For example, when pressed about whether *The Cryptogram* is autobiographical, he completely sidesteps Susan Stamberg's question but responds with a startlingly clear statement of his aesthetic: "To be an artist is to deal with an amalgam of something that either happened or something that might have happened or something that one can imagine happened or some mish-mosh of the above. And I've never felt it particularly important to separate those strands in my work. I mean, it's sufficient to have an idea, whether that's prompted by fantasy or memory is really irrelevant."[12]

Given his prodigious body of work and interviewers' and audiences' curiosity about it, I have included those interviews with Mamet that took place during or prior to theatrical productions or the release of films and publications, which contain the most substantive discussion of his works. I have also selected interviews in which Mamet's remarks are not limited to specific plays, or even to the theater, and to this end I have included brief conversations that offer piquant insight or incisive repartee. In fact, the extended interviews, such as those with *Playboy*, John Lahr, Charlie Rose, and Jeremy Isaacs conducted in the 1990s, not only reveal Mamet's impressive craft and agility in the interview mode; they afford us glimpses into the life and experience that animates his art. I regret that several valuable interviews, including some of those I cite in this introduction, could not be included in the collection because of space limitations and copyright constraints. Among these are "David Mamet: An American Playwright Speaks," a conversation with Sylvie Drake published in the *Los Angeles Times*, February 5, 1978, Calendar sec., 54; "Art: The Painter and the Playwright, American Dreamers," a conversation with Donald Sultan and David Mamet conducted by Robert Becker and published in *Interview* 13 (March 1983): 56, 58; "Thoughts From a Man's Man," a conversation with Bruce Weber published in the *New York Times*, November 17, 1994, sec. C, 1, 10.

David Mamet in Conversation presents a broad selection of interviews that reflects both the consistency and the evolution of the writer's aesthetic principles first voiced in Ross Wetzsteon's now prescient profile essay published in 1976. This telling exchange, and other early interviews in this collection, capture the mood and mindset of a young playwright confident of his talent, who, having won an Obie Award for *Sexual Perversity in Chicago* and for *American Buffalo,* is both enthused about having plays in rehearsal in Chicago and New

York and wary of critics misunderstanding his work. Similarly, interviews in ensuing years give voice to Mamet's mature artistic vision, his insistence on morality and truth, and his view of theater as celebratory. Although the young playwright interviewed by Wetzsteon at the beginning of this collection appears worlds apart from the screenwriter/director who has established a reputation as an accomplished filmmaker, the attention fostered on him by film critics recalls the heady period when *American Buffalo* premiered in New York in 1976. Paralleling the Wetzsteon piece, this collection begins and ends with profiles that incorporate several questions and answers put to Mamet, a format that he especially favors. The final interviews, then, with Robert Denerstein, who interviewed Mamet at the Sundance Film Festival where he introduced *The Spanish Prisoner,* and Renée Graham, who spoke with him about *The Winslow Boy,* are representative of numerous conversations with Mamet, who seems eager to sit down, however briefly, to chat about melodrama, Hitchcock, the light thriller, and period drama which has captivated his interest of late.

But, whereas the writer in early interviews talks about the well-made play, Midwest virtues, a pantheon of writers whom he admires, his disinterest in writing for Hollywood or television, and Stoical philosophy, in later discussions he is likely to speak openly about his ethnicity, the art of acting, favorite productions, directing movies, turning fifty. He also acknowledges new directions that his career has taken and the overtly personal terrain that his later works disclose. Over the course of his career these conversations are notable for the writer's confidence, erudition, strongly worded opinions, and occasionally vulgarity.

David Mamet in Conversation includes an extended conversation with *Playboy* in which Mamet discusses *Oleanna,* with Charlie Rose in which he talks about his novel *Old Religion* and the American Dreyfus case that was its impetus, and with Jeremy Isaacs in which a discussion about his family and youth in Chicago provides insights on *The Cryptogram* and *Old Neighborhood.* In his discussion with John Lahr, "The Art of the Theater," Mamet speaks about his attempt to write tragedy, the trick of dramaturgy, why the trickster and confidence artist people his works, and his fascination with genres other than theater.

I have arranged the interviews, whether brief or extended, in chronological order to reflect better the consistency and the evolution of Mamet's thinking. This arrangement also provides ample evidence that in recent years Mamet has generally become more relaxed and voluble in interview, fielding questions with aplomb, so that one finds words like *rectitude,* evidence of his early training in se-mantics, tempered by *golly.* Always pensive and often reserved, his later interviews frequently reveal an alternating rhythm of epigram-matic phrases and soliloquy.

To that end *David Mamet in Conversation* contains interviews with the playwright published in diverse venues, many of which are not readily available. A quarter of these conversations aired on radio or television or before a live audience and have not previously been tran-scribed or published. In editing the previously unpublished inter-views, I have made every effort to transcribe Mamet's remarks as close to the original. And with the permission of interviewers I have taken the liberty to correct usage and spelling, eliminate repetition, and cut material to accommodate additional interviews in the collection. Es-pecially in the live performances, I have retained those features, such as audience—or interviewer—laughter, pauses to reflect and rephrase responses, and repetitions that illustrate the spontaneous dynamic of the interview process.

These conversations complement Mamet's significant body of work, offering scholars and aficionados a retrospective and perspec-tive on the playwright's dramaturgy, artistic vision, attitudes about American culture and society, varied interests and influences, and intentions. As Paul Delaney has similarly noted of Tom Stoppard's "interview talk," Mamet's comments on his work "in no sense consti-tute the last word on the subject."[13] Conversations with Mamet are, finally, rewarding not for what they reveal about his life but for what they reveal about his work and the aesthetic principles that under-gird it. Indeed, his best interviewers uncover the pleasure, allure, and invaluable insights to be gleaned from listening in on the cir-cumspect, oftentimes comic, and always engaging Mamet in conver-sation. If the last decade has revealed anything about this writer, it is that much can be learned about Mamet *from* Mamet—from a wide range of genres, not the least of which is his interviews.

NOTES

1. Polly Ullrich, "Mamet: He's Still a Chicagoan," *Chicago Sun-Times,* Febru-ary 6, 1977, np.

2. John Lahr, "Fortress Mamet," *New Yorker,* November 17, 1997, 72.

3. Michael VerMeulen, "Mamet's Mafia," *New York Observer,* October 7, 1991, 1.

4. Minty Clinch, "Mamet Plots His Revenge," *Observer* [London], January 22, 1989, 49.

5. Imogen Edwards-Jones, "Man of Few Words," *Sunday Times*, May 16, 1998, 16.

6. Michael Lerner, "David Mamet on 'The Old Religion,'" *Tikkun* 12, no. 6 (November–December 1997): 10.

7. Graham Fuller, "April's Favorite Fooler," *Interview* 28, no. 4 (April 1998): 66.

8. John Lahr, "David Mamet: The Art of Theater XI," *Paris Review* 39, no. 142 (Spring 1997): 59.

9. Steven Dzielak, "David Mamet: An Interview," *Manhattan Arts Review* 8 (February–March 1978): 13–14.

10. Richard Stayton, "David Mamet Turns Out to Be a Funny Man," *Los Angeles Herald Examiner,* November 27, 1987, C1.

11. Sylvie Drake, "David Mamet—An American Playwright Speaks," *Los Angeles Times,* February 5, 1978, 54.

12. Susan Stamberg, *All Things Considered,* National Public Radio, February 6, 1995.

13. Paul Delaney, ed., *Tom Stoppard in Conversation* (Ann Arbor: University of Michigan Press, 1994), 8.

David Mamet: Remember That Name

Ross Wetzsteon

Ross Wetzsteon, a highly respected drama critic for the *Village Voice,* met with David Mamet in Gramercy Park in New York shortly after the young playwright won his first Obie Award for *Sexual Perversity in Chicago* and *American Buffalo,* both of which were running in successful productions off-Broadway.

Already only half a minute into *Sexual Perversity in Chicago,* the dialogue has given the male characterizations razor edges, cutting as caricature, yet sharply defined as personalities. Already in the most trivial interchange, you know you're listening to a playwright with an acute ear for the rhythms of speech . . . for vocabulary as characterization . . . for conversation as action . . . for comedy not in gags but in the way we speak . . .

Now listen to the language of the man who wrote this scene:

"Theater is the area of the evanescent. The very nature of theater is always to be dying. By that I mean the theatrical urge is the very antithesis of the urge toward institutional survival. You see it ineluctably throughout the entire history of drama—form outliving its original aesthetic impulse."

David Mamet pauses. We're sitting on a bench in Gramercy Park, and he leans down, picks up a handful of gravel, and gently lobs one pebble after another into the midst of a half-dozen skittering pigeons. "Jesus, I have a feeling this piece is going to make me sound pretentious." He grabs another handful of gravel. "I mean, once you get a certain recognition . . . I mean, you tend . . . People begin to see you as spouting." He tilts his hand, and the pebbles slide off to the ground. "Oh, what the fuck," he laughs, "let 'em."

Listen to his characters again—Don and Teach, in *American Buffalo,* have agreed to burglarize an apartment later that evening, and act 1 ends as they say good-bye.

"Some of my favorite writing is at the end of act 1," Mamet says. "That 'see you later' scene. I'm so glad you liked that. That's exactly the kind of thing I'm trying to capture in my plays. Have you ever listened to two people trying to say good-bye on the phone? Especially in a business situation? They just *cannot* say good-bye. And the language is so revealing of their relationship. All those quid pro quos. Who owes what to whom? They can end up saying 'okay, okay, okay,' for half an hour. I think I have a gift for that kind of attenuated scene."

Mamet laughs, amused at himself, the laugh of a young man who understands his weaknesses as an artist and yet is secure in his talent. "One critic in Chicago says I write the kind of plays where a character wakes up in act 1 and finally gets around to putting on his bathrobe in act 3."

Of course, some of the great plays of the twentieth century would have the character *pondering* whether or not to put on his robe by the end of act 3. In any case, the critics on the Obie judges committee were more impressed and last month voted Mamet "the best new playwright of the year for his plays *Sexual Perversity in Chicago* and *American Buffalo.*"

And, speaking of language, we were rather more careful in our wording than might appear at first glance. There's a new generation of unheralded playwrights about to burst forth with major works— one thinks, for instance, of Marsha Sheiness, William Hauptman, Dennis Reardon, Corinne Jacker, Albert Innaurato, and Steven Shea—but most of us felt that only Mamet had done work worthy of major critical recognition at this point, and recognition not so much for his plays as for the potential they represent, especially in his careful, gorgeous, loving sense of language. In fact, I'd go so far as to say that at the age of twenty-eight Mamet is the most promising American playwright to have emerged in the 1970s and that he has the most acute ear for dialogue of any American writer since J. D. Salinger . . .

Mamet is surprisingly thoughtful, even self-conscious about dialogue. "I fell in with a good group when I was young. I mean I came from a very bourgeois background—my father was a lawyer, *you* know—but in Chicago I was always exposed to a wider variety of lives. Summer jobs, the steel mills, factories, that kind of thing. I washed windows and drove cabs and spent time in the Merchant Marine."

Another handful of pebbles. "The first thing I learned is that the exigent speak poetry. They don't speak the language of newspapers. I heard rhythms and verbal expressions that dealt with an experience not covered in anything I'd ever read. Then I read Mencken, and I became fascinated by the notion of a native American language. And then through my dad—he was interested in semantics—I read Stanislavski. That's when I first learned the correlation between language and action, that words *create* behavior, which is crucial if you want to become a playwright."

"Actually, my main emphasis is on the rhythm of language—the way action and rhythm are identical. Our rhythms describe—no, our rhythms *prescribe* our actions. I became fascinated—I still am—by the way, the way the language we use, its rhythm, actually determines the way we behave, more than the other way around. Everything I am as a playwright I feel I owe to Stanislavski—I mean, Jesus, every playwright should be forced to read him just on consonants and vowels alone!"

I mention how sensitively he picked up on the way we often omit words from our daily conversation.

I tell Mamet I *shiver* in the theater, listening to this dialogue—the quick alternation between the elevated and the obscene, the fucked-up syntax, the characterization by language—and how his ear gives us lines at once idiosyncratic and universal.

"Yeah, I love that kind of thing," Mamet says, still lobbing pebbles. "And I just heard a great thing on the elevator today. This one old lady turns to another and says, 'Nice weather, aren't we?'"

Of course, verbal accuracy, no matter how acute, doesn't go very much further in making a playwright than pertinent jokes, no matter how funny, go in making a comic artist. *American Buffalo,* with its echoes of Hemingway's "The Killers," is partly about the relationship between language and behavior, but it's also about loyalty and responsibility, about the relationship between money and business and violence . . .

The central metaphor, a rare Buffalo nickel worth several hundred dollars, is one of those clean, precise, yet resonant images an artist can spend a lifetime looking for. Don, who runs a junk shop, sells it to a stranger for ninety dollars, only to realize he's been taken. He and Bob, his gofer, decide the stranger must have a valuable collection of coins and plan to burglarize his apartment. But Don's friend Teach, a more experienced burglar, convinces Don to drop Bob from the deal, to take him along instead. The play ends in frustrated violence, in a kind of spiritual entropy that stunningly evokes the contrast between the open-sky, spacious, whoopingly rapacious violence of the American past (the buffalo) and the airless, petty impotence of the bourgeois culture it grew into (the junk shop).

"What I was trying to say in *American Buffalo*," Mamet says, "is that once you step back from the moral responsibility you've undertaken, you're lost. We have to take responsibility. Theater is a place of recognition, it's an ethical exercise, it's where we show ethical interchange. That's why Don's exclusion of Bob from the deal is so crucial. In a way the second act is a mirror image of the first—Bob tries to buy his way back in. As Marx says, other people have objective reality to us only insofar as they possess something we want. Their possession of it denies it to us—that's the only way we see them."

Mamet suddenly grins. "If that's not too *precieux*. Anyway, it's not a Marxist play or anything like that. I'm more interested in what Tolstoy said—that we should treat human beings with love and respect and never hurt them. I hope *American Buffalo* shows that, by showing what happens when you fail to act that way."

But, with all this in mind, I ask him about accusations of some critics that *Sexual Perversity* is a misogynist play.

Mamet bristles. "I disagree profoundly. I'd even say . . . No, never mind."

"What were you going to say?"

"Never mind."

"That it's the characters who're misogynist, not the author?"

"Look. All the characters in *Sexual Perversity* are losers. To me it's a play about insight. Insight not acted upon leads to all our impedimenta." He tilts his hands back and forth, shifting gravel from one to the other. "To me it's a play about four different ways of dealing or failing to deal with insight. Joan intellectualizes everything, Debbie uses catch phrases, Danny jokes things away, and Bernie tries to overpower everyone."

He grins and tosses the handful of pebbles away. "I'll probably read myself saying all this and think it's all wrong, but what the hell. Look at it this way. James Bond fucked up my sex life for years. It's the way we perceive each other. If you say *cunt* or *cockteaser*, what you say influences the way you think, the way you act, not the other way around. It's a play about deferred action."

A sudden melancholy tone enters his voice. He slowly shakes his head from side to side. "Why don't men and women get along?"

One reason, the play suggests, is because men, in both their language and behavior, regard women as objects of conquest, as beings who possess what men want yet refuse to yield it. Notice the skillful blend of yearning and hostility in the final scene of the play, on the beach, as Bernie and Danny ogle women.

The production at the Cherry Lane, by the way, which I panned two weeks ago, has improved immeasurably. A series of fuguelike vignettes that depicts the sexual misadventures of four Chicagoans, two of whom have an affair, and their two swinging single friends who coach them from the sidelines, it's raunchy as hell, hilarious and despairing, occasionally callow, gorgeously written, and now at last decently performed.

The ending, I notice, has been changed to cast a melancholy glow back over the action, but this sad-happy ending (happy in the sense that the male characters finally gain a hint of insight into their fatuity) seems to me to violate the dominant tone of the text, with its emphasis on the comedy of failure to learn. (Oddly enough, the original ending, more ruthless, was also more liberating.)

But it's the delicious, lovely, uncanny accuracy of the dialogue that—but, no, I've got to stop quoting, I've got to stop quoting, or soon we'll be verging on infringement of copyright! In any case Mamet's extraordinary promise resides not so much in his insights into male-female relationships, or in the comic manipulations of his understanding, as in the exhilarating perfection of the language with which he expresses it. It's a rarity in theater to find the insights, the action, so deeply embedded in the dialogue itself.

It's a terrible burden to place on a writer, but, if Mamet can continue the astonishing advance in achievement from *Duck Variations* (1971) to *Sexual Perversity* (1974) to *American Buffalo* (1975), I feel confident his next leap forward will give us nothing less than an American masterpiece.

"I want to change the whole nature of American theater," Mamet says calmly, and for a moment I think I have the lead to my piece—until I realize he's talking less about aesthetic vision than institutional theater. Having been an actor himself, he talks with some passion about "the degrading life of performers, especially the way, like all op-pressed groups, they internalize the prejudice society holds against them. They're like slaves who weren't allowed to learn to read. I mean they have no say whatsoever about the artistic conditions of their work. They should go out on strike not for higher salaries but to gain more control over their artistic life. 'I won't do this shit anymore'—that should be their demand. Not a theater run by unions, producers, backers—all that crap."

So, the changes he advocates in the structure of American the-ater would have as their goal the liberation of every theater artist to pursue his own vision, a revolution for multiplicity, for diversity, not any single kind of theater—especially not, Mamet insists, so that his own artistic credo can become a rallying point for a new American theater. (He's even glad to discover that his favorite writers, Hem-ingway and Wharton in particular, can sometimes "write such trash—it shows that making art isn't magic but hard fucking work.")

It's a rare writer indeed who by the age of twenty-eight has *both* such a distinctive voice and such a wide range of subject matter (from metaphysical reflections on death to sexual farce to an exploration of the relationship between money and violence in American culture).

"I remember something Kenneth Koch said," Mamet comments when I ask him about the astonishing ease with which he avoids re-peating himself. "You can't lose your talent, but you have to *follow* it. To always write 'my kind of dialogue' would be the kiss of death. I be-lieve you should always try to tell the truth in a way that taxes your ability to tell the truth."

"When I saw Elizabeth Wilson singing at the third-act curtain of *Threepenny Opera,* well, I was just proud to be a member of our an-cient profession. That's theater—someone on stage, putting their life on the line to tell the truth as they see it."

What about his future plans?

A fall production of *American Buffalo* ("though I may have to kid-nap the offspring of some producer to get it on") and a play "about love" to open in Chicago, "happy in the sense it's a tragedy." (It's clear what he means from his earlier talk about theater as an arena for ethical demonstration—to learn from tragic experience is as much happiness as anyone can aspire to.)

"Do you ever learn from critics?" I ask finally.

"Let me put it this way—someone once told me never to listen to advice from anyone who doesn't have a vested interest in your success."

But, supposedly, a critic has a vested interest in the ability of theater to tell the truth, to tell it with beauty, dignity, and humanity—and, in that sense, wouldn't it be fair to say that a critic has a vested interest in any playwright's success?

"In that sense, sure, but what I mean is that you never learn anything from critics—and especially you don't learn from raves or pans. 'The theme is weak'—okay, so next time I'm supposed to make it stronger. What the hell does that mean? The trouble with most critics is that they don't know enough about the inner working of theater to actually *teach* you anything. Before anyone's allowed to be a critic, he should be made to be a gofer for two years—keep your mouth shut and your eyes and ears open."

Mamet's still lobbing pebbles, one by one, looking as innocent as an undergraduate, and for some reason when I write his comment down on my pad I add the phrase: "The only thing we learn from the mistakes of others is what mistakes we're going to end up making ourselves."

And, when I remember him talking about his reluctance to take advice, I realize I have none to give. Because when I think of what he's accomplished by the age of twenty-eight and the riches I'm confident he'll bring to the American theater, I decide that as far as David Mamet goes, instead of giving him advice, I'll take his—and keep my mouth shut and my eyes and ears open.

Solace of a Playwright's Ideals

Mark Zweigler

In 1976 Mark Zweigler sat down with the young Chicago playwright on the verge of achieving national recognition to discuss his work and the response of New York critics. The double bill of *Duck Variations,* and *Sexual Perversity in Chicago,* was receiving its first New York production directed by Albert Takazauckas. Opening at the St. Clement's Theatre, off-Broadway, it transferred in January 1976 to the Cherry Lane Theatre, where the production featured Peter Riegert and F. Murray Abraham. In March 1976 Gregory Mosher's New York production of *American Buffalo* opened at the St. Clement's Theatre starring Michael Egan, Mike Kellin, and J. T. Walsh.

"It was never anything I set out consciously to do" is the way David Mamet, a young Chicago playwright on the verge of national recognition, describes how he first got started in playwrighting. As an undergraduate student in English literature at Goddard College in Vermont, Mamet was required to write a thesis. He had been spending most of his time in theater, however, so he asked his professor if he could write a play instead. To Mamet's surprise his professor said yes, so he did. The name of the play was *Camel,* a semisatirical review influenced by Mamet's experiences at Second City, where he worked as a busboy when he was a teenager. Although he never performed in the Second City company, Mamet later spent time in New York, testing his additional talent as an actor. "I lived in New York for about a year and a half," he explains. "I took time out from my undergraduate work at Goddard to study acting. I had a great time. I worked my ass off as a student. I also worked for about a year with *The Fantasticks* off-Broadway. I ran the lights, and I was house manager for a while. It was a wonderful experience."

On graduating from Goddard, Mamet returned to Chicago. "I was working at some sort of—I don't know, I think I was driving a cab. Since I had had some experience as an actor, I wrote a letter to some of my friends at Marlboro College, asking if they wanted an actor for their summer theater. They said no, but the fellow who ran the drama department was leaving on sabbatical, and he asked me if I would like to teach. I said I'd love to. He wrote back asking if I had anything specific to recommend me, and I said I had just written a new play. I hadn't, but he said that was great and that I could come to Marlboro and produce it. In the interim I worked on a bunch of notes concerning my stint in the Merchant Marine and made them into a second play, called *Lakeboat.*"

After successfully producing *Lakeboat* at Marlboro, Mamet returned to Chicago, working in a real estate office, "selling property to unsuspecting elderly people." Meanwhile, he wrote a third play and asked Goddard College if they would like him to come back and produce it. After seeing the play, Mamet recalls, "They hired me for a short term, and I started teaching an acting class. I ended up staying for two years as an artist-in-residence and wrote about three or four more plays. It was probably the most precipitous point in my career as a playwright, because it gave me a laboratory to constantly produce. It was invaluable."

Pausing for a moment, Mamet asks if I've seen his most recent play, *American Buffalo,* premiered at Goodman's Stage 2 in Chicago and showcased at St. Clement's Theatre in New York, where two of his other plays, *Duck Variations* and *Sexual Perversity in Chicago,* opened at the Cherry Lane Theatre in June. I tell him I've seen *Buffalo* and that I'm interested in getting a specific statement from him about the theme of the play. "That's a good question," he says. "I don't know if I can give you a good answer." Concentrating for a minute, he begins, "I think it's concerned with the mythology of America, which is that we've always been susceptible to exhortations to do what is right, but we've never been susceptible to exhortations to *think* what is right and to arrive at our own conclusions. We're always on the verge of fascism. We're incredibly myth prone in our culture, incredibly semantically unsophisticated. I think the theme of the play has to do with the corruption of heartfelt moral knowledge for the sake of a mythological ideal, whether that ideal is patriotism or loyalty.

"I was certainly writing about a society outside the law, which means the theme would probably be more focused there. But I think in a larger sense we're all outside the law. It's about the same thing Nixon and all those people were doing. It's not that much more sophisticated."

Mamet seems to enjoy digging into the subject of playwriting. He seems to love involvement, so I ask him how much influence he has over the casting of his plays. "I have a fairly large amount of influence," he answers confidently. "It's not a question of contractual stipulation so much as it's a matter of interaction between the director and the playwright. Some of the projects need a lot of involvement; some of them don't. With Gregory Mosher, who directed *American Buffalo,* there was very little involvement. I would come in and do rewrites and then come back four or five days later and do some more. I wasn't there breathing down his neck.

"Sometimes the actors felt good about rewrites; sometimes they felt bad. Sometimes they felt excited; sometimes they felt hocked. It bothered them to have to rememorize; an actor will always feel that. But I think there's a dedication to the script as a whole that usually supersedes it. I know a lot of times in *American Buffalo* I'd cut out lines, and the actors would come back and say, 'Jeez, I loved that fuckin' line, may I please have it back?' A lot of times I'd say yes, a lot of times I'd say no.

"A lot of the rewrites had to do with the through-action of the play. The characters and dialogue were no problem. But the through-action had to be strengthened and solidified so that what happened in the play became not reasonable but inevitable. It's the first full-length, nonstop two-act play I've written. The others have been very episodic, like a Brechtian culmination of scenes."

Those "others" include two plays Mamet wrote last year for the Center Youth Theater at the Bernard Horwich Jewish Community Center. One of them, *Mackinac,* was a children's play about life on Mackinac Island; the other was a play called *Marranos,* about life under the Inquisition in sixteenth-century Lisbon. *Duck Variations* was aired this spring on Chicago radio, a couple of Mamet's other plays were performed in New York in small workshop productions, and the St. Nicholas Company, with which Mamet has been associated for a number of years, presented *Lakeboat* in Chicago. Altogether, Mamet has written fourteen plays and several TV screenplays, one of which—a reworking of *The Man without a Country*—was commissioned by NET in Chicago but was never seen because the producers decided it would be too expensive to film and because, unknown to Mamet, it had been done with Cliff Robertson in 1973.

Mamet confesses it takes him "a long, long time" to develop his ideas. He jots down phrases or writes short scenes or character sketches. "I have the first act of about two hundred and fifty plays in my trunk," he reveals, telling me how satisfying it feels to have so much material he wants to develop, despite a certain amount of frustration. "I'll be involved in about five or six projects, and then something else will begin to interest me," he complains. "I find it very unprofessional to keep accruing beginnings. Sometimes I really have to force myself to finish a project."

When a writer creates under pressure, his work can sometimes lack spontaneity. Mamet admits there's something to be said for "freshness" as a writing value, "but the playwright's job is to be able to meld the spontaneity of creation with the technical skills and knowledge that will make his play sustain itself for one theme, for one idea, for one action over the course of two hours. Like Robert Edmund Jones said, 'The difference between a play and an imitation play is that real plays are not written but wrought.'"

"Do you find it difficult to sustain a theme when you're writing?"

"I think there are two extremes," Mamet asserts, poking a finger into the arm of his chair. "One extreme is to make it brilliant and nonfulfilling, and the other is to make it incredibly boring and tendentious. The beautiful play has to contain both elements. Each moment must exist for itself; each moment must be beautiful. Each moment must also put forward and contain the action, which is difficult. I'm fascinated with teaching myself how to write, because I've always been able to do the one, which is to write dialogue, but the other is very difficult for me. I'm striving in that direction. I know a lot of playwrights have exactly the opposite problem. It was said of O'Neill, for example, that he was a playwright of great genius but no talent."

"Have you ever gone through much anxiety when you're writing a play, wondering if anyone's going to care about it?"

"Not while I'm writing, usually, because then I can't do anything but get drunk or get laid or go to sleep. Most of the artists I know are incredibly manic-depressive. They say, 'Jesus-God, am I great. Why have I had this talent visited upon me?' Or they say, 'What a piece of shit I am. I don't deserve to live. I'm kidding myself.'"

"Do you think you'd give up writing if you ever understood why you do it?"

"That's the question Sandy Meisner used to use on actors in New York. When he'd interview students at the Neighborhood Playhouse he'd always ask them, 'Why do you want to be an actor?' He said that the ones who answered glibly were usually discarded. But a handful would say, 'I—ah—fuck, I don't know.' And they usually turned out to be good. But he also said that anybody who didn't give up the theater at least once every fortnight probably wasn't worth anything. I think that's the difference between an artist and a hack—the incredible self-criticism—which is the other part of the contract of being given some sort of talent, whether it's talent in perception or talent in being able to work, to suspend one's self-consciousness long enough to get something done. Reviews can drive you nuts, money can drive you nuts, or acclaim, or failure. If you write something good, that's all that matters."

In the November 10 issue of the *New Yorker* Edith Oliver, in her review of *Duck Variations* and *Sexual Perversity in Chicago,* called Mamet "a true and original writer." Remembering this, I ask him how he reacts to positive and negative reviews. "A friend of mine called me up from New York the other day," he says in a confidential tone. "The *Soho News* had just come out with a review of my double bill at St. Clement's, and the woman who was reviewing said that *Duck Variations* was the best one-act play she'd ever seen and that *Sexual Perversity* was the mark of a sexually mature person. So, I told my friend to write her a note saying, 'Would you say that *Hamlet* was the work of an indecisive person?'" Smiling candidly, he shifts in his chair, continuing, "Of course, any artist who's worth his salt is going to be alert to critics who tell him to stop fucking around, to stop serving himself, to stop being so goddam whimsical or so goddam esoteric. On the other hand, sometimes I think a critic's praise can be overblown. A good review can be just as subjective as a bad one. I was taught as an actor to devote myself to the theater, not necessarily to the American or the contemporary theater but to the metaphysical idea of a place of recognition, of a place where people can come to see what they know and hear what they know. In the last analysis, where I'd like to get—and I think perhaps I will in time—is where I can say, 'Hey, these critics are men and women just like myself. They're writers. That's what they do for a living. Sometimes they're right, sometimes they're wrong.' Nevertheless, it's still terrible to be humiliated in front of five million people. Lillian Hellman once said that nowhere in the world is the reward or the castigation so immediate as for the playwright. I spent four or five years in the theater as a professional actor, as a second-class citizen. To find myself catapulted through no conscious effort of my own into being a playwright—which is a very respected position in the theater—has come as quite a shock."

From what Mamet says, I assume he knows where he stands as a playwright. The question is, does *he* know where he stands? "There's a schizophrenia in my writing," he claims. "On the one hand, I like to write very esoteric stuff. Some of it makes Tom Stoppard look like Paddy Chayefsky. I've written several plays like that. I also like to write neorealist plays like *American Buffalo*. My true métier lies somewhere in between. I'm really into language as poetry. I think it has to be poetry. If it's not poetic on the stage, forget it. If it's solely serving the interest of the plot, I'm not interested. As a consequence, I go overboard the other way."

I hesitate to pose the next question, because it has been discussed so often, but I proceed anyway, hoping Mamet won't take offense. "Do you think the American theater's dying?"

"Well, like somebody said," he remarks a little satirically, "the theater's always dying. The theater was dying in the 1930s when the WPA and the Mercury Theater rescued it for a certain amount of time. The theater was certainly dead in Russia in the 1890s when Stanislavsky and Danchenko rescued it. The theater was dead in Germany when Brecht and Reinhardt rescued it. I think it's always dying. It's the responsibility of those with vision to save it."

"Maybe you'll be one of our rescuers," I conclude, thankful for Mamet's response.

"I hope so. What I discovered as an actor was that the theater was such a terribly exacting profession and such an appalling life that it's actually easier to strive to change it than it is to try to suffer under it. It really is. Because, at least then, one has the solace of one's ideals."

Buffalo on Broadway

Henry Hewes, David Mamet, John Simon, and Joe Beruh

In this round-table discussion David Mamet, the young playwright who had taken New York by storm, sat down with critics Henry Hewes and John Simon and the producer of the Broadway production of *American Buffalo*.

HEWES: I am delighted that *American Buffalo* is with us. The playwright who revealed himself last year in *Sexual Perversity in Chicago* and *Duck Variations* is obviously one of the most gifted of all the playwrights we've had. He introduces a dialogue that is at once realistic and at the same time has a poetry in it that is touching, a rhythm that takes it deeper than just in the surface dialogue . . . a play about the betrayal of individuals, about the morality that people use words to escape from.

The words are almost like traffic islands in this play. Sometimes the dialogue hides violence; sometimes it is the trigger for violence. The play is funny, and, no matter how much you disapprove of it, any part of it, no matter how impatient you may be that there is not more plot, you're constantly held by this play in a way that few others do. I have a certain reservation about the circular shape of the play, because at the end of it I don't think an awful lot has happened in the sense of plot. However, an awful lot has happened in the sense of emotional tides being turned loose and then damned up again.

SIMON: I must confess that, glad as I am to see David Mamet on Broadway, I shall probably be gladder with future plays than I am with

From Ira Bilowit and Henry Hewes, "Round Table Discussion: Henry Hewes, David Mamet, John Simon, and Joe Beruh," conducted by Ira Bilowit, *New York Theatre Review* (Spring–Summer 1977): 29–33. Copyright © Ira Bilowit 1977. Reprinted by permission.

this one. . . . In those earlier plays he dealt with more sympathetic figures, and we therefore had a kind of automatic sympathy for two old
Jewish farts on a bench or, conversely, for four silly but still ultimately
likable young people. Well, not so likable but at least recognizable . . .
whereas here we have three totally unsympathetic characters caught in
a very static situation, involved in some kind of mumbo jumbo whose
ultimate meaning escapes us . . .

How about plot? Well, I don't think that that's a Broadway re-
quirement when you say that we've become used to plot and story. I
think it was Aristotle who was the first to hazard this aspect or need
or element of drama as one of the crucial and necessary elements.
Now, Aristotle wasn't God, and Aristotle may have been wrong. Nevertheless, his ideas have worked pretty well for the theater for a good
many centuries, not to say eons. And it's a little risky to futz around
with that. Mind you, some great artists of the theater have done that
and gotten away with it. But there's another problem at work . . .

I think that what has happened somewhere toward the end of
the nineteenth century—I think it begins with the poetry of
Stephane Mallarmé, whom I admire very much—is that the arts became self-referential. More and more, poetry was about the writing
of the poet, painting was about the painting of a picture, so that with
the abstract expressionists, finally, it's no longer what is on the can-
vas that matters, but the action of putting that stuff [on the canvas]
becomes of primary and visually artistic significance, hence the term
action painting. Well, I think a little of this goes a very, very long way.
And I think the human mind should experiment with everything
possible and available. But it should also call it quits when something
has been exhausted, when it has become a glut and a source of nausea. . . . Because, finally, it is *not* of consuming interest to the world
how a poem is written or how a play is put together or how the words
of a play become the totality of that play. . . . I think it's perfectly alright, especially because he's so very young, for Mr. Mamet to experiment with these things and to achieve his small successes with them.
But I think for bigger things he will need to expand his horizons.

HEWES: Referring to what you said about self-referentialness, I
don't think people enjoy his plays because they can see the workings
of how they're made. I think people enjoy his plays because they are
very funny and because the dialogue is so good.

Now, in these days when playwrights tend to live more on grants
than they do on royalties, we've encouraged a whole generation of
playwrights to whom we say, "Write the way you want it," just the same

way you'd say to a painter, "Paint it the way you want it." Whereas the authors of previous generations, if their plays failed on Broadway, they were very receptive. You had Tennessee Williams up in the hotel room rewriting his second act. Which is better?

MAMET: I certainly wouldn't quarrel with the notion of Aristotelian unities. I take no issue with anything that Mr. Simon says, with the possible exception of the fact that it pertains to my work.

Aristotle comes along, and he says that as a proscriptive formula we have to have unity of action in a play. And Stanislavski comes along at the beginning of the twentieth century and says perhaps this is not a proscriptive formula; perhaps it's a descriptive formula. And he describes the process of perception that one goes through when one views a play. That is to say that not as any God-given fiat must we have a unity of action in a play but solely because the audience comes in and the curtain goes up, they see a play for two or three hours, and they come away. We're going to internalize that experience, as a totality, and because of that, because of that, because of the nature of perception, you'd better jolly well make sure that you have a unity of action in a play . . .

SIMON: I'm not asking for unity of action. I'm asking for any bloody kind of action whatsoever.

MAMET: And right you are to ask for it. I think it is absolutely essential that every beat in a play put forward the action, that every word in a play put forward the action. And any word of a play that does not put forward the action must be excised from the play. And that at any point in the play where the action takes too great a leap or turns back on itself, that point in the play must be corrected. I believe that, completely, strongly . . .

Those points at which the attention of the audience will lag, where the audience will in effect nap, those points, no matter how brilliant the dialogue is, no matter how exciting the stage action is, those points that are not essential to the action of the play—to what happens next—must be corrected. I completely agree; I couldn't agree more. I don't, however, feel that it applies to *American Buffalo*.

HEWES: In this case [*Buffalo*] you have three ineffectual people using these slogans so that they become patently absurd, whereas when you have [Richard] Nixon and [H. R.] Haldeman and [John] Erlichman doing it [in the Watergate break-in and cover-up] it's not so absurd.

MAMET: But that's the American myth again, Henry. The question is, here are people who are engaged in theft, and you say that they are absurd because they failed. The question is, would they be more laudable if they succeed?

HEWES: They're see-throughable immediately by the audience and almost by themselves.

MAMET: Well, God bless them, then, if they are. Because it's the same thing that goes on in board rooms all over this country. It's the same thing that goes on in advertising agencies, eh? How can we get the American people to bend over. If we win, eh, if we win, we're successful, and we give ourselves awards in advertising, and we give ourselves awards in the motion picture academy, eh? And we give ourselves awards in a weekend at Palm Beach. And, if we lose, we're on the unemployment lines, and we're having food stamps, and poverty comes in the door, and love goes out the window. But what's the difference? I mean, *what* are we trying to succeed in aid of?

My point in the play is that as much as we might not like to think so, these people are us. And, as Thorstein Veblen says, the behavior on this level, in the lumpenproletariat, the delinquent class, and the behavior on the highest levels of society, in the most rarefied atmospheres of the board room and the most rarefied atmospheres of the leisure class, is exactly identical. The people who create nothing, the people who do nothing, the people who have all sorts of myths at their disposal to justify themselves and their predators—and they steal from us. They rob the country spiritually, and they rob the country financially.

HEWES: I certainly would agree that there's a common denominator between all of us and the people in this play. Even though we're more educated and live with a different lifestyle. And certainly the things that happen in this play . . . transfer to me very easily . . .

SIMON: I hate to be excessively Brechtian here, but I think there is such a thing as hiding the lowest common denominator so successfully that no one can find it. . . . Not for nothing did Brecht ask for a certain alienation, so that the moral message can come through more clearly. Here I think the funniness—which is not my kind of funniness, I must confess, but seems to be other people's—is such that underneath the jolly scatological and obscene phraseology, which I'm sure accounts for 50 percent of the play's success, possibly more, people don't look for anything more. They're so happy to hear those *fucks* and *shits* come at them in a shower of obscenity that they're perfectly content to lose any other meaning that may be there . . .

MAMET: Now let's retract for a second. Either the play has a meaning, or it doesn't. If it doesn't have a meaning, then the play can't be served by the language that I've employed to put forward the meaning. . . . Having acquiesced that there is in fact a meaning to the play, what you're saying is that the meaning is inaccessible, eh?

SIMON: Yes.

MAMET: Okay. Now, in doing so, I think what you're doing is making one of the errors, to my mind, in reasoning, which is at the essential core of the play. Which is that human behavior is something that someone else does. . . . You seem to be playing two sides of the street on a number of issues, John. What I think is an important point, and I'm not going to characterize your attitude as totalitarian, is the attitude that the moral and the aesthetic are separable, that it's possible to appreciate the play on a moral level, on a philosophical level, on an ethical level, and to appreciate it in a completely different way on an aesthetic level. And I think what Aristotle is saying, and certainly what Stanislavski is saying, in speaking of the unity of action in a descriptive way, is that the two are interlocked, that the two are inseparable, that the ethical interchange is an aesthetic interchange. Which is a rule for a precept upon which I'm willing to let my play be judged.

A Man of Few Words Moves
On to Sentences

Ernest Leogrande

Ernest Leogrande interviewed Mamet in New York just prior to the Broadway premiere of *American Buffalo*. The much-touted production, which opened February 28, 1977, ran concurrently with *A Life in the Theatre*, which at the time of this conversation was in rehearsal for its upcoming production at the Goodman Theatre, Chicago. Directed by Gregory Mosher, *A Life in the Theatre* featured Mike Nussbaum and Joe Mantegna, who would collaborate with Mamet on numerous stage and screen projects over the next two decades.

An acquaintance with David Mamet's plays might leave the impression that he will talk the way his characters so often do in staccato plain speech: "Oh no." "Yes." "Oh no." "I'm afraid so." Or this example, "What's that?" "That." "This gun." "Yes."

Instead, met in person, he has a colorful gush of words, a plenitude deriving from youthful energy—he's twenty-nine—or else from having a mind that outraces his tongue.

"I've worked with Ulu [Grosbard] on the script for four months," he said, gulping club soda in a West Side restaurant, "and it's more fully achieved now. Certain things in it had been left disquietingly unachieved, in a French sense. Like Helmut Newton photography. Or some of the things you see in Paris *Vogue*. They suggest but don't resolve."

He was talking about his play *American Buffalo,* directed by Ulu Grosbard, opening Wednesday at the Ethel Barrymore Theatre. It has a three-person cast—Robert Duvall, the memorable *Godfather* lawyer, Kenneth McMillan, and John Savage. This will be Mamet's first time on Broadway.

His successful off-Broadway double bill, *Sexual Perversity in Chicago* and *Duck Variations,* has been running at the Cherry Lane since last June.

American Buffalo was showcased a year ago off-Broadway at St. Clement's. . . . He won an Obie, the off-Broadway award, last year as the best new American playwright. Now his *American Buffalo,* in a polished version, is ready to take on the big-time.

"I could revise forever to make them rhythmically perfect," Mamet said. "It's better than biting my nails."

Lest the dialogue quoted at the beginning be misleading, Mamet also uses multisyllabic words and long sentences in his plays. It is the terse crosscut exchanges, however, a distinguishing factor in his writing, that have won him critical acclaim for his ability to capture rhythms, intonations, and idiomatic peculiarities of living speech.

"I studied music all of my life," he said. "I've played the piano, and I've studied theory and composition, and my writing is influenced by musical ideas, resolution, phrasing. I think it becomes less and conscious the more I do it."

He said the rhythms of the dialogue in *Sexual Perversity* exhibit another influence: television. "It's written for a time format, in five- and eight-minute scenes," he said.

However, television is not a medium he wants to write for. "My main objection," he said, "and I'm not talking about public television, is you can't overcome—an incredibly pompous thing to say— you can't overcome the tacit assumption of either the creator or the audience. It's ineluctable that every eight minutes you are being sold soap. It's like having a date with a prostitute. No matter how interesting or loving or boring or completely achieved the exchange is, you know it's always done for money."

Duck Variations was an exception to his polishing compulsion, he said. "From the time I wrote it until it was produced I changed only two lines. And I was tricked into dropping a third line."

"The director for a production of the play in Saratoga [New York] felt the line, which got a laugh, was out of place. He believed it inhibited the completion of the scene," Mamet said. "He took me to lunch at Sardi's one day, and he plied me with drinks and lunch, four hours. As we were leaving, I realized I had been conned. I said, 'This whole thing was just a set up just to change that one line, wasn't it?'"

For the record, in the play one man [Emil] says, "Hay, barley, mushrooms, rye, stuffed full of abundance, enough to feed the nations of the world."

The other man's [George's] rejoinder—since restored for the Cherry Lane production—is "We'll have 'em over. We don't get enough riff-raff."

Mamet's turtleneck, glasses, and boyish haircut conveyed the physical appearance of an undergrad as he talked enthusiastically about his work, an impression reinforced by the occasional remark with the ring of a required reading list.

"I was thinking of what Thorstein Veblen said," rolled off his tongue, for instance, as he hurried into the description of a Veblen theory of how we keep searching for new objects to replace old ones in a fruitless try to satisfy our desires.

"America is a very, very propaganda-prone nation," he said. This willingness to be sold constitutes some of the basis for the actions of *American Buffalo,* a play about two men and a youth who join in an inept plan to commit a burglary.

"Americans have always been very susceptible to exhortations to do what is right but never to think what is right," Mamet said. "Gene Debs said it beautifully, 'Even if I could I would not lead you into the promised land because if I could lead you in someone else could lead you out.'"

Mamet hopes to branch out more into the world of directing, a field he's already tried, but acting—an area that he has also explored—he leaves to actors. "I think acting is the greatest thing in the world," he said. "As Tairov said, 'It's the most difficult art to master, and it looks like the easiest.' I wouldn't want to sully the art by being a dilettante." (Checking the required reading list, that would be Alexander Tairov, a contemporary of Russian director Konstantin Stanislavski.)

John Simon, a critic known for his deadly skewer, has acknowledged—with Simonesque qualifications—that Mamet is a man to listen to, with a future to be watched. Treading the eggshells of this and other critics' praise, Mamet obviously is aware that his reputation is building, not solidified, and so the occasional modesty that bobs up in his remarks can be seen as a protective device.

As an example, in discussing another play of his to be done at the Chicago Goodman Theatre, *A Life in the Theatre,* a play that was still in rehearsal at the time of this interview, he described its theme as "the pursuit of the ephemeral" and then added quickly, with a hex-removing remark, "That'll keep 'em away in droves, won't it?"

I Just Kept Writing

Steven Dzielak

Steven Dzielak's conversation with David Mamet took place in 1977. In this interview Mamet speaks passionately about those who have influenced his writing for the stage, about stoic philosophy, aesthetics, and the responsibility of the playwright to convey the truth rather than engage in political statement.

Is there any strong specific philosophical undercurrent to your writing?

Well, I once heard a medical lecture at Harvard about the concept of life, and I was thinking about stoic philosophy, of which I know nothing other than the meditations of Marcus Aurelius, and it occurred to me that there's an idea that Dreiser promulgates, and that Tolstoy's always talking about, that everyone always tries to do good, but no one succeeds. This is seen concretely for the first time in Stanislavski's concept of the method of physical actions. He takes this notion that has always operated in the writing of great plays and refines it down to make it understandable for the actor to fit himself into the mode of the play. This is the schematic into which the actor can fit himself; you can be taught to act, but you can't be made to act, and this is one way to fit yourself into the exigencies of the role and to understand the role. This way everyone is capable of perceiving how the play operates and how the actor operates in the play.

When you first read Dreiser and Tolstoy, did you conceptualize this notion as some sort of inspiration to write?

No, as a matter of fact, I had been a writer for a couple of years

From "David Mamet: An Interview," *New York Arts Journal* (February–March 1978): 13–14.

before I read them. I actually started writing in college because I had been active as an actor; for a while I actually supported myself as an actor. I think I then perceived that I didn't have the talent for it, but the words came easily, so I resisted the urge to quit and just kept writing. I just stopped looking for inspiration, because that will fuck you up all the time; just sit and write, that's all. I'm just writing out of my head, as I think of it, but, when I have to complete something, I'll just go with the deadline. That's the wonderful part about theater—we have such exigent deadlines; if it's wrong, it *has* to be made right, it *has* to work, you *have* to have the inspiration. I think you need to find a kind of Zen way of learning not to look for inspiration and letting things flow and percolate. As an actor, you ask a director, "Should I pick up the phone in this scene with my left or right hand?" The director says, "With your right." He or she doesn't know why consciously; they just know "right hand" because they've been training to make that decision for years; it's the same with the writer. Peter Brook says it's like being a samurai because you train for years and years so that, if you need this technique once in ten years, you'll have it.

Do you live the way you write?

No, my life is a shambles, my writing is pristine. My apartment is neat, but it's only my apartment. I'm actually trying to get more and more disorganized. John Barth says you should break a habit once a week just for the habit of breaking one. My days do seem to fill up, though; I like to shoot the shit with the merchants on Eighth Avenue, maybe play a little gin for an hour. I also like to read and go running and travel, and I wait for my new couch to be delivered a lot.

I understand you've almost completed a screenplay of Sexual Perversity in Chicago. *Do you feel that you or your writing have been affected by the commercial demands of Hollywood?*

It's not really a question of letting yourself be fucked up by commercial demands; just letting yourself write is an answer to those demands.

Writers like F. Scott Fitzgerald and Nathaniel West were deeply affected by their Hollywood experiences. Have you had any such experiences?

Actually, I've had no need and no desire to go there to work, but I have met some of the studio people. They're all nuts; I mean, they really are. Everyone I've met in California is zonkers. I really laughed out loud when, in *Annie Hall,* Woody Allen said that California's greatest cultural contribution is the ability to turn right on a red light. He may be right.

Are you a moviegoer yourself?

Yeah, I go a lot. My favorites last year were *Orca the Killer Whale* and *Grizzly*, especially *Grizzly*.

Do those films have any special significance for you, or are they just escapes from daily pressures?

No, actually I like them because they have big animals that kill a lot of people. Really, I love that kind of film because it's not pretentious. Lately there's been a rash of absolutely horrendous, pretentious films. I love to eat popcorn and talk back to the screen.

I get the feeling you may have also been a television freak as a kid. Were you?

Oh sure! But no longer; it's just so boring. Once in a while in a hotel I'll turn it on, but it's just so fucking boring, especially ABC. That's the wave of the future—all those cartoonlike shows. It seems that the networks pander to the lowest tastes. It's a little frightening, but that's okay; it had to happen to this country, anyway. We're definitely becoming Germanic and Teutonic and entrenched in our idealism.

Do you see any of these things happening in the theater?

No, no; historically, when the country becomes more fascistic, the theater becomes more alive. It happened in the early Soviet period in Russia, in Germany in the 1920s, there was a resurgence of theater in this country in the 1930s, and in postwar Britain. At a time of social upheaval and unrest and austerity the theater has more to answer for.

Do you have any strong political inclinations?

I sent Jimmy Carter a telegram when I thought he was going to pass the B-1 bomber; I told him I was very disappointed, but politics don't particularly interest me.

Were you an activist in college?

Not particularly; I went on a few marches and signed a few petitions. I wish I'd been more of an activist.

Have you ever made any strong political statements in any of your writings?

No, but neither did Hogarth.

Can I have a translation of that?

Seriously, the theater is a most useful political tool; it's a place where we go to hear the truth.

Do you think the theater is the strongest medium for conveying truth?

Sure, the difference with theater is that people go to participate in it as a community endeavor; they seek that by nature.

Do you see that function of theater ever being superseded by television?

33

No, TV is like masturbation. If you do it, you do it by yourself in a dark room. Theater is completely opposite; you do it with all of your fellows in an atmosphere of love, watching people on stage who've come for the same purpose you did—to celebrate something. It's the difference between a birthday party and a car crash.

In March of this year you were quoted by a syndicated television colum-nist, William Raidy, as saying, "Fuck television. I don't want to write for tele-vision. The obstacle of commercial breaks every seven minutes is too great to surmount. If people sit down and watch a play interrupted by exhortations to buy soap, then that's what the play's about to them: buying soap." Yet here you are starting on a TV project. Is it noncommercial TV?

No, as a matter of fact, it is commercial. I'm also doing a non-commercial children's play, but the drama is commercial. I'm going to get my wick wet, as it were. Something changed my mind; I don't know what it was, though. I guess I was in a bad mood that day. Every-thing I said there is true, but I'm going to try it anyhow.

A final quasi-political question: what do you think of plays David Rabe has written? Will they have meaning for people who will have forgotten what Vietnam meant?

Well, you know what Marcus Aurelius says, "There's no such thing as posthumous fame." In answer to your question, I don't know—it's possible.

Among others, the name of Albert Innaurato is often mentioned with yours . . .

There's no truth to the rumor; we're just friends. Actually, I have great respect for his writing. He's done some beautiful hometown stuff about south Philly [Philadelphia] that I just love.

How do you feel about your work being discussed and given meaning you never intended?

That's okay; I subscribe to the theory "You write it—you bite it." Or, to put it differently, having it on stage with my name on it, people can say what they wish. It's certainly their right. You know what [Rudyard] Kipling says,

If you can bear to hear the truth you've spoken,
twisted by knaves to make a trap for fools,
and see the things you gave your life to broken,
and stoop and build them up with worn out tools.

The poem "If . . ." could've been written by Marcus Aurelius. I'm a big fan of Kipling; basically, he was a stoic philosopher. Take your

34

shot; do the best you can day-to-day; don't hurt nobody; listen to the best part of yourself, and do those things that make you happy. In a larger sense it is probably good for mankind, and you'll never know, anyway. Did you now Kipling was a Midwesterner?

No, I didn't.

Well, he really wasn't; I just like him so much, I imagine he must've been born in Indiana or somewhere.

So far you've quoted novelists, but you write plays—why not novels?

I can't write novels. Anyhow, it's not just the form that touches a person; plays do that also, at least for me. The play succeeds by exquisiteness, the novel by brute force, by repetition, by elaboration. It makes a different kind of impression.

Who were the playwrights whom you were influenced by?

I was influenced by the same people everyone was influenced by: [Harold] Pinter, [Clifford] Odets, [Samuel] Beckett, [Eugene] O'Neill, Lanford Wilson. You know, I don't have any theories about how to write plays; that's something you can't possibly learn from reading a book of plays. You do it by doing it. You can sort of be guided in the pursuit of this knowledge by what other people have done and by what you see happening on the stage, but you have to teach yourself. I mean, if the technique in Beckett were so blatant as to be abstractable upon reading, it couldn't possibly be that beautiful. It took him fifty years to write that play.

You don't feel writing can be taught?

Most of the time at Yale I talk about acting or about aesthetics. I don't think you can teach playwriting at all. You can work with somebody's script and try to apply some generalized principles to it in a way that might help them better understand the nature of writing; on the other hand, you might be ruining their play. I go back and rewrite things of my own and find that I've ruined them, and I certainly understand my work better than I understand someone else's, so that the prospect of taking someone else's writing, even as the best influence in the world, and changing it is intimidating. You have to be more than careful.

What about revising your own unstaged works?

You have to look at and refine what you've done. The play generally won't support much embellishment.

Is this also the case with works already staged?

Yes, now and again, absolutely.

How about a major work such as American Buffalo? *Is that complete as far as you're concerned?*

For the moment. It's just being published. I was thinking the other day that there are lines in it that I'd change if I could when I get the galleys back. I'll probably get to that sometime.

Do you think your revisions are ever influenced by the way you personally feel that day?

Let me ask you a question. Could you conceive of an airplane pilot of a flight crashing the plane into a mountain because he had a bad day? It's certainly not impossible, but it's rather unlikely because of the responsibilities and training he has. In terms of revising something, I doubt that I'd render it useless because I didn't feel good that morning. When I talk about revising, I'm talking basically about a small section. As I've said, the play has a life of its own; beyond a point you can't touch it. You can make the rhythm a little more perfect, you can make it a little more exact, reduce embellishment, but past a certain point you can't rework it.

At which point, you feel it's out of your hands?

To the largest extent, yes.

Is this because you feel a sense of responsibility toward someone or something in particular?

I'm writing for the stage, you know. You have to understand, it's not what it looks like. I'm writing words for actors to say and for the audience to hear. So, yes, I do feel a sense of responsibility toward them. But you wouldn't say to a surgeon, "When you're operating on someone, do you think that you'll fuck up this operation for the children that this man or this women will never have?"

Specifically, how do the routines of your personal life affect the creation of your plays?

I don't think it does much good to describe the process because it's not something I'm completely aware of, and I certainly have had the experience of being warped by writers' descriptions of what it is they do. Things like "Do you get up in the morning and write, or do you get up, eat breakfast, and then write?" As silly as it sounds to say, I've been influenced by those things, like hearing about Hemingway standing for three hours a day at his typewriter or Georges Sand working eight hours a day whether she felt like it or not. The important thing is what the piece is about; I think, everything else is subordinate to that. If you're a writer you'll do what you have to do to write it; if you're not, you won't. Some plays take a couple of years to write, and some are written in an afternoon. It's not just the discipline of sitting at the typewriter that's important, because that in itself accomplishes nothing. The discipline lies in trying to write *every* line as best you can, to stick to the action. It also helps to unplug the phone and to get away now and again.

Currently, several playwrights such as Robert Wilson are conveying their thoughts on stage by using other media in the play as visual metaphors to break the linear concept of story and staging. Do you have any feelings about this development in theater?

To me, a writer has to write. Really, the only tool he has is the dialogue and the absolutely essential minimal stage directions; the rest of the staging must be the province of the director. What the characters say to each other must contain and give birth to what they do to each other. There are always attempts to get away from that, but you can't, because every time you do you end up with garbage. There are always trends, but basically there's nothing new in theater. It always has been, and always will be, just actors and audiences, no matter how many fucking lasers you put in. You can't get beyond the beauty of actors on a stage. Nothing will make that more beautiful if they're correct, and nothing will save that if they're incorrect.

Would it be fair to say that you'd rather stick to basics?

No, what I'm saying is that experimentation is, per se, a nonregenerate idea; it has to be experimentation related to what the script says about ourselves, and how best to achieve that. A different kind of experimentation, which is crap, is: how do we use this technology? Who cares? I'm not saying that technology is out of place in theater; I'm saying it has no intrinsic value. It's most times a distraction.

You've written about twenty plays, most of which have been or are being done in regional theater. Now that you're known, is there more interest in doing them?

People definitely want to do them. For stuff that a couple of years ago was called inconsequential or unfinished, people are now beating down my door. But that's the way of the world.

Has success, especially of American Buffalo, *changed you in any way?*

No, I've always been an asshole, and I see no reason to change now. But the basic difference is that agents will talk to me now. When I call them about casting, I don't get put on hold while they go off to Majorca, as they are wont to do.

How do you deal with the phone as an interruption?

Well, I sometimes pretend to be my Japanese houseboy and sometimes the French agricultural attaché, but most times I just leave the phone off the hook. Actually, I'm a bit of a jolly prankster on the phone. I used to sell on the phone, and every chance I get to abuse the hospitality of Ma Bell I avail myself of.

What did you do to support yourself besides acting when you were young and struggling?

Oh, I did everything, notably selling land or carpets or books by phone, driving a cab, waiting tables, dishwashing—name it. That's how life always is.

Many of your characters are working-class people, as in American Buffalo. *Do you have more of an interest in them than in other socioeconomic groups?*

Yes, my new play *The Woods* is about the middle class, but in the main that's true. There's not very much interesting about the middle class—dramatically, not socially, that is. We've already had a bunch of plays about the middle class; in the 1950s we were very concerned with the idea of newfound prosperity and the onus that it put upon us to be happy and "why aren't we happy?" Personally, I don't give a fuck at this point. Maybe the upper class would be interesting, but who's going to write about them?

You previously made references to fascism in this country. Does that connect with some of your characters, like Teach in American Buffalo?

Yeah, he's a good American, he's an intellectual; at least that's how he views himself. But I think that's definitely true. He doesn't communicate many of his feelings very well, but neither do the intelligentsia, nor does the middle class. He certainly makes his desires known rather vehemently. I've always felt that all three characters in *American Buffalo* are rather transparent in that there's nothing occult about their desires.

Did it ever seem to you that the bluntness and crudity of those characters might disturb viewers who see in them a resemblance to themselves?

Maybe. A lot of people saw it only as slice-of-life realism, but I do know that a lot of businessmen didn't understand *American Buffalo*.

Certainly, there was more going on than a story about three small-time crooks; you seemed to be commenting on capitalism and hustling for profit, but would you be willing to elaborate?

No, I won't talk about it. I wrote it—there it is; it's not hidden. People looked at Beckett and at O'Neill and asked "What the fuck is he trying to say?" I've done my part; now it's up to you guys.

The Postman's Words

Dan Yakir

Dan Yakir's conversation with David Mamet is the playwright's first lengthy discussion on writing for film. Although the interview takes the form of a profile, which Mamet favors until the 1990s, the playwright enthusiastically discusses his admiration for James Cain's novel *The Postman Always Rings Twice* and the differences in the creative process between stage and screenplays,

"It is much easier to write great dialogue than to write great plots," David Mamet wrote in a *New York Times* article last year. "So we playwrights do the next best thing to writing great plots: we write bad plots. And then we fill up the empty spaces with verbiage. . . . Working in the movies taught me . . . *to stick to the plot and not to cheat.*"

The plot to which Mamet had to stick for his first Hollywood assignment was a classic: James Cain's *The Postman Always Rings Twice*. It's a story that Mamet considers "quintessentially American," not unlike his own plays (most notably *American Buffalo* and *Sexual Perversity in Chicago*) or the previous films of director Bob Rafelson.

"When I write a play," says Mamet, "I start from the inside out. I write scenes, with characters, but I have no idea who these characters are. Only later do I try to decide what they do. When I write a movie, it's the other way around: I start with the structure and work backwards."

There's a reason for these differences in the creative process: "Film is basically a narrative medium, in the sense that it conveys one

From *Film Comment* (March–April 1981): 21–24. Copyright © Dan Yakir. Reprinted with permission.

person's perception—for instance, that of the camera. By contrast, the stage is a dramatic medium: the characters interact, and there's friction, because they want things that contradict each other's desires. The drama is in this interaction of opposites."

Perhaps because *The Postman* is an adaptation, Mamet's work on it resembled less his own description of screenwriting approach than it would had it been an original script. With the "structure" pretty much a given, "it was a lot like writing a play, in that I was constantly trying to determine for specific moments—after isolating the events—what the characters do. I compared them in order to understand what their 'through action' was and then worked backwards to see how that influenced the various moments. It was a process of refining.

"When I submitted the first draft, there were a number of people—Rafelson wasn't one of them—who said, 'What is this? It doesn't make any sense!' I answered, 'You're nuts! It's the best screenplay you've seen in the last five years!' But then it dawned on me that I wrote it the way I wrote my plays. I never write any adverbs. To me, the dialogue is self-explanatory. So I added *savagely* or *feelingly* after each character's name—and they said it was a great screenplay.

"It's a 4,000-year-old story: the aging man with the young wife, who wants to precipitate some violence, sexuality, regeneration, and so takes on a younger, more virile stranger to their house. Sidney Kingsley's play *They Knew What They Wanted* is about an Italian immigrant who becomes rich and owns a vineyard in California. He has a mail-order bride who falls in love with a drifter. It's the same story—and *it's* based on a Greek play about the king of the Rainy Country who finds himself in a bind: he can't reproduce, and the country is barren. A young drifter comes along, etc. . . . It's a mythological story.

"It's really a 'black' novel—about people deluding themselves, creating a *folie à deux* to justify their passion for each other. Each touches a secret spring in the other, something that neither of them would have foreseen happening.

"And Cain's is a beautiful vision of the country in 1933. It's not picturesque or sentimental. It's like the wonderful evocative photographs of Dorothea Lange or Walker Evans. It's about killing and screwing and betraying each other—and under all this very cynical vision is a crying need for human contact in a bad, bad world."

"I'm of the Aristotelian school: characters are nothing but habitual action. You don't create a character; you describe what he does. To me it's the story of a drifter (Jack Nicholson) who's happy living by his wits and off the land until he meets this woman (Jessica Lange). He tries to exploit her and leave her but can't. He finds himself bound to her. And to have her, to be able to keep her, he commits a murder. It's the story of a man who gets caught up in spite of himself.

"She wants a have a home—a woman who came to California, having won a screen test, and ended up as a semi-whore. She married this Greek man (John Colicos) at a time when she had a very low opinion of herself and needed someone to protect and anesthetize her. She resigned herself to this life with a man she doesn't love. Then the drifter comes along and awakens in her the possibility of having a fulfilled life—excitement, sexuality, and perhaps children. That's what she tries to do throughout the movie.

"Her husband is an interesting character. In the scene where he goes to town and leaves them alone—and they decide to run off—he wears jodhpurs, a white alpaca jacket, and a Tyrolian hat. That's his image of being the lord of a manor. He has a lot of the ambivalence of the successful foreigner. On the one hand, he's a European man, much more intellectual than the people around him—he comes from a great tradition of learning—and, on the other, he's not as intelligent as he thinks he is. He enjoys being the 'foreigner' because it gives him something to kvetch about, yet he thinks that people are always taking advantage of him. He's very much the prototype of the first-generation American: he wants to succeed, is good at business, but feels a bit of an outcast. And enjoys it.

"This book—I love Cain, and this one is his best—has a great plot: just when other books would have ended, this one begins. It's what happens *after* the murder that's the interesting part. I accepted almost everything in the book. Once I started working on the script with Rafelson, the challenge was to dramatize the narrative sequences—how to take something that's basically narrative, which is an interior monologue whereby the character is telling you his feelings, and translate it into drama, where all you see is what the character does.

"For example, when the character says, 'I looked at the car, and I knew if it went down the road I'd never see her again,' Cain is delineating the choices in a narrative fashion, but you can't put that on the screen. They used to—very badly. One thing about the great silent films is that they're completely visual: they don't rely on narrative material for advancement of the plot, which is a mistake most films today make. That's why they're wretched. First of all, you can't determine what people want from what they do. Second, by relying on literary content—the little pussycat in the window, next to the picture of her master . . . that's not drama. That's shorthand, a program note.

"The movie is structured in the screenplay almost along classical lines of suspense, and no question is really answered in any single sequence. It makes a very productive use of the medium of cutting, which the book really doesn't. There he makes a decision and then goes and carries it out. For example, he's presented with the alternative of the woman and finds out she's married and then decides to leave the diner. When he's going down the road, he stops for a car, and the guy opens the door, and he stands there and glances back at the diner. There's a point-of-view shot of the diner and then a cut. In the next shot he's working on a tire. . .

"There's a great vignette in *The Last Tycoon* when the protagonist Monroe Stahr tells a playwright who can't write movies, 'A woman is in a room. She looks at the door, goes to it, and locks it. She takes two black gloves out of her purse, looks around the room, and sees a fire in the grate. She takes scissors and cuts the gloves to pieces and then throws them into the grate. The telephone rings. She freezes in fear. She goes to the phone. 'Hello,' she says. 'No, I'm sorry, I don't have a pair of black gloves.' And the playwright asks, 'What happens then?' And Monroe Stahr answers, 'I don't know. I'm making it up. That's how you write movies.'

"One thing that narration always tends to do in literature is to make you cease asking that question. We talked for a while about putting narration into the movie, and I said I was completely against it, because it relieves the audience of . . . it tells them someone is taking care of their problem—putting a frame on the movie, making it a flashback. It implies that *somebody* knows the end of the story, so it gives the audience the signal that they can care about it that much less.

"I tried to put the audience in the same position as the protagonists: led forth by events, by the inevitability of the previous actions. They don't know what they're going to do next either. They find out after they've done it.

"The major stumbling block was motivating the murder: how to put the people in a trick bag, so that to commit murder will become inevitable—that it's not really a choice. It's easy to do it if you're going to narrate it. In the book he does it with one line: 'I looked at her and I knew I had to have her if I hung for it.'"

"*The Postman* is written so beautifully as a 'hard-boiled' novel that it makes Raymond Chandler look rather sissified. But I didn't preserve the dialogue. It doesn't work. His dialogue is brilliant but not actable. Stanislavski once was doing a play about a terrorist at Yalta. He imported to Moscow, at a terrible expense, real palm trees, but when he put them on the stage they looked phony. So he had to make artificial ones that would look real.

"For example, after they've just tried to kill the husband in the tub, the lights go out, and a cop comes by, and they have to make a quick story about what happened. In the book Frank says to Cora, 'We just got to sell him a story, that's all. You were in here, and the lights popped, and you heard him slip and fall, and he didn't answer when you spoke to him. Then you called me, that's all. No matter what he says, you got to stick to it. If he saw anything, it was just his imagination, that's all.' What we're doing here is describing something the audience is seeing, which in the movie becomes boring, so you take it out. All he has to do is turn to her, grab her arm, and say, 'He slipped in the tub, got it?'

"The essence of dialogue is always to make a point. To go on and on is to betray your objective. Lee Strasberg used to say that the difference between a book and a movie was: in a book the character would say, 'Would you like to go to the movies?' which would be followed by something like: She turned in a swing, her hair kind of whispered in the summer breeze and her mouth curled up in a corner, slightly, in a yes-no grin. She looked at him, lowered her eyelashes. 'I don't know. Perhaps,' she said. That's a book.

"In a film he'll ask, 'Would you like to go to the movies?' to which she'll answer, 'I don't know' and the actors will fill up the rest.

"I love writing dialogue. It's a lot of fun for me. We were able to take a lot of 'hard-boiled' types and flesh them out with dialogue. One of my favorite characters is Katz, the crooked lawyer. He's basically all made-up on my part, which is also why I like him. He tries to convince Barlow, an insurance investigator, to drop his charges against the couple, Frank and Nora."

"An interesting thing I noticed when I'm writing is that my dialogue is much closer to Raymond Chandler. It's punchy, catchy, and funny—very close to the way the Fred MacMurray character talks in *Double Indemnity*. But you can't really film Cain's stuff, while Chandler is a brilliant writer of dialogue that's all meant to be spoken. That's

43

why you love him. You read him, and you hear it, and you understand the people from what they say to each other, while in Cain you understand them from what they say about themselves.

"A very common rule of writing that everybody breaks is: never write anything in the first-person narrative. But Cain did, and the most successful Cain film is *Double Indemnity* because Chandler wrote the screenplay. You really needed that. That film was a great inspiration to me. It's one of Billy Wilder's great films and certainly one of the best MacMurray and Stanwyck ever did. That and *The Blue Dahlia*. You can watch them any number of times.

"In John Houseman's book *Front and Center*—he produced *Dahlia*—he tells about Alan Ladd trying to get Chandler drunk to get him to solve the killer's identity. But, finally, the plot in *Blue Dahlia* is silly. The beautiful thing is that there are two people who could have committed the murder: William Bendix and Howard da Silva. If Bendix committed the murder, you hate the movie because he's such a nice guy and a looney. And if it's da Silva, you hate the movie because he's the bad guy and has a pencil-thin mustache and you *know* he did it. And then he brings out the third guy—because you've got to leave the theater smiling. What a movie!

"Chandler as a dramatist really demands acting. Rather than giving actors the answers, he incites them—by leaving out steps—to act."

"My own experience in Hollywood was very good. Rafelson is a great perfectionist, in terms of planning and logistics. We spent almost a year working on the structure of the script, trying to make it fascinating and give the audience a treat. Someone once asked Vakhtangov, the Russian stage director, 'How is it that every time you stage a play it becomes a hit? It's impossible!' And he replied, 'I always imagine that the audience is there with me at the rehearsal; I put myself in their place.' To a great extent that's what Bob does. He's not patronizing. He *becomes* part of the audience. We must have done ten drafts of the damn screenplay! When I was on the set, I was rewriting scenes that were to be shot the next day.

"In terms of style *The Postman* is classical. Rafelson's style is always the motivated camera; it doesn't move gratuitously. It's very fitted to a film of that period—very straightforward, almost Hitchcockian. A lot of judicious use of inserts but nothing gratuitous.

"The Tay Garnett version of *Postman*? I never saw it until after the third draft of my screenplay. It's very emasculated. It uses all sorts of late 1940s and early 1950s sign language for sex and violence—

for anything that's a real expression of emotion. It's rather uninteresting that way.

"I was very impressed by the atmosphere on the set; it's like the atmosphere on stage when one is dedicated to a project. That's one thing I like about Hollywood—about this movie, anyway—everybody seemed to have the idea that what's good for the movie is good for them and for the industry. There was no waste; Bob is a great fan of cost accounting. I hope to do another movie with him at some point. It was a very happy experience."

Something Out of Nothing

Matthew C. Roudané

Matthew C. Roudané's conversation with David Mamet took place on December 4, 1984, in New York. Earlier that year *Glengarry Glen Ross,* directed by Gregory Mosher, had received its American premiere at the Goodman Theatre, Chicago, and transferred to the Golden Theatre on Broadway, where it garnered the Pulitzer Prize, the Drama Critics' Award for Best American Play, and four Tony nominations. Principally focused on Mamet's dramaturgy, specifically as it pertains to *Glengarry Glen Ross* and *American Buffalo,* Roudané's interview is the first such scholarly discussion with Mamet.

ROUDANÉ: The myth of the American Dream seems central to your artistic vision. In *American Buffalo, The Water Engine, Lakeboat, Mr. Happiness, A Life in the Theatre,* and *Glengarry Glen Ross* a whole cultural as well as spiritual dimension of the American Dream myth is present. Could you comment on why this myth engages you so much?

MAMET: It interests me because the national culture is founded very much on the idea of strive and succeed. Instead of rising with the masses, one should rise from the masses. Your extremity is my opportunity. That's what forms the basis of our economic life, and this is what forms the rest of our lives. That American myth: the idea of something out of nothing. And this also affects the spirit of the individual. It's very divisive. One feels one can only succeed at the cost of

From Matthew C. Roudané and the editors of *Studies in American Drama, 1945–Present* 1 (1986): 73–81. Copyright © Matthew C. Roudané. Reprinted with permission.

someone else. Economic life in America is a lottery. Everyone's got an equal chance, but only one guy is going to get to the top. "The more I have the less you have." So one can only succeed at the cost of, the failure of another, which is what a lot of my plays—*American Buffalo* and *Glengarry Glen Ross*—are about. That's what Acting President Reagan's whole campaign is about. In *Glengarry Glen Ross* it's the Cadillac, the steak knives, or nothing. In this play it's obvious that these fellows are put in fear for their lives and livelihood; for them it's the same thing. They have to succeed at the cost of each other. As Thorstein Veblen in *Theory of the Leisure Class* says, sharp practice inevitably shades over into fraud. Once someone has no vested interest in behaving in an ethical manner and the only bounds on his behavior are supposedly his innate sense of fair play, then fair play becomes an outdated concept: "But wait a second! Why should I control my sense of fair play when the other person may not control his sense of fair play? So hurray for me and to hell with you."

ROUDANÉ: What are your thematic concerns in *Glengarry Glen Ross?*

MAMET: If there are any thematic concerns, they must be blatant. The play concerns how business corrupts, how the hierarchical business system tends to corrupt. It becomes legitimate for those in power in the business world to act unethically. The effect on the little guy is that he turns to crime. And petty crime goes punished; major crimes go unpunished. If someone wants to destroy Manhattan for personal gain, they call him a great man. Look at Delorean. He completely raped everybody in Northern Ireland with that scheme; he made a car that wasn't worth the money—and that wasn't enough. He started dealing in cocaine—and he walked. He walked away because he "suffered" enough.

In *Glengarry Glen Ross* it's interesting to watch Aaronow. He's the one who comes closest to being the character of a *raisonneur,* for throughout the whole play he's saying, "I don't understand what's going on," "I'm no good," "I can't fit in here," "I'm incapable of either grasping those things I should or doing those things that I've grasped." Or his closing lines, "Oh, God, I hate this job." It's a kind of monody throughout the play. Aaronow has some degree of conscience, some awareness; he's troubled. Corruption troubles him. The question he's troubled by is whether his inability to succeed in the society in which he's placed is a defect—that is, is he manly or sharp enough?—or if it's, in effect, a positive attribute, which is to say that his conscience prohibits him. So Aaronow is left between these two things, and he's incapable of choosing. This dilemma is, I think, what many of us are facing in this country right now. As Veblen, who's had a big influence on me, says, a lot of business in this country is founded on the idea that, if you don't exploit the possible opportunity, not only are you being silly, but in many cases you're being negligent, even legally negligent.

ROUDANÉ: At the close of *American Buffalo* I sensed a felt compassion, some sense of understanding between all three men, but especially between Don and Bobby. However, at the close of *Glengarry Glen Ross* I sensed little compassion, no resolution, little sense of redemption. Could you talk about these two plays in light of this?

MAMET: *Glengarry Glen Ross* is structurally a very different play from *American Buffalo*. *Buffalo* is a traditionally structured drama based on tragedy, whereas *Glengarry*, although it has aspects of tragedy in it, is basically a melodrama—or a drama. Endings in tragedies are resolved. The protagonist undergoes a reversal of the situation, a recognition of the state, and we have a certain amount of cleansing. This is what Don experiences in *American Buffalo*. But this doesn't happen in *Glengarry Glen Ross*. So the structure is different, it's not as classical a play as *Buffalo*, and it's probably not as good a play. But it is the structure of each that affects the characters and the endings.

ROUDANÉ: What engages your aesthetic imagination in *American Buffalo*?

MAMET: I was interested in the idea of honor among thieves; of what is an unassailable moral position and what isn't. What would cause a man to abdicate a moral position he'd espoused? That's what *American Buffalo* is about. Teach is the antagonist. The play's about Donny Dubrow. His moral position is that one must conduct himself like a man, and there are no extenuating circumstances for supporting the betrayal of a friend. That's how the play starts. The rest of the play is about Donny's betrayal of the fellow, Bobby, who he's teaching these things to. The same is true to a certain extent of Levene in *Glengarry Glen Ross*. All throughout the play Levene is espousing the professional doctrine of technique. What he's saying is that I am therefore owed certain support because of what I've done, because of who I am. And at the end of the play Levene betrays himself.

ROUDANÉ: I think one of your major contributions to the stage is your "language": clearly you have an ear for the sounds, sense, and rhythms of street language. Could you discuss the role of language in your plays?

MAMET: It's poetic language. It's not an attempt to capture language as much as it is an attempt to create language. We see this in various periods in the evolution of American drama. And when it's good, to the most extent, it's called realism. All realism means is that the language strikes a responsive chord. The language in my plays is not realistic but poetic. The words sometimes have a musical quality to them. It's language that is tailor-made for the stage. People don't always talk the way my characters do in real life, although they may use some of the same words. Think of Odets, Wilder. That stuff is not realistic; it is poetic. Or Philip Barry: you might say some part of his genius was to capture the way a certain class of people spoke. He didn't know how those people spoke, but he was creating a poetic impression, creating that reality. It's not a matter, in *Lakeboat* or *Sexual Perversity in Chicago* or *Edmond* or my other plays, of my "interpretation" of how these people talk. It is an illusion. It's like when Gertrude Stein said to Picasso, "That portrait doesn't look like me." Picasso said, "It will." It's an illusion. Juvenile delinquents *acted* like Marlon Brando in *The Wild One*, right? It wasn't the other way around. It was life imitating art! So, in this sense my plays don't mirror what's going on in the streets. It's something different. As Oscar Wilde said, life imitates art! We didn't have those big pea soup fogs until somebody described them.

ROUDANÉ: Despite your social exposures of human folly, one could argue that you're a playwright concerned with existentialist themes. That is, you seem fixed on objectifying certain crimes of the heart: the failure to communicate authentically with the self and the other. Possible? What do you think?

MAMET: Concerning ourselves with the individual's soul is certainly the fit province of drama. I really never understood what existentialism meant. I've tried a whole long time. It has something to do with sleeping with Simone de Beauvoir, but other than that I'm kind of lost. But I suppose my plays are about the individual's inner spirit. I think that's what it's about. The purpose of the theater, to me, is to examine the paradox between the fact that everyone tries to do well but that few, if any, succeed. The theater concerns metaphysics; our relationship to God; and ethics or our relationships to each other.

ROUDANÉ: Whereas many contemporary playwrights create antimimetic plays, you seem to rework a more classic, Ibsenesque dramatic form: the well-made play. Could you discuss the dramatic form of your work?

MAMET: I'm sure *trying* to do the well-made play. It is the hardest thing to do. I like this form because it's the structure imitating

49

human perception. It is not just something made up out of old cloth. This is the way we perceive a play: with a clear beginning, a middle, and an end. So, when one wants to best utilize the theater, one would try to structure a play in a way that is congruent with the way the mind perceives it. Everybody wants to hear a story with a beginning, middle, and end. The only people who don't tell stories that way are playwrights! Finally, that's all that theater is: storytelling. The theater's no different from gossip, from dirty jokes, from what Uncle Max did on his fishing trip; it's just telling stories in that particular way in which one tells stories in the theater. Look at *Sexual Perversity in Chicago* or *The Duck Variations*. To me recognizing the storytelling dimension of playwriting is a beginning of a mark of maturity. That's why I embrace it. Nobody in the audience wants to hear a joke without the punch line. Nobody wants to hear how *feelingly* a guy can tell a joke. But we would like to find out what happened to the farmer's daughter. That's what Ibsen did.

ROUDANÉ: Has your cinema work—the screenplays for *The Postman Always Rings Twice* and *The Verdict*—helped your playwriting technique?

MAMET: My work in Hollywood has helped me very much. The good movie has to be written very clearly. The action has to be very clear. You can't take time out to digress to the highways and the byways of what might happen. You've got to tell the story. And I am trying to do this in my plays. I mean, I wrote a lot of plays about feeling slices of interesting life. Nothing wrong with that—I just didn't know any better. I'm talking about my earlier plays—*Lakeboat,* for example, and others with those episodic glimpses of humanity. Those were fine, but now I am trying to do something different.

ROUDANÉ What's the effect of Hollywood and mass media on the theater today?

MAMET: It ain't good, but it doesn't make any difference. They're flooding the market with trash. The taste and the need for a real theatrical experience, which is an experience in which the audience can come to commune not so much with the actors but with themselves and what they know to be true, just increases. Everyone's pallet has been dulled to an extraordinary degree by the mass media. But that's just the way it is. Television, of course, isn't an art form. It might be, but nobody's figured out how to make it so. It's not even a question of doing good work on television, which happens once in a while. It's that nobody seems to understand the essential nature of the media. I certainly don't.

ROUDANÉ: Could you elaborate on the actor's relationship with an audience?

MAMET: The young artist has to get better every year, or the audience doesn't grow just numerically. It's not even a question of growing spiritually. What happens if the audience doesn't grow is that everything deteriorates. You don't have enough income coming in to support the artists. So, you start having to appeal to a larger and larger audience, which means you start getting worse and worse. This is exactly what happened to Broadway. You have to take advantage of people; rather than appeal to a native constant constituency, you're appealing to people who ain't never going to come back, who don't really have any expectations but know they better get something for their forty-five dollars. So we show them a hundred people tap dancing on stage instead of *Death of a Salesman*.

ROUDANÉ: You've said that acting has nothing to do with emotion but with action: "Stick to the action" and "Practical aesthetics." What do you mean?

MAMET: The action is what *is* the character doing. That's what the actor must do. Acting has absolutely nothing to do with emotion or feeling emotional. It has a little to do with emotion as playing a violin does. You have to study emotion. People don't go to the theater to hear the emotion; they go to hear the concerto. The emotions should take place in the *audience*. It just doesn't have to be dealt with from the actor's viewpoint.

ROUDANÉ: How might you answer the charge that your plays tend always to focus on the negative, cynical side of experience?

MAMET: I've never heard that charge, so I say that's interesting. But it's easy to cheer people up if you lie to them. Very easy. Acting President Reagan says he's not going to raise taxes. Of course, he's going to raise taxes; he has to raise taxes. Although it's easy to cheer people up by lying to them, in my plays I'm not interested in doing that. I'm not a doctor; I'm a writer.

ROUDANÉ: In *A Life in the Theatre* Robert and John undergo a role reversal: John's career rises; Robert's declines. What were you suggesting about the theatrical world in this play?

MAMET: The play is not so much about the theatrical world, although that's the metaphor. The play concerns how youth and age talk to each other. John and Robert show something about our inability to communicate experience. While this notion isn't really present in *The Duck Variations* because George and Emil are the same age, it's there to a certain extent in *American Buffalo* and in *Lakeboat*.

51

ROUDANÉ: Could you talk about the way in which form and content coalesce to generate the creative process within your plays?

MAMET: My real concern always is with the play as a whole, with writing the play. There's a curious phenomena that happens when you compose a play or movie. The creation very quickly takes on a life of its own. I have no idea why; it's just words on paper. But the art I can compare it to in my experience is carving wood. You start to carve wood, and very quickly the thing takes on a life of its own. Part of the wisdom of wood carving is to realize when the wood is telling you where it wants to go. Obviously, it's going to be a duck if you start out to make a duck, but the kind of duck it's going to be is largely dictated by the kind of wood. And there is a similar phenomenon in writing drama. You start out with an idea, it becomes something else, and part of the wisdom is learning to listen to the material itself. Much of the material, of course, is in the subconscious.

ROUDANÉ: What is your artistic response to what some may call a "Business as Sacrament Ethic" in America?

MAMET: One has to learn something that can't be taken away: you have to learn your craft. As Sherwood Anderson said, a man who has a trade is a man who can tell the rest of the world to go to hell! If you want to become a commodity, which is what most actors and actresses tend to become, then you have to rely on the goodness of others, not only for your bread but for your happiness. That's not very much fun.

ROUDANÉ: As a writer, you're confronted with a universe that is largely hostile, even absurd. Flux, struggle, the precariousness of existence itself is the norm. Given this reality, what is your artistic response to such a world?

MAMET: My response is always the same thing; it's never any different. Tolstoy said it's a mistake to think that human nature ever changes. This is the only world that I live in, so (a) it would be silly for me to say something else because it isn't something else; and (b) I am part of it. So, the ability to perceive the problem doesn't necessarily mean that one is not part of that problem. Of course, I am part of the problem. It's the same thing as people driving home from the country on Sunday night. Look at all these assholes driving, getting in my way! It's modern life. I *am* one of those assholes.

ROUDANÉ: Do you see yourself, as a writer, as one who shatters illusions or as some kind of truth-teller?

MAMET: No. I am just a storyteller. Keep in mind that playwrights—O'Neill or Albee or myself—know as little about what we do as anyone else. We're just storytellers, that's all. It just so happens that society rewards some of us in extraordinary ways because the society is desperately betting that one of us is going to say something that might offer some comfort. Our job, as writers, is to do our jobs. I was thinking the other day, I have trouble sometimes finishing a lot of plays. But then I always try to remind myself it took Sophocles eighteen years to write *Oedipus Rex;* that's also because he wasn't trying to write *Gigi*.

A Matter of Perception

Hank Nuwer

Hank Nuwer met with Mamet over tea at the Drake Hotel in Chicago, where Mamet's one-act play *The Spanish Prisoner* and *The Shawl* were being staged at the Briar Street Theatre.

NUWER: A memorable line from your play *The Water Engine* states, "The mind of man is less perturbed by a mystery it cannot explain than by an explanation it cannot understand." Would you say that your plays deepen the mysteries of life?

MAMET: I don't think so. I think the purpose of theater is not to deepen the mysteries of life but to celebrate the mysteries of life. That's what a good play does, and that's what a good play has done for ten thousand years.

NUWER: Your purpose is not to try to explain the mysteries?

MAMET: You *can't* explain them; that's why they're mysteries. The purpose of the theater is not primarily to deal with social issues; it's to deal with spiritual issues.

NUWER: Saint Paul said that one must put away the things of a child when manhood is reached. Does it seem to you that making a living out of creating theater in effect allows you to continue playing with the things of a child?

MAMET: I don't think they're the things of a child at all. It [the theater] is the *most* essential aspect of modern life. What is missing from modern life is spirituality—the connection to the greater truths of the universe. What is missing is the feeling of knowing our place and a sense of belonging. It's the theater's job to address the ques-

From "Two Gentlemen of Chicago," *South Carolina Review* 17, no. 2 (1985): 9–14. Copyright © Clemson University. Reprinted with permission of Clemson University.

tions of "What is our place in the universe?" and "How can we live in a world in which we know we're going to die?"

NUWER: What is the premise behind *Glengarry Glen Ross*?

MAMET: This play is very much about work and about how one is altered by one's job.

NUWER: The main characters are real estate salesmen whose job is peddling worthless property. Are you dumping on such salesmen?

MAMET: I don't write plays to dump on people. I write plays about people whom I love and am fascinated by. A lot of times I want to write letters to newspapers to dump on people, but, gratefully, I can usually resist that impulse.

NUWER: *Glengarry Glen Ross*'s characters are all frustrated in their struggles to attain success. Are you optimistic that an individual can get what he wants out of life?

MAMET: Sure. The only person who *can* get what he wants is the individual man. You can't do it as a race; you can't do it as a culture. In the theater an individual has to come to terms with what he wants and how capable he is of getting it. Making peace with the gods— that's what drama's all about.

NUWER: The sales manager [Williamson] in *Glengarry* never regards his salesmen as human beings. Can you say you hold no dislike for him?

MAMET: I felt he was doing his job—doing the job of a sales manager. The job of a sales manager is not to empathize. Irrespective of whether or not it's a "good" job or whether he likes his job is not the point; his job is to inspire, frighten, tempt, cajole, and do any other thing he can do to increase sales. When things fall apart he indulges in the very human propensity to play "catch-up ball" because people have been abusing him throughout the play.

NUWER: At a given time how many ideas for plays lie dormant in your notebooks?

MAMET: Always a few—between two and three or four and five. It's easier to come up with ideas than execute them. I have millions of ideas in my trunk. They're not good for anything but ballast.

NUWER: Do you like to read biographies of other writers and playwrights—Eugene O'Neill perhaps?

MAMET: No. After all, everybody had a childhood. I take that back. I did like Ted Morgan's biography of Maugham.

NUWER: Are you a voracious reader, however? What about your contemporaries? What playwrights today do you admire?

MAMET: I read everything. I'll read this table if there's nothing else to read. There are several of my contemporaries I'm very impressed by. My particular taste runs from Richard Nelson, Wally Shawn, and Romulus Linney to John Guare and David Hare.

NUWER: Are you a good self-editor?

MAMET: Oh, yeah.

NUWER: Does your wife [actress Lindsay Crouse] ever edit what you write?

MAMET: Oh, she's a much, much better editor than I am. When it comes to prose, she's the real thing. She's my best editor. My wife had a classical education in New York and at Radcliffe.

NUWER: Can you reveal a bit about your lifestyle with your wife? Maybe give a voyeuristic tour of your home perhaps?

MAMET: We live in Vermont in an old house—a simple farmhouse with simple furniture, soap on the sink, and a small alarm clock on the mantelpiece. Basically, it's a city boy's dream.

NUWER: Anything else?

MAMET: I don't want to talk about my personal life [*chuckles*]. I came to talk about me.

NUWER: Are you concerned about your "public image and stature" as a playwright?

MAMET: All those things are really secondary. The older I get the more I like to think about my life than my career. I'm a writer; I write for a living. I have a certain high profile for the moment; that seems to be how the universe has turned. My job is to write: it's not unpleasant by any means. I've always been interested in what's happening about me—that's what I write about. I don't do "research."

NUWER: Would you rather discover a truth out of your own mind or your own experiences?

MAMET: Well, to discover a truth is to have it come out of your own mind. It's not an objective reality. The line between seeing someone do something in a restaurant and imagining what their motives might have been and seeing someone *almost* do something in a restaurant is not that great. It's a matter of perception. Finally, writing is expressing a perception about the way things are, irrespective of whether or not you've seen things concretely be that way.

NUWER: Ever act out any destructive impulses?

MAMET: Oh, yeah—going to work for a living and satisfying the impulse to stay in school. I was never much of a student.

NUWER: How do you feel about all that lost energy of the 1960s that seems to have found few authentic voices out of all that potential?

MAMET: Depression. Obviously, it wasn't enough to be angry at the way the world was. The important thing about the 1960s is the same thing that Christ was telling us two thousand years ago. It's not our job to change the world. It's our job to act according to precepts we perceive to be right.

NUWER: Do you feel your end has been preshaped by destiny?

MAMET: Destiny shapes everybody's end. Don Marquis said that the ultimate reconciliation of the free world and the doctrine of pre-destination is that man is free to choose to do whatever he wants—and that whatever he chooses to do will turn out wrong [*laughter*].

NUWER: Is there anything you have trouble tolerating?

MAMET: As Mr. Wilde said, "I can stand anything but discomfort."

NUWER: Would you have been an equal success in some other field?

MAMET: I think so. I've always been driven. I've read about a lot of hustlers with admiration, I think, because in moments of stress I lack those skills that I can write about.

NUWER: Among your many jobs in Chicago while working to-ward recognition as a playwright was a stint at Hugh Hefner's *Oui* as an editor. Did you enjoy that job?

MAMET: I had a great time; I had a wonderful time. I had a beau-tiful cork-lined office that had these blue lines—stats (photocopies of issue pages before printing) of naked women. I used to stare at the naked women until I found something interesting to say about them. It was a great job.

NUWER: Was the Midwest a good place to grow up?

MAMET: The Midwest was a *great* place to grow up, especially for a writer. It nurtures virtues that are good for a writer, at least for me and many twentieth-century writers: keep your eyes open, your mouth closed, work hard, be a part of the community, and tell the truth.

NUWER: The South is said by writer Barry Hannah to like its writ-ers dead or away. What about Chicago? Do you feel appreciated in your hometown?

MAMET: Oh yeah, very much so. Chicago's always been the best town in the country for writers. Chicago's always honored its writers, and the best writers always came to Chicago.

NUWER: While you were growing up, did you have an imaginary friend similar to the one you call Rain Boy in *Dark Pony*?

MAMET: Basically, that's what a politician is to grown-up people—an imaginary friend. We endow them with the qualities of per-ceptiveness, strength, and caring. They frighten us that they might

57

withdraw their love. Doctors are imaginary friends. We endow them with curative powers—endow them with a concern they don't really have. The same is true of the legal profession [*grins*]. Plays are very real friends. Nina, in Chekhov's *The Seagull*, over the years has attained real reality for us. If you read *War and Peace* fifteen times the people in *War and Peace* become your imaginary friends. In the illusion we see something of ourselves, and it supplies something we need.

NUWER: Do you have any diversions to speak of that interest you?

MAMET: I have diverse and sundry hobbies that keep me from my work.

NUWER: Are you ever bored watching actors mouth your lines?

MAMET: I'm never bored watching actors, especially in rehearsal. You see them do things that break your heart all the time.

NUWER: Do you notice any difference in audiences, say Chicago as opposed to New York as opposed to London?

MAMET: No, not a lot. I think audiences are basically the same all over. It helps not to have an audience prejudiced against one for whatever reason. In Chicago we prize the virtues of continuity. The Goodman [Theatre] audience knows it is going to see something that has a modicum of integrity to it because they're familiar with the playwright's previous work. This means that they're going to be relaxed when they come to the theater. But this doesn't mean I cultivate a specific audience.

NUWER: Do you work well when you need to flatten back your ears and rework a play just before its opening?

MAMET: Oh, sure. That's when I work best. It's instant gratification. Someone will say to you, "You did that in a half-hour?" and you'll shrug, "Oh yeah, yeah!" [*laughter*]. Most plays I'm rewriting until the critics come and sometimes thereafter. Many times an audience will help figure how to get a play right. You might think there is something they might not understand, and so you're overly clear about it. If they understand before your explanation is over, you're ruining your play. You've got to cut that explanation. Or there might be a point that's clear to you but unclear to them. That point has to be clarified.

NUWER: Ever look in the mirror and imagine your hair receding and wrinkles everywhere to figure out what kind of "Grand Old Man of the Theater" you'd make?

MAMET: I always thought I'd be a great "Grand Old Man of

the Theater." I look forward to being a crusty yet kindhearted curmudgeon.

NUWER: Let's say you've been invited to write your own epitaph for your death sometime late next century. What would you write?

MAMET: I think all of us would like to write our own. We'd tell everyone the same thing: "I *told* you that you were going to miss me."

Celebrating the Capacity for Self-Knowledge

Henry I. Schvey

Henry Schvey's interview with David Mamet was conducted in New York on January 2, 1986, following a performance of a Mamet double bill, *The Shawl* and *Prairie du Chien*.

You grew up in Chicago?

Yes. And then came to New York, to study acting at the Neighborhood Playhouse, a school of theater where I came back later to work as an actor and director. I kind of stumbled upon a career as a playwright. I became a playwright because I was an actor, and I started directing because I wasn't a very good actor, and I started writing because I was working with very young actors, and there was nothing for them to do. I started writing because nothing existed for twelve twenty-three-year-old actors to do.

And where did you study drama and dramatic literature?

I studied at the bookstore. But the Neighborhood Playhouse was founded on the teachings of Stanislavski, who was very influenced by Aristotle: most of the Stanislavski system is a practical aesthetic for the actor based on the Aristotelian idea of unity.

Which playwrights made the deepest impression on you?

Well, Pinter and Beckett really made the most impression on me, because I discovered them at the time when I had no connection with any sort of dramatic literature—my late teens and twenties—and this was the first exposure to drama as literature, drama

From Henry I. Schvey and the editors of *New Theatre Quarterly* 4, no. 13 (1988): 89–96. Copyright © Henry I. Schvey. Reprinted with permission.

as a living expression of things that people felt. It was kind of a revelation.

You grew up in the 1960s, and what was fashionable then was a much less verbally oriented kind of theater. And on one level at least your plays are fairly static—though not at all in terms of the emotional drives that lurk underneath. Do you attribute this again to the influence of Pinter and Beckett?

Well, a play is not a dance. Unless you're going to have a sword-fight, you're not going to have a lot of jumping around: the action in the play means the progress of a character toward a goal on the stage, because that is the convention of the theater—to reach up and grab a ring to uncover some truth, which usually takes a lot of talk. I have always thought that mixed media and performance art was basically garbage, very decadent, and the sign of a deep unrest, the sign really of a cultural disease—a turning of one's back on a regenerative cultural institution in favor of novelty. The whole idea of performance art, people covering themselves with chicken blood . . .

Do you feel that it served a purpose as a phenomenon in the 1960s?

What do you remember about what happened then? Nothing at all. It had purpose in the way a guy goes into McDonald's, pulls a gun, and kills a bunch of people. Obviously, there is some meaning. But it's not very constructive. The trick of the light was that we looked for ways in which these phenomena were constructed because they seemed to want to be described in aesthetic terms because they seemed to partake of theater. But really they don't, I think. It's like criticizing somebody's bad draft of a play that should have been thrown in the wastebasket instead of on to the stage. And the real answer to the playwright is, "Yes, there is something there and you should be looking at the work. Why don't you throw it out and attack it again?"

Does your antagonism to these experiments lie in the fact that they did not establish any sort of structural pattern?

The proof of it is in the eating. People remember nothing of the happenings of the 1960s and will remember nothing of the performance art of the 1980s. They have no capacity to move, whereas the purpose of the theater is to transcend the individual conscious mind, to put the spectator in a communion with his or her fellows on the stage and also in the audience, so as to address problems that cannot be addressed by reason. It's not that the problems are absurd, which the performance artist would say, but, rather, that they are so deeply subconscious that they must be treated symbolically.

61

All of us read Artaud, we're very influenced by Artaud, but finally it does not work. It is like black people trying to be white or white people trying to be black. There is a certain learned, habituated, perhaps even genetic cultural need for the rituals of the culture in which you exist and which is your culture. You might try to escape it by wishing that you could, and that's a kind of fascistic wish fulfilment: you have to ignore a hell of a lot to enjoy yourself at such a performance. You have to pretend that you are something that you are not.

You have to become a child, uncivilized, without two thousand years of Western civilization?

Yes, you've got to become the noble savage. And the test of it is the very critical reaction, which is obliged to be so abstract, and to intellectualize about events that are supposed to be the very opposite of that impulse. Robert Wilson or Christo—I mean, those people would sneer if you tried to apply traditional critical norms to their work.

Have you seen any works by Robert Wilson, for example?

Yes. I like his style. I like *Einstein on the Beach.* I saw it at Carnegie Hall.

That would seem to be the epitome of the performance art of the 1980s, and yet you have said that you liked it . . .

I saw it as an opera. I can sit through *Tristan;* that is pretty long, too.

It reminded me very much also of Wagner, with its delayed resolutions. So, you did enjoy it, then, as opera, as visual spectacle?

Yes, but it is the sign of a very decayed and decadent society that we no longer apply ourselves to the old norms to renew ourselves but have to find new ones. We are so frightened. Those things that have sustained us for two thousand years we no longer retreat to. We have to find new ones.

You've described your own work as being regenerative. In what sense do you see contemporary drama, specifically your own plays, as having that sort of sustaining function?

Well, the function of drama, as Stanislavski said, is to bring to the stage the life of the human soul so that the community can participate therein, so we can celebrate those things that we really know to be true. Some of those things are funny, and some are sad, and some are shocking, but that is traditionally the purpose of drama.

In fact, you see your own work as being this collective celebration, just as many of the people involved in performance art would also see it—as celebratory?

I see it as trying to partake of the ideal of theater, and that is what the ideal of theater is.

And yet a lot of your work is focused on the exposure of hypocrisy. Cutting through facades, cutting through surfaces. Manipulation is very important in your plays—as, indeed, it is in Pinter.

Well, as it is in Shakespeare. Drama is basically about lies, somebody lying to somebody.

When I met Arthur Miller recently, he was extremely pessimistic about the course of American drama. How do you feel about the direction that American drama is taking?

Well, American drama is just taking the same direction that American culture is taking. I mean, it would be rather surprising if we had a flourishing, happy theater in this country.

On the other hand, your plays are being seen and appreciated. They are being increasingly recognized, and plays by Sam Shepard and Lanford Wilson are being performed in New York City and attracting audiences. Serious drama seems to be finding some sort of audience in this country.

Well, yes and no. Not for those of us who lived through the off-off-Broadway era in the early and mid-1970s, when there really was a flourishing theater that allowed all sorts of voices to be heard. What is happening now seems dull as dirt. Society has, as it usually does in moments of stress, elected a couple of people more or less by lottery, to stand for the presence of theater. In the 1970s there would have been fourteen or twenty or forty theaters needed to put on plays. We don't have that anymore. Broadway theater is a joke—the prices are too high—and rents are too high for the off-Broadway theaters to exist. *And* rents are too high for young actors to live here in New York.

You're better off in Chicago.

Sure.

Doesn't it take considerable courage to buck the system of the New York establishment?

Well, I wasn't bucking it. I had my own theater in Chicago. We were putting on plays all the time, so I wasn't bucking the system. It was paying the rent. One had to do what one knew how to do. And that is how we both got the audience and kept the audience in Chicago. From being identifiable we brought them something that we also wanted to say.

It is exciting that a number of people involved in Chicago theatre have made tremendous breakthroughs now in New York. Do you yourself feel excited about that and about your double bill (The Shawl and Prairie du Chien) being chosen to reopen Lincoln Center?

It's lovely. But the resurgence of Chicago theater has been going on for a long, long time, and the first big wave was in the 1960s. A lot of people not just from one Chicago theater but from several Chicago theaters burst on the scene. And then it happened again in the late 1970s. It doesn't have anything to do with me—I just happened to be there. There were different schools, playwrights, theaters, companies, all with very separate identities. There was a little bit of crossover, but mainly what they indicated was that Chicago as a community likes to support new theater.

Glengarry Glen Ross *was a watershed in terms of your work. Do you see it as an artistic breakthrough as well? Or more as a continuation?*

Well, it's kind of . . . a bastard play. It's formally a gang comedy in the tradition of *The Front Page* or *Men in White*. And the first act is episodic, although like a detective story, almost gothic. The second act is a very traditional formal last act of a comedy drama.

What makes it different, though? Why did it get the response it did?

I don't know. It's not as good a play as *American Buffalo*—say, for example, by Aristotelian standards . . . and the poetry isn't as good. But I guess it speaks to something that is current in the collective unconscious of the country at this time: the idea of the difference between business and fraud, what's permissible in the name of getting a living and what isn't.

In that sense, do you see it as a continuation of the themes of American Buffalo? *I mean,* business, *of course, is a keyword in* American Buffalo *as well . . .*

Yes, I think in many ways it is.

The language of Glengarry Glen Ross *struck people as being something new. I don't know if you saw it that way. I don't mean simply the use of obscenities but the poetry of the play.*

I kind of thought that was how I was writing all along, but if people want to appreciate it I am certainly not going to stop them! The play got a lot of lovely response from all sorts of different people. That's nice.

But, seen in terms of the plot, Glengarry Glen Ross *could be perceived as a fairly mundane exercise, a "whodunnit."*

Well, so is *Hamlet* a whodunnit. But *Glengarry* really isn't a whodunnit; it is a gang comedy, which is a play about revealing the specific natures and the unifying natures of a bunch of people who happen to be involved in one enterprise.

Did you want us to be sympathetic to the figure of Roma, the slickest salesman?

I think so. I always want everyone to be sympathetic to all the characters. Because when you aren't, what you are doing is writing a melodrama with good guys and bad guys. Drama is really about conflicting impulses in the individual. That is what *all* drama is about. And with the birth of the antagonist you get two people on the stage. What you are doing, just as in a dream, is taking one individual and splitting him into two parts. And, with the further elaboration of drama into more characters, always what is happening is the splitting of the nature of one individual into many more parts. In the gang comedy what you are doing is again splitting one individual into many, many more parts. Because it is a comedy as opposed to a tragedy, or even a drama, the confrontation is between individuals and their environment much more than between individuals opposed to each other. So, what you are doing, unlike in a drama or a tragedy, is splitting one individual into a protagonist and an antagonist. And cloning off aspects of the character of the individual.

So, all the characters in that play are aspects of a single person?

Sure. Just as they are in a dream or in a myth. And, as I said, the difference between a comedy and a drama is that in the drama or the tragedy the two major aspects would be two vehemently opposed aspects of one individual. In the comedy what they are is many, somewhat dissimilar renditions of the same attitude. Which I think is true in all gang comedies, and it is certainly true of *Glengarry.*

Some of your plays, notably Glengarry, *in their attitude toward big business, have been compared with Arthur Miller's* Death of a Salesman.

Yes, but *Death of a Salesman* is really not concerned with big business. That is the difference: *Death of a Salesman* is a tragedy. The gang comedy is really concerned with the effects of the specific environment, which in a gang comedy is almost always the workplace, on the people engaged—whereas in *Death of a Salesman* Miller is concerned with the family. It is a tragedy about a man who happens to be a salesman.

A lot of great American drama is family drama, yet this is something that you have not really written very much . . .

Reunion is about the family. *American Buffalo,* sneakily enough, is really a tragedy about life in the family—so that is really the play that is closest to *Death of a Salesman,* though it's something I only realized afterward. Formally, the two are very closely tied.

I thought that The Shawl *exploded with constant surprises in a way that I find a play should, constantly overturning the audience's expectations.*

Oh good! This goes back to writing for movies. Writing for movies is really all about revealing information: when and how you reveal information. Structurally, that is how you are thinking all the time. That is all there is in a movie—structure.

What makes a play like The Shawl *so effective, like the way that the first scene is totally undercut by the second scene, is the underlying structural irony that makes it really spring to life in the mind of the audience. And so too with* Glengarry? *The idea of exposure? Seeing the real motives that are behind apparently honest responses?*

Yes, but I mean this goes back to Aristotle. It's really a twentieth-century version of the idea that what the hero is following and what he ends up with may be two very different things, but they are nonetheless related in the subconscious. The older guy in *The Shawl* wants to teach a lesson to his young lover and ends up experiencing a true psychic vision. But both of them are really part of the same objective, just as Oedipus wants to find out why there is a plague in Thebes and then ends up finding out that he killed his dad and screwed his mom. What happens at the crucial moment, as Aristotle says, is that the protagonist undergoes both recognition of the situation and a reversal of the situation. And that is what strikes the responsive chord in the audience—that what is revealed to have been the low objective is transmogrified into the high objective. And we realize that the high objective is carried in the low objective all the time. That is how Aristotle says that tragedy works, and that is the essential celebratory element of theater. That what we celebrate with the audience is the capacity for strife, the capacity for revelation, and the capacity for self-knowledge.

Both in ourselves and in the character?

If we celebrate it in the character, we *will* celebrate it in ourselves.

I found it very exciting how the different levels of irony are gone through in The Shawl. *First, we assume that events are as they seem, that there is an actual introductory meeting preparatory to a seance, then we see the man simply as a charlatan, and then, of course, we see something more. Yet you leave it open at the end as far as the audience's response is concerned.*

I think I do to a certain extent. The guy is expatiating throughout to his young friend. And that is what he is saying to the woman too, that you cannot overcome your skepticism because our nature finally protects us. Finally, we have to make up our own mind about what it is that we have seen.

But you believe, then, that he had had some sort of moment of intense clarity?

Yes, I think so.

Tell me about how you got interested in the subject matter used in The Shawl.

I am very interested in magic, and I have a good friend who is a magician and a scholar of magic—a curator of a prestigious magical collection in addition to being a performer. And what he said to me was he found both the séance in *The Shawl* and the mentalism act that I created very interesting, although I had had no exposure to the craft. I did do a certain amount of research on mentalism and on cold reading, which is what *The Shawl* is about. But I had never actually seen these things done. And so I had to go back to square one and create them myself. I think the same is true of me as a playwright. I did not have a lot of exposure to dramatic literature until later in my life. All I had was an exposure to Aristotle, an exposure to the rules of acting and the rules of directing, and so I had to create plays "on the hop" as I went along.

The Shawl *could easily be read as a play about fraud, about charlatanism. And on one level, of course, it is. But, in fact, the play is ultimately extremely optimistic about the possibilities of self-exploration and is not a cynical play at all. Do you think that that is true of other works of yours as well?*

I hope it is true of all of them.

In what way would you apply that to Glengarry Glen Ross *or to* American Buffalo?

Well, *American Buffalo* is classical tragedy, the protagonist of which is the junk store owner who is trying to teach a lesson in how to behave like the excellent man to his young ward. And he is tempted by the devil into betraying all his principles. Once he does that, he is incapable of even differentiating between simple lessons of fact and betrays himself into allowing Teach to beat up this young fellow whom he loves. He then undergoes, as I have said, recognition in reversal—realizing that all this comes out of his vanity, that because he abdicated a moral position for one moment in favor of some momentary gain, he has let anarchy into his life and has come close to killing the thing he loves. And he realizes at the end of the play that he has made a huge mistake, that, rather than his young ward needing lessons in being an excellent man, it is he himself who needs those lessons. That is what *American Buffalo* is about.

Often your plays involve a very close relationship between two people, probably more than those of anyone else writing now. A Life in the Theatre *is another example of this very intense concern with the relationship between characters . . .*

Yes, but it is a different kind of a play. To me, *A Life in the Theatre* is about the necessity, the desire, the impossibility, of communicating wisdom. It is about the relationship between young people and old people. Or let's say that to a certain extent the form it takes is epic, in which one scene is played over in different guises thirty times.

What about Edmond? *How do you see that play fitting into your oeuvre so far?*

Edmond is a morality play about modern society. Jung said that sometimes it really is *not* the individual who is sick but the society that is sick. I don't know whether I believe that completely or not, but that is what *Edmond* is about—a man trying to discover himself and what he views as a sick society.

Which plays of yours do you think have been least well understood?

People do not understand *The Woods* very well—I think partly because it is a play about heterosexuality, which is just not a hot theatrical topic over here. It is something that you look at in the popular media, a subject that people would rather not address—why men and women have a difficult time trying to get along with each other.

What about the tone of the play? It is a rather lyrical play in contrast with other things you have written. Do you think that that may also have affected its reception?

That may be so. We don't have a great tradition of liking American poetic drama. It is a play that is going to be appreciated much more in the coming years, because it is a wonderful play, a very well-written play . . . because it has a lot of meaning. It is a dreamy play, full of the symbology of dream and the symbology of myth, which are basically the same thing.

Are there any other plays that you'd like to see come in from the wilderness?

If people like everything you do, then you are doing something wrong, I believe. That is especially true if you are rather prolific, as I am. People sometimes find it hard to make an honest evaluation of your plays based on objective critical standards. They would be horrified to assume that the vast majority of what I write, taken as a body, can be any good, because there is too much of it. This is one of the downsides of being prolific.

Perhaps you have to establish an audience that is able to respond to extremes like Edmond, *on the one hand, and* The Woods, *on the other?*

I don't know whether one ever does establish such an audience. Some people are going to like one kind of play; some are going to like another. Some are going to overlap, but no one is going to like all of them. So, I don't even know whether I would want to bring a play back and ram it down people's throats. I have gleaned a whole lot of praise and appreciation and respect for various different projects in different quarters. And a whole lot of flak for others. I have nothing to complain about.

What about the temptations of cinema? You have already written several very successful screenplays, including The Postman Always Rings Twice *and* The Verdict, *and apparently your next work is going to be a film. Do you see cinema as being in competition with drama in America? I mean the lure of fabulous sums of money, tempting certain playwrights away from the stage?*

I have made a lot more money from writing plays than I have from writing movies, although I must say that I am in the minority in terms of being able to make money in the theater. What cinema offers is an outlet for production in a way that the theater doesn't. For example, I wrote three movies last year—I can get them put on, and that's fine. If I wrote three plays, as I used to do, I would get lambasted because nobody in the critical establishment or in the community wants to see three plays by one person in one year.

What are the different requirements of the media as specifically related to your own vision, to your own work?

It's like painting and sculpture: some of the ideas are very much the same, but . . . well, when you write a movie, you have got to describe pictures, that's what it's for. If a movie were to be *the* excellent movie, it would have absolutely no dialogue in it. But with a play everything takes place in dialogue; all the action that takes place between two people has to take place right there.

Well, you can change the scene, of course . . .

Aristotle says that you can't.

Do you go along with that?

Sure, I mean you've seen my plays.

So, you are writing very much in the tradition of Aristotelian drama, concerned with the restrictions it places on you?

Sure. It makes better plays.

Where do you see your own future direction? Combining cinema and theater? You are not going to abandon one or the other?

I hope to direct a whole bunch of movies and maybe come back and direct a whole bunch of plays. And write some more plays, too.

69

As a director, obviously you have definite ideas about how your plays should be done. Are you pleased with the way your plays have been directed?

Probably there are things that I would have changed had I done the directing, but I cannot think of what they were.

What particular elements, from the directing standpoint or from the acting standpoint, should one bear in mind when working with your scripts?

Keep it simple: that's the beginning and the end of it.

Concentrating on the actors' voices, on the language, particularly?

No: concentrating on what the characters *want*. But, when in doubt, don't do anything. That is what I think. My plays really don't call for, nor will they support, a lot of invention. I always think of something Stanislavski said—that any director who has to do something interesting with the text does not understand the text. So, that would be my dictum, along with Stanislavski. Don't be "interesting." If you are doing Shakespeare, it does not make any difference if you put it in evening clothes or the Wild West to the audience's enjoyment of the play. Because what they're following are the actions of the characters.

But with your plays, surely, the setting is very important.

Yes, it is important in *American Buffalo*, for example, that the setting is a junk shop.

Right. But does it make any difference whether American Buffalo *is set in a realistic space or not?*

Well, finally, it is a play. The audience is going to know it's a play. The important thing is—what does the junk shop mean to the play? What is the active aspect of the junk shop? Is it a place where people can support themselves, a place where they can be alone? Having made that election, then you know what kind of junk shop it should be.

How important, say, would a box set be for American Buffalo?

It depends on the theater. And also on what the set *means*. And then you know how it should look.

Do you think that the set means restriction, claustrophobia, in that play?

I don't know. I never write stage directions. I don't care about them. I figure that most of what needs to be said is what is being said in the dialogue. Beyond that, decisions are going to be made by the director and designer anyway.

Do you think America is a particularly fertile place to emerge as a playwright today, as compared with the exciting days of the 1960s?

I don't even know whether it was like that in the 1960s. I think I just kind of got lucky.

70

That would tend to make one feel very pessimistic about the state of dramatic art in the United States. Would you share that view?

Absolutely, sure. In a very, very strictly structured, increasingly authoritarian environment, which is life in this country, if one pursues a career one of the main aspects of which is being an iconoclast, one is not going to have the happiest time of it.

You see your own plays as being iconoclastic?

Sure. In the sense of tearing down the icons of American business and some of the myths about this country. This is one of the jobs of the writer.

To force people to question accepted values?

Not to force people to question but to question for themselves.

Would you consider yourself a political playwright? Is that a label that means anything?

No, I don't think I am a political playwright. I think I probably have as good a chance of ending up in jail as anybody else, but I don't think I am a political playwright.

Comics like Me Always Want to Be Tragedians

David Savran

David Savran interviewed David Mamet in New York on February 11, 1987.

What led you to become a playwright?

I was an actor, and I started directing actors. Then I was teaching and directing students, and I started writing, really, to illustrate the points that I was talking about as a teacher. I started a theater company, and we didn't have any money to pay royalties. And that's how I started playwriting.

Before that, what got you interested in theater?

There was a community theater in Chicago, and I spent a lot of time hanging out at Second City. At that time in Chicago it was just in the air.

During that period what playwrights particularly influenced you?

Lanford Wilson was a big influence on me—the collections of his early plays, like *Rimers of Eldritch* and *The Madness of Lady Bright*. There was also a book from the New American Library—I think it was called *New Voices in the American Theatre*—that was a major influence on all of us who were young in the 1960s. It included *Mrs. Dalley Has a Lover* and *Upstairs Sleeping* and a play by Murray Schisgal. *Waiting for Godot* was the most influential play. A lot of the plays from Grove Press in the 1960s—Pinter's *A Night Out* and *Revue Sketches* and Ionesco's *Rhinoceros*—were a great antidote to all those wretched

British series of modern European theater with their bad translations of mediocre plays.

In Godot *Beckett places the main action in the traditional sense— Pozzo's blinding—offstage. That's a strategy you use a lot as well, placing the conventionally dramatic event between the scenes, as in* Glengarry *or* The Shawl.

A very good rule of dramaturgy is that you can't show the unshowable. You can't dramatize "They waited for a long time" better than by having a cut. If the event in *Glengarry* is not the robbery but, rather, something closer to the through-line of the protagonists, a condition rather than a dramatic action, the robbery doesn't have to be shown. You can just cut past it. That's a lesson we all learned from cinema.

And this has the effect, as Beckett and Pinter have taught us, of redefining dramatic action.

Well, maybe. I don't know. Take a play like *Betrayal,* a brilliant play that just puts everything backward. But Pinter curiously doesn't redefine the dramatic action. He uses the dynamic between the traditional dramatic structure and the audience's perception of it to create, almost in a cinematic way, a third reality. But the rules of dramatic structure, redefine them how you will, are based on the rules of human perception. That's what enables deviation from them to work. That's what enables so-called performance art to function. There's really nothing there other than randomness, in a lot of instances, but it works because the human mind will always impose order.

What about Tennessee Williams? You refer to him in Writing in Restaurants.

He had a great impact on me but not until later. In the 1960s his work was viewed, at least in my community, as classic rather than contemporary. Although, of course, he was a contemporary writer. I became very interested in the work of Tennessee and also Arthur Miller. I started working my way backward through dramatic history.

What about Miller?

I think he has a very different view of writing from mine. He sees writing as a tool of conscience. His stuff is informed by the driving idea that theater is a tool for the betterment of social conditions.

How does that differ from what you do?

I just write plays. I don't think that my plays are going to change anybody's social conditions. I think Mr. Miller's always thought, and it's a great thought, that his plays might alter people's feelings about real contemporary events. My view is very, very different because

73

we're different people from different generations. I think the purpose of theater, as Stanislavski said, is to bring to the stage the life of the soul. That may or may not make people more in touch with what's happening around them and may or may not make them better citizens.

So it might indirectly have a political impact by making people more aware?

Yes. I wished that I could write that kind of play. I tried it once in a while. *Edmond* is an example.

What about Brecht?

He influenced me a great deal. *Edmond,* again, is a good example of that. I used to teach the works of Brecht and was fascinated by him. All that nonsense he wrote about his writing I think is balderdash, a direct contradiction of the writing itself—which is the most wonderful, charming, involving, quintessentially dramatic writing. It's wonderfully whacky.

To some extent Brecht the theorist wanted to deny what Brecht the playwright was doing.

All of the comics like me always want to be tragedians. I think the same was true of Brecht. Historically, his plays fall under the wide aegis of comedy. His stuff is brilliant.

Did your training in New York under Sanford Meisner have a greater effect on you than any other work?

Absolutely. The most important thing I learned at the Neighborhood Playhouse was the idea of a through-line, which was Aristotle filtered through Stanislavski and Boleslavsky. That idea is a couple of thousand years old. Also the idea from Stanislavski of the subjugation of all aspects of the production—not just the script but the acting and the plastic elements—to the through-line of the play. That has stood me in very, very good stead in film directing.

In your plays the through-line is so strong that the characters can be saying things that are very, very different from what is really being communicated in the subtext.

That's why theater's like life, don't you think? No one really says what they mean, but they always mean what they mean.

And the subtext is always about power, buying and selling.

Why not? Lately I've developed a real love of Thackeray. The thought occurred to me that almost every English novel I know, whether it's *Vanity Fair* or *Pendennis* or *Howard's End* or Orwell, is all about the guy trying to raise the money to get his bowler hat out of hock so he won't be embarrassed when he goes to the party. They're all about people being embarrassed about their lack of money. And I guess most American literature—the American literature that I love, that I grew up on—is about business. That's what America is about.

Also, in acting subtext is usually defined as a power dynamic.

I've been teaching acting for about twenty years now, and I love it. It's all about two people who want something different. If the two people don't want something different, what the hell is the scene about? Stay home. The same is true for writing. If two people don't want something from each other, then why are you having the scene? Throw the goddam scene out—which might seem like an overly strict lesson to be learned in a schoolroom but is awfully helpful in the theater. If the two people don't want something different, the audience is going to go to sleep. Power, that's another way of putting it.

All of us are trying all the time to create the best setting and the best expression we can, not to communicate our wishes to each other but to *achieve* our wishes *from* each other. I think awareness of this is the difference between good and bad playwriting. Whether it's a politician trying to get votes or a guy trying to go to bed with a girl or somebody trying to get a good table at a restaurant, the point is not to speak the desire but to speak that which is most likely to bring about the desire.

How do you write a play? What do you start with—character, dialogue, plot?

Well, there's an old cowboy's trick. The herd is coming through fast, and one cowboy asks another how you estimate the number of cows so quickly. The other cowboy says: "It's very easy. You just count up the number of hooves and divide by four." That's how you write a play. You do a lot of writing to figure out what the hell the play's about and throw out three-quarters of it and write it again and look at it and find out what *that* play's about and throw out three-quarters of it and write it again.

Most playwrights have spoken of the importance of letting the unconscious material out first and then going back and working on what has been released. Is that a fair description of your process?

I think so. I have my processes of writing a play. But technique is training to break down the barriers between the unconscious and the conscious mind. That's true whether you're playing Ping-Pong or writing. After a number of years one attains a certain amount of technique, which enables the unconscious to respond, in the case of tennis, faster, or in the case of playwriting, perhaps better, than the

75

conscious mind could. The bad side is that you tend to do things in the same way. That's called habit.

Do you ever work from an outline?

Sure. When I write movies, I always work from an outline. When I write plays, at some point I work from an outline. I may have several thousand pages of dialogue before I decide it's time to write an outline.

You've generally chosen your director for a first production?

Yes.

You've worked with Gregory Mosher a great deal.

We did a bunch of plays at the Goodman from 1975 to 1985. We're doing a new play next February at Lincoln Center, *Speed-the-Plow*.

Do you always attend rehearsals for first productions?

It varies. There have been plays with Gregory where I was there every day. We had conferences deep into the night. For example, *American Buffalo*. And then there were plays where I went to the first rehearsal and said hello to the cast and showed up at the opening. For example, *Edmond*. That was the most brilliant production I've ever seen on any stage. The whole thing was done with two or three chairs and a table. It was devastating.

Is there some quality in a good production of your work that you would identify as a David Mamet style?

No, I don't think so. I think that, as Vakhtangov told us, we shouldn't rush to scenic solutions—they should follow the essential solution, which comes out of a consideration of what the play is about and what the character is doing to get what he wants. What I want in my productions—or in any production—is honesty, simplicity, and directness.

When you attend rehearsals, do you do much rewriting?

Sure. If the audience beats you to the point, take it out. If they don't understand, put it in. If the structure's wrong, fix it.

What about after first productions?

Sometimes you don't get it right, and you're never going to get it right, and it's useless to kill yourself over it. It's better, past a certain point, to learn a lesson for the next play rather than give yourself the luxury—if, indeed, it is that—of working something forever. Sometimes I've got to say, "There's an answer to this problem, but I don't know it."

Any other favorite productions, besides Edmond?

John Dillon's production of *Lakeboat* at Milwaukee Repertory Theater with Larry Shue. Wonderful, beautiful, unforgettable. I go to the theater to enjoy myself, just like anybody else.

How do you feel when you go to see theater that's more confrontational?
Like what?
Like Aunt Dan and Lemon.

I feel confronted. You seem to have the notion that in my estimation there must be a right way and a wrong way to do things. But I don't think that that's true. There are as many different kinds of theater as there are playwrights. I went to see Jackie Mason last night—a brilliant, brilliant evening. I felt very confronted at times. That's the point. It's nice that ABC Television is having all this brouhaha about *Amerika*. I want to see that. I hope I feel very confronted.

Your plays are confrontational only indirectly, insofar as they're about asking questions rather than providing answers or delineating a mystery.

In *Writing in Restaurants* I say that the purpose of the theater is to deal with things that can't be dealt with rationally. If they can be dealt with rationally, they probably don't belong in my theater. There are other people who feel differently and who work that way brilliantly. One of them is Arthur Miller. *Incident at Vichy, The Crucible,* also his new play, *Clara.* Or Wally Shawn, in *Aunt Dan and Lemon.* Or Fugard, for example.

In your essay, "Decay: Some Thoughts for Actors," I was surprised to read your statement that "the problems of the world . . . are, finally, no more solvable than the problems of a tree which has borne fruit." I find that a rather despairing attitude—an attitude I don't get from your plays.

I didn't feel in despair when I wrote that. I felt despair *before* I wrote it—like a lot of people today, I felt frightened and confused and very anxious. Looking around and saying, "Well, this is what's happening," I felt, *after* I wrote that essay, rather calm—somewhere between hopeful and resigned.

Do you have any idea, or any guess, as to how change will take place?

If you read the paper, you see that the world is trying to determine which of the many alternatives for decay and dissolution will work. One is a plague. Another is a nuclear accident or a war. Another is economic catastrophe. I think it's going to be something rather surprising. I was talking to Greg Mosher about it just the other day, and he says that he's kind of looking forward to it. I think a lot of people are.

Your plays often draw a connection between a brutal social network and a particular economic framework. Glengarry *is perhaps the purest example. Do you think it's possible that a change in the economic structure would lead to a radical change in society?*

I don't hold to that view. Of course, that's a very Marxian view. I think that the economic system is not susceptible to change but that it is an outgrowth of the intrinsic soul of the culture. You can't change the economic system. They changed it in Russia, and sixty years later they're back where they started.

When you say soul of the culture, *do you really mean* human nature?

Not human nature. Because I think that human nature is altered by certain essential aspects of life in a given place, at a given time. For example, the same people live in California and Vermont, but the human nature is conditioned by such factors as the different flow of the seasons, the difficulties of earning a living from the soil. So, although human nature remains the same, it's tempered by different climates and different locales. The economic system is an outgrowth of this conditioning.

Do you think it possible to create an economic system that isn't brutal?

Sure. I think it's been done in the past. At various times in history there was a sufficient stasis, a sufficient equilibrium between that which people possessed and that which they desired. It's kind of an anarchistic view, in that these people I'm thinking of lived in small communities and were capable of making their own ad hoc logical rules and regulations. I live in a small town in Vermont where people can do business by giving their word, leaving a check at the post office, calling up the bank and saying, "Will you send me this money?" One reason they can do this is common sense. If you live in a community where you're dependent on the same people day in and day out, then it's common sense that those people would deal honestly with each other.

And isn't that what it comes down to, this sense of community? That's the message in The Water Engine.

"All people are connected." The other view of the theater is that it's really a great time to go in and kick some ass because people are so starved. As I said, I saw Jackie Mason last night. I hadn't realized how long it's been since we've all sat in the theater and laughed because we shared the same values.

You say that, as a writer, you don't have a political agenda. Then what effect do you want to have on your audience?

When I write a play, what I'm trying to do is write that play. As for the effect . . . it's not that it doesn't interest me, but it's really not my job to manipulate the audience, whether for a political motive or to get them to "like" my play. My job with the play succeeds according to its own logical syllogism. If this, then that. That's the difference between a playwright and a writer of advertising. The writer of advertising should be concerned, as Mr. Ogilvy tells us, solely with the effect it's going to have on the reader or the viewer, to persuade him or her to buy the product or service advertised. If the writer of advertising is worried about the awards that he or she is going to win or the esteem that he or she is going to win in the advertising community or even the aesthetic beauty of the ad—absent its ability to influence the viewer—that person is not doing his or her job. Playwriting is exactly the opposite. Somebody said that, if everybody likes everything you do, then you're doing something wrong.

How do you see the relationship between your work for stage and screen?

Hollywood people are very, very cruel and also very, very cunning. One of the things that they will say to me and to other writers, if they don't understand something or if it's not bad enough for them, is, "It's very theatrical. It's too theatrical." That is used as a curse word. Also as an irrefutable statement. What are you going to say? "It's not theatrical"? I try to write the best I can for whatever medium I'm engaged in. We all know that we should stay away from Hollywood, but we don't. I try to do the best job I can, because, in addition to my own love of the work, I'm getting paid for it as a working man.

Do you read the critics?

Once in a while.

Do you take them seriously?

There are good critics and bad critics, well-meaning and depraved critics. I'm like anybody else in the world—I'd rather be praised than criticized. There are some people who may write about my work and make very, very good points about it, but I'll be goddamned if I'm going to pay any attention to it. They don't speak in a kindly and respectful fashion, the way that I would speak about them if it were my job to criticize them. So fuck 'em, in short. And that, I think, sums up my feelings about critics.

Many of the playwrights I've spoken to have commented on the sorry state of the American theater.

America is in a sorry state. We're at a very difficult time. Our culture has just fallen apart and is going to have to die off before something else takes its place. So, whether you say American theater or American car production or the American standard of living, they're all in the same boat. Theater is not an aspect of our civilization to be separated out. It's part of the body politic.

Broadway has become like Las Vegas. It's very rare that a serious play is able to run there.

I don't think it will ever happen again. It's just life. If someone went to Provincetown in 1920, he could have seen some great theater on the wharf, had a moonlight stroll down the beach, had some magnificently fresh and inexpensive seafood, and breathed the clean air. If that person came back to Provincetown today, he would say, "Wait a second. What happened to this beautiful community? Why are there so many people here? Why is everything so expensive? What happened to that theater?" What happened is that the world changed. Theater went someplace else. Cheap seafood went someplace else. Good air went someplace else. The same is true of Broadway.

What about the regional theaters?

I don't know anything about them. I got a lot of bang for my buck out of regional theaters in the 1970s, had some great times working at the Goodman and Actors Theater of Louisville, The Empty Space, Yale Rep, Milwaukee Rep. I don't know what's happening with them now.

When you direct your own work on the stage or the screen, do you work on it any differently than you would someone else's?

No, not at all. You ask the same questions, reduce it to a through-line: What does the protagonist want? What does he or she do to get it? What does the play mean? That's all. Someone else might know different questions to ask, but I don't. Whether I direct them myself or whether they're directed by, say, Greg, a lot of my productions tend to be incredibly austere. Which I like. Which I love, as a matter of fact. Other people may have a more pronounced visual sense. The questions that I ask in terms of the plastic elements are: Where does this take place? What does it mean to the play?

So everything is determined by the life on stage.

Greg did a play of mine called *The Disappearance of the Jews*, which takes place in a hotel room. It was designed by Michael Merritt, who's designed many of my plays and movies. We kicked around what the hotel room would look like, and finally I said the scenic element essential to the dramatic thrust of the play—why this room rather than another room?—is that this is a place where these two guys can be alone and be intimate with each other. That's what we came down to. So we said, well, what if we take everything away except for the two chairs and a little cigarette table between them. Then Greg said, "If we really want to say that's all it means, and we don't want to over-characterize, let's reupholster the chairs in white muslin so that we take away the distracting element of the particular choice of fabric." So we aren't asking, what kind of hotel is it? The important thing is, it's a hotel. It was a brilliant set. I think Merritt's sets for the Miller plays that Greg directed are absolutely brilliant.

Is there any theater you've seen recently that you particularly admire?

I haven't gone to the theater much over the last year. I've been working on *House of Games*. I admire Greg's work on the Miller plays at Lincoln Center. I admired *Platoon* and *A Room with a View* and *Crocodile Dundee*. I liked *Radio Days* very much.

What is Speed-the-Plow *about?*

It's a play about my experiences in Hollywood—two producers and secretary. I also may be directing a new movie that I wrote with Shel Silverstein.

Where do you think the hope for the future of theater lies?

I think it's a great time to be a young person in the theater. All bets are off, as in such times of social upheaval as the 1920s in Germany, the 1960s in Chicago, the period from 1898 to 1920 in Russia. Traditionally, these are times when new theatrical forms arise. That's what all this garbage about performance art is about, to a large extent—it's young people in the culture experimenting, casting about for a new form.

Certainly, the political scene has become increasingly polarized over the past six years, and I think that holds true for cultural products as a whole.

I think the lines will become more and more sharply divided. I think we're going to start putting people in jail again for what they write. People have been subconsciously afraid of expressing themselves because the times are so tenuous. And the reality will follow that feeling. So that will be exciting.

And frightening.

And very frightening, sure.

And you don't see a gentle way out of this state of polarization? You believe there will be a radical change?

It's like the weather. People get oppressed by the heat and humidity; it's got to rain before it's going to clear up. There are ebbs and flows in any civilization. Nothings lasts forever. We had a good time. We had Tennessee Williams. We had the hula hoop. We had the Edsel. All kinds of good stuff. The Constitution. To name but a few. Shelley Winters. Now you've got to pay the piper. Big deal.

Pulitzer-Power Playwright Takes on Screen Challenge

Ben Brantley

Ben Brantley spoke with Mamet in New York in the summer
of 1987 when Mamet was in preproduction for his first film
as writer/director, *House of Games.*

On screen the poker game begins and stops and begins again, an er-
ratic repetition of tightly framed images and phrases that suggest the
hypnotic poetry of the gambler's patois. The scene—which is being
played and replayed in tantalizing snippets for sound mixing in a studio in midtown Manhattan—is the centerpiece of *House of Games,* the
movie that marks David Mamet's debut as a film director.

It is enacted by a corps of performers who must have seemed re-
assuringly familiar to a man doing an unfamiliar job: The tense kib-
itzer, and only female at the table, is Lindsay Crouse, Mamet's wife;
the man betting over his head is Joe Mantegna, a veteran of many
Mamet stage productions; and three players are Mamet's real-life
poker cronies, nonactors who live near his home in Vermont.

The last group was flown specially to Seattle, where the movie
was shot, and during breaks from filming the players would adjourn
to a table off the set, where the cards were ready for a real game of
poker. It became difficult, one of the actors on the set recalls, to distinguish between the true and fictitious games.

Before an interview David Mamet is viewing the results on this
Pirandello-ish slice of movie making through a horizontal slot of a

window in a small chamber behind the screening room. He keeps his eyes fixed soberly on the screen except when he is answering a question, which he tends to do in fairly short order.

"God, it's odd to be talking to you and to see this," he says, in a voice still wrapped in the foggy tones picked up in his hometown of Chicago. "It's like watching a Fritz Lang film, *Contempt,* or something. I'm talking to you, and they're showing the movie."

It seems appropriate that the conversation that follows is also in a way distinctly removed from reality—something that is shaped and edited as it goes along. When reading a Mamet script—with its ingeniously ordered American street phrases and cadenced slang—you can immediately hear it, as if it were being spoken; when listening to Mamet talk, you feel as if you're reading a script.

He speaks slowly, in short, deliberate, and measured phrases that are less likely to trail off in ellipses than conclude with the polished finality of an epigram. His language is a careful blend of laconic blue-collar machismo and academic references. The tone ranges from pedantic to flippant ("Although there may be some evidence to the contrary," he says, about creating female characters, "I think women are people, too. I just don't understand them as well as I do men. But, on the other hand, that's been the source of much diversion and trauma in my life.")

One would be unlikely to mistake Mamet for one of the bumbling thieves or con artists whose voices he has rendered with such resonance in plays such as *American Buffalo* and the Pulitzer Prize–winning *Glengarry Glen Ross.* But it is very easy to perceive the particular intelligence of the craftsman who created them.

This is an intelligence that—with its unique aptitude for dialogue, strong self-propelling story lines, and bracingly original moral vision—is keeping Mamet busy. Last winter he published *Writing in Restaurants,* a collection of essays, and the first Mamet television script was aired, a snappy "Hills Street Blues" episode. In summer came *The Untouchables*—a new corruption-conscious take on the Eliot Ness legend directed by Brian DePalma—and *House of Games* (with screenplay by David Mamet from an idea he developed seven years ago with comedian Jonathan Katz) is scheduled for release this fall.

He then hopes to polish up the screenplay of *Glengarry Glen Ross* and move directly into preproduction of his second directorial effort, *Things Change,* which he cowrote with Shel Silverstein. Mamet also hopes to complete a play that would be directed by longtime collaborator Gregory Mosher next year at Lincoln Center. "I never quite

83

feel I'm really, really, really working if I'm not writing for the theater," he says. The subject of the play in progress: Hollywood.

Movies are virgin territory for Mamet as playwright, although he has been stockpiling observations through his early days, a decade ago, of pushing story ideas to unreceptive producers and, more recently, as the successful screenwriter of *The Verdict* and the remake of *The Postman Always Rings Twice.*

"I kind of think it's just like cops and crooks," he says of the film industry. "I don't think that the cops are there to protect society so much as the cops and crooks are both there to give each other something to do. And I kind of think that about Hollywood. It's a whole race of people who are not quite writers—and some who are—and there's a whole race of people who are not quite executives, and they're both out there to give each other something to do." Despite this view of show business, Mamet has reached the point where, he says, "I can do just about as much as I want."

This has meant, among other things, the opportunity to write the screenplay for *The Untouchables,* a project that allowed Mamet to draw from his enduring fascination with the city in which he grew up and the gangster mythology that it spawned. "I always loved gangster films because they were very virile," he says. "They're about a guy who wants something and would do anything to get it and eventually learns his lesson and ends up seeing the error of his ways and wishing he could've gotten back together with 'Mary.' It's a very American form, a broad, melodramatic form." The film's theme, as he succinctly describes it: "the education of a gunfighter; in this case, Eliot Ness."

The fact that he is now directing films is something he takes in ostensibly easy stride. "It was like a whole new aspect of life opened up," says Mamet of directing *House of Games,* the story of a rigidly self-controlled psychotherapist (Crouse) who finds herself magnetically attracted to and eventually betrayed by a group of con artists who embody her fantasies of a less inhibited existence. "It can be lonely. But it's nice being in the midst of a hundred people, who, because of professional hierarchy, are always asking you something."

Although Mamet says that, in directing his first film, "the main problem that I talked to myself about a lot was being frightened," Mantegna says there was little evidence of insecurity on the set.

"Of course, there were times when David was learning by doing," says Mantegna, who's known Mamet since the early 1970s, when they were both starting out in Chicago. "But I was amazed at just how much confidence he exuded during that period." That is, Mantegna continues, simply the sort of person that Mamet is. "People say it must be something for David to go from being a banging-around, nobody-knows-him playwright to a Pulitzer Prize winner. My feeling was the Pulitzer Prize caught up with him. David never doubted, even for an instant, that he had that kind of talent."

Mantegna also points out Mamet's wisdom in surrounding himself largely with actors who were extensively familiar with his work, a group, incidentally, that Mamet intends to use for *Things Change.* It includes, in addition to Mantegna, three actors who also appeared in *Glengarry Glen Ross* and a number of young performers from the Atlantic Theater Company, which was created by former acting students of Mamet's.

There is also, of course, Lindsay Crouse in the film's central role. "The shoemaker's children do go barefoot," says Mamet, on directing his wife. "And the children of psychiatrists are all nutty. Looking back on the movie, I think the only instances when I didn't deal with the actors with the attention they deserved was probably in talking to my wife, because she was my wife."

The world portrayed in *House of Games,* as in most of Mamet's plays, is not a particularly sunny one but, rather— in a vision Mamet shares with his favorite writer, Kurt Vonnegut—"a bizarre, and in many ways terrifying, and in many ways ironic and diverting place." It is populated principally by predators—the overwhelmingly dominant image of the film is that of the con game—and triumph over such people, the film suggests, comes only through personal corruption. "This movie attempts to be very frank, perhaps to the extent of being upsetting," he says. "But I don't think it's negative, any more than it would be if you were diagnosing someone and saying, 'You have *x, y,* or *z.*"

He remembers when his play *Edmond,* a dark fable of urban decay, was performed several years ago: "It got some really vicious press in New York City. Looking back, I think it was kind of inevitable, because it was a view that no one wanted to embrace. It is difficult for people with a vested interest in the continuation of a certain aspect of culture to look at a person who says, 'The world is disintegrating around me,' and identify with that."

"People are frightened," he says at another point. "No one knows what's going to be next in our culture. Increasingly, people know it's gotta be something, and it's gonna be a vast change. Hell, I become afraid when I have to go away for the weekend. . . . There's a lot of frightened people out there, myself included."

A Community of Moviegoers

Jim Lehrer

David Mamet spoke with Jim Lehrer in October 1987 on the "MacNeil/Lehrer NewsHour" on an evening in which the hard news included Vice President George Bush's declaration that he was an official candidate for president. The release of Mamet's first film as writer/director, *House of Games,* and his promotion of it were the impetus for their conversation.

LEHRER: You seem to be very excited about making movies. Why?

MAMET: When I started off in theater about, approximately twenty years ago, you could get together, and you could do theater in the church basement; you could do it literally with no money. And I came to New York, and off-off-Broadway was in flower, and again people got together and said, "What about this?" and went over to a church or a community center, and the next week it was on. And those times, at least for people in my generation, seem to have gone for a number of reasons. One is that real estate in the big city has gotten so expensive, so theater's gotten expensive. The other is that people who were twenty when I was twenty are now forty when I'm forty, and it's tough to assemble a cast of friends of yours to work cheaply and quickly, because they're all off paying their mortgages just like I am. One of the many reasons I'm excited about movies is they give me an opportunity to get together and work time after time with the people who I'd been working with before.

LEHRER: But you're one of this country's leading playwrights.

You're not suggesting that you have trouble getting people to do your plays, are you?

MAMET: No, it's not that so much. Well, for example, I had my own theater company in Chicago for a number of years, and I would put on five of my plays in the course of a year. Nobody in Chicago or anywhere else for that matter wants to see if I can write that many plays anymore or wants to see that many plays by me. My interests have changed over the years, and I would rather now spend three and four years working on a very, very closely structured traditional play—it takes a long time to write—rather than dash off a bunch of episodic plays. So, what am I going to do in the interim? Movies are a wonderful thing for me to do.

LEHRER: Why? Why are they wonderful?

MAMET: Well, you get to work with your friends. You get to appeal to a broad audience. The theatrical audience—at least people in my generation—seem to be shrinking year by year. A healthy theater is really an outgrowth of community, just like a healthy church. Only the church is made up of theological principles which are passed down from generation to generation, and the congregation, which is fixed, cares about each other enough to apply those principles to each other. It's the same with the theater. You don't take a job in a church to talk to the congregation, and you don't take a job in a theater to talk to a community. A theater must be an organic outgrowth of the community, because all a theater is, is people talking to themselves about themselves. New York has become a city of transients; what has been traditionally the hub of American theater really is no longer. Although there is still theater here, because the theater now in New York caters to transients, there isn't a theatrical—there isn't a community of playgoers in New York, as there was fifteen years ago. But there is a community in this country of moviegoers. As a country, we go to the movies, and they are our theater.

LEHRER: So, somebody sitting in Texas and Illinois and New York and California, they're all going to see the same movie on the same night, and that ties them together?

MAMET: That's right. Sure. Because the movies are a huge conglomerate, which is elected by the—if you want to take a Darwinian view, it's elected by the country at large to talk to the country at large. Every time we buy a ticket, we cast our vote in a very, very real way for the people that we want to see next.

LEHRER: All right. You did *The Untouchables*—you were the screenwriter for that. What's it like just to be the screenwriter?

MAMET: It's like being somebody's aunt, you know? Being an aunt is not a very responsible position. You want to go out there and be the best aunt you can. Nobody cares much. And that's what it's like—

LEHRER: Did you feel valued as a writer in Hollywood around movie people, just as a writer?

MAMET: No, there's a tradition in—I was treated, and am treated to this day, exceedingly well by—for a screenwriter by Hollywood standards, which is to say badly. In the theater the playwright is kind of Yertle the Turtle. The playwright traditionally chooses the director and through that the cast. And influences what happens in all aspects of production, which is kind of nice if you're the playwright. And then to go from there to being a screenwriter, as Scott Fitzgerald says, they treat you like a secretary—the only difference being that they call you "sir," because that's just not the tradition in Hollywood. The tradition in Hollywood is the director makes the movie, the star sells the movie, and, if the screenwriter doesn't work, throw him out. Get another one.

LEHRER: When did you decide you also wanted to try your hand at directing?

MAMET: When I first went out there as a screenwriter, I think is the answer to that question [*laughter*].

LEHRER: When you first were treated badly, because you realized that's where the power was if you really wanted to make a movie?

MAMET: It wasn't that I was treated badly; it's just that I wanted to be able to take things on to their logical conclusion. Like if you ever worked with an architect or a designer or something like that, there comes a time when you take the architect's, the designer's, plans, and you say, "That's great, but I think I would rather like the walls striped rather than solid in color," and you see this look in their eyes, these people whom you've hired. It says, "This man doesn't know what he's doing. This man is wasting his money. If he wants to get my advice, why doesn't he follow it through the whole way?" Which is kind of what it's like being a screenwriter.

LEHRER: And now you've done *House of Games,* which you not only wrote, but you also directed. It's your movie, isn't it?

MAMET: Well, it's my movie to the extent—somebody—Andrew Saris on the *Village Voice* made up this theory years ago called the Auteur Theory, which as far as I can determine means that the director is the author of the movie. I don't think the director—having been a screenwriter for a number of years—I don't think the director is the author of the movie. He is, on the other hand, the director of the movie. And this movie that I just did, *House of Games*, I did both, and I really enjoyed it.

LEHRER: Whether it's *House of Games, The Untouchables,* many of your plays, particularly *Glengarry Glen Ross,* there is always—there's something in there about business—that crime, con, whatever, is the American way of business. Do you really believe that? Or is that just something that your characters—explain that to me. Is that—?

MAMET: Well, I think that there is a lot of fraud in America—there's probably a lot of fraud in every country's business, or sharp practice, anyway. I happen to be an American, so it's the only country I know anything about. I think that when times get hard as they are now, people become frightened, and it becomes more difficult for them to be—some people—to be ethical. I think everybody at any time when faced with the possibility of getting something for nothing is tested, and I think when people are frightened or people are worried that sometimes they don't pass the test so well. I think that's certainly the case in America now.

LEHRER: I get the impression in *House of Games* that your con men were essentially saying, "Hey, look, we're just playing by the rules. We're playing by the same rules that—" they didn't say it, but the implication was that General Motors—fill in the blank—were also playing. Is that a correct reading of what you're saying in a lot of these things?

MAMET: Yes. Which is not to say that I espouse that view. I once worked in a fraudulent land sales organization—I was very young—and I was faced with two choices, either get over your scruples or get out of the job. And at that point I got over my scruples, and I did what was a job of questionable legality in selling bad land over the phone to people who could ill afford it. And what happened to me, I remember, as I'm sure what happens to most criminals, is they'd say, "Well, these fools, they deserve whatever happens to them." It's a way of protecting yourself.

LEHRER: When you sit down to write something, do you sit down to write with a theme in mind or with people in mind, or where do the germs usually come from?

MAMET: Well, I get my ideas the same way as anybody else. You know, everybody walks down the street talking to themselves. They say, "If I could just go back there again, what I'd say to that son of a gun" or "You know what happened to that guy who won the lottery? Boy, if I won the lottery," etc. So, I think we all have a very—I know we all have a very active fantasy life. And being a writer or being maybe any kind of artist, I don't know, is just being aware of it, is not discarding that idea: what if—

LEHRER: Are you nervous about how *House of Games* is going to be received, whether it's going to be a "successful movie"?

MAMET: Oh, sure, one is always nervous. It—the interesting thing to me is over the years it doesn't make any difference if you're doing a reading in a church basement that you just rehearsed that afternoon or putting a play up on Broadway, people—I'm one of them—like to be liked and love to be loved.

LEHRER: If you don't care about it, it would be hard to do, wouldn't it?

MAMET: Yeah, one cares very, very deeply—of course, over the years you develop a certain protective way of dealing with criticism.

LEHRER: How do you deal with it?

MAMET: I swear quite a bit at bad reviews. I make up speeches about—I have this fantasy—there's a couple of critics in New York who—if people would write to you care of this address, I'll be glad to give you the names and also some of the speeches, as a matter of fact. And I have—see, this is my fantasy—but somebody doesn't know what I think about these swine and that I'm invited to introduce them at a Rotary luncheon or something like that. So, that's one of my fantasies; I'm going to write that speech. That's one way of dealing with criticism [*laughter*].

LEHRER: If you and I sit down five years from now, what would you like—and we're talking only, say, we can't talk about anything that happened before right now, what would you hope that we would be talking about?

MAMET: That's a very good question. Maybe—I'd like to start another theater company. So, I would hope that perhaps we'd be talking about that. I love teaching, and I love directing and working with the same people time after time after time. And the nice thing about working in theater and movies is that you can just flip-flop from one to the other, and the change is not only as good as a rest but better than a rest. So, I'd like to start in a few years flip-flopping my energies back into working on—where in a theater, it's as I say, I can't write all the time—what I'd like to do is direct and teach in the theater.

LEHRER: And maybe a couple or three more movies, too, in the—

MAMET: A little bit can't hurt, right?

Things Change for Mamet

Jay Carr

Jay Carr, film critic for *The Boston Globe*, sat down with the writer in his office in Cambridge, Massachusetts, in early October 1988 to discuss *Things Change*, whose opening was set for October 21. For this profile, however, Mamet was also anxious to talk about his love of movies, his adaptations of Chekhov's plays *The Cherry Orchard* and *Uncle Vanya*, and *Sketches of War*, the Vietnam Veterans Workshop benefit which Mamet was directing. *Sketches of War* featured a performance of his play *Cross Patch* and staged readings by Al Pacino, Michael J. Fox, Donald Sutherland, and Christopher Walken, who read selections from Shakespeare, Kipling, David Rabe, and Dalton Trumbo.

"Why do Americans love crooks and con men and lowlifes? Because we get used to seeing them in office," says film maker David Mamet, deadpan-frisky. *Things Change*, Mamet's new film due October 21, is a comedy in which low-level mobster Joe Mantegna takes shoemaker Don Ameche to Lake Tahoe and learns a few things. It's played out against a landscape rich in venality. Film maker Mamet? Mamet's new film? These are terms the media are getting used to, after two decades of referring to Mamet almost exclusively as a playwright whose lapidary way with street talk tapped dark American currents and returned language's magic to the theater. But while there's no shortage of talk that falls upon the ear with wonderful concreteness and resonance in this new film, Mamet says, "You must be able to tell the story with the sound off."

Not that Mamet is giving up playwriting. After his impressive debut film, *House of Games,* he sent *Speed-the-Plow* to Broadway. *Crosspatch,* a new short play of his, will be unveiled tomorrow night at the Vietnam Veterans Workshop benefit at the Colonial. "It's one act, 25 minutes long. It's a play I wrote a while ago, after I went to a Soldier of Fortune convention for *Esquire.* That's where it's set. Kevin Bacon is the narrator, W. H. Macy is his assistant, Mike Nussbaum, Don Ameche, and Robert Prosky are speakers at the convention."

Mamet, interviewed at the Cambridge office from which he is overseeing the benefit, likes the idea of shuttling between stage and film, he says. "A change is as good as a rest. One is very solitary, the other very communal. Playwriting takes place over an unspecified amount of time. Making a film is more structured, compressed, intense. It's like creating little 10-second plays. But the family aspect of it is fun." In Mamet's case, the word is apt. Mamet has been working with actors Mantegna, Macy, Mike Nussbaum, J. J. Johnston, and a handful of others for years, starting in his native Chicago. He met Johnston when both played animals in a children's play there. He met Nussbaum when he was a backstage gofer, before he began writing plays.

"I started about 20 years ago," Mamet says, "I had always been interested in theater. I started writing sketches when I was working backstage for the Second City improvisational troupe—5–8 minute blackouts. Then I started teaching at Goddard College. I went to school there in the turbulent '60's. I was teaching acting, and I wrote things for my students. How did I get from Chicago to Goddard? When it was time for me to go to college, only one school accepted me. That was Goddard. So I went to it. At the time, there were only two courses—sex and drugs—and even they weren't required. I remember vividly only the death of Janis Joplin. Other than that, the whole thing is a sort of orange blur.

"I've always liked films. In Chicago, I remember there was this great theater on Clark Street, open all night. They'd run Jimmy Cagney festivals, S. Z. Sakall festivals, Yakima Canutt even. You'd go at 3 in the morning when you couldn't sleep and meet all your friends there. I wrote scripts of two of my own plays—*Sexual Perversity in Chicago* and *The Water Engine.* No one would produce them. When they finally did film *Sexual Perversity*—it was called *About Last Night*— they fired me off the movie and used another script!" When Mamet's wife, actress Lindsay Crouse, was signed for a film, he asked her to ask the director, Sidney Lumet, "to give me a job writing the movie." That was in 1982, the film was *The Verdict*, and Mamet's first screenplay was nominated for an Oscar.

Later came screenplays for *The Postman Always Rings Twice* and *The Untouchables*. He's written a new screenplay, *Homicide*. It's about cops, not crooks. Its star, when filming begins next year? Mantegna. There'll be more plays, too, and more translations, an enterprise he began with Chekhov's *The Cherry Orchard* in Chicago and continued with Chekhov's *Uncle Vanya* for the American Repertory Theatre in Cambridge. While living in New York, Mamet taught at the NYU's Tisch School of the Arts, where in 1985 he established the Atlantic Theater Company, a traveling repertory company whose performers he cast in his films. He and Crouse remain on the troupe's board of directors and run a summer acting school in Vermont, near a home they bought shortly after they were married 10 years ago.

Although polite and articulate, Mamet does not care to dwell on his personal life, preferring to live as quietly as possible in Cambridge with Crouse and their two daughters, aged 5 years and 8 months. Why did he move from Manhattan? "You been there lately? I want my family to live in a nice place, and so did my wife. New York is changing. I think it wasn't quite as pleasant a place to live in as it had been. Too many people. Too many 3-story buildings being replaced by 300-story buildings. Also, I got spoiled living in Vermont. It was kind of fun going to the bank and the hardware store and the post office and not have to grit your teeth."

One of the facets of Mamet's working life in Cambridge involves ongoing work with the ART [American Repertory Theatre]—adapting and directing other classics and shaping new work, including his own. "Would I do a new play of mine here? Sure. Absolutely. In a while. A while may be somewhere between soon and never. I liked working on Chekhov. He's very, very funny, and I've never read a translation that reflected this. I think I sensed how funny the plays must be from reading the short stories. I don't understand Russian. I worked from literal translations of his texts. He always said his plays were comedies. That's not always a reliable guide, but in his case I think it's there."

Mamet says he was pleased when ART artistic director Bob Brustein asked him to do *Vanya*. "I'd like to direct Shakespeare, too, and I've lately been interested in French plays. I'd like to try Giraudoux's *Madwoman of Chaillot*. I'd also like to do Molière. And my wife

93

is hocking me to do a translation of Beaumarchais. I'm looking forward to doing a lot more theater in the Cambridge/Boston area. I have work I want to do and intend to do and enjoy it. I just finished a children's book with my wife, *The Owl,* published by Grove Press. When I was growing up and being influenced by Pinter and Beckett and reading the Grove Press editions of their plays, it was my dream to have something published by Grove Press."

Mamet also is working on a second book of essays. His first, *Writing in Restaurants,* is urgent, funny, impassioned, invigorating, filled with high-minded gusto that seems almost paradoxical in view of the cultural decay he regularly notes. One of the essays is even called "Decay," and it caused more than a ripple when Mamet delivered it at Harvard in 1986. Far from being Spenglerian in outlook, though, Mamet takes an almost Eastern view of decay, seeing it as cyclical, the first step in a possible rebirth.

"The decay still holds," he says. "It's still our life. But confronting it is a way of getting over being frightened by it—admitting it rather than denying it." Could these reflections on decay perhaps have proceeded from Mamet's own fear of growing older? "I kind of like getting older," Mamet says. "I turned 40 last year. I feel I'm doing a lot of things I never did before. I'm even lifting weights! It has to do with being more relaxed, coming to terms with oneself. There are benefits in not having to refer things to a contrived sense of self. I'm glad I live here now."

Mamet never has gone in much for the interviewing game. He never did many. Now he does almost none. For this one, he's patient and obliging about posing for a photograph—but he draws the line at smiling on cue. He's perhaps most revealing in his essays, two of which are devoted in heartfelt myth-making ways to pool and poker, two activities Mamet says he doesn't have as much time to enjoy as he used to. Ditto for cigar-smoking. Male bonding rituals and mentor relationships recur in such plays as *Sexual Perversity in Chicago, American Buffalo, A Life in the Theatre, Glengarry Glen Ross,* the new *Things Change,* and even the film that preceded it, *House of Games,* in which, for the first time, a woman enters traditional male preserves of pool, poker, and scamming—with lethal effect.

While acknowledging the presence of mentor figures in his works, Mamet cautions against generalizing. "I think this isn't a story about a mentor figure," he says of the new film. "It's about two aspects of a personality. There are two heroes—one who's kind of resigned to not getting his dream and the other not getting what he

94

feels he deserves. The others have outward similarities, too, but they all have different stories. *Sexual Perversity in Chicago* is about a fellow learning bad lessons. The most important thing my father ever told me was, 'Don't trust an expert.'"

"No, my mother and father weren't in show business. My uncle Henry was an actor. I remember him telling us he had a part in *Panic in the Streets*, with Richard Widmark. We've looked, but couldn't see him. We also have pictures in somebody's cellar of Uncle Henry as a model, next to a 1941 Packard." Mamet retains the roll-up-your-sleeves-and-let's-get-on-with-it approach to work. Without seeing his desk, you know he's no certain-number-of-sharpened-pencils-in-a-certain-jar-in-a-certain-corner-of-the-desk writer. Where does he write? In restaurants? In his Vermont retreat? In Harvard Square? "All over. Work habits have nothing to do with the work. It has more to do with habits of thought. I never remember writing anything," he says. "It's tough to write, when I'm doing something, like making a film. Otherwise, I write all the time. If you have a technique, you should be able to do it anywhere."

A Mamet Metamorphosis?

Richard Stayton

Richard Stayton, to whom Mamet has granted numerous interviews, characterizes this discussion as a conversation with
a soft-spoken "sunny optimist." It took place at Harrah's
Casino, Lake Tahoe, during a promotion blitz for *Things
Change,* replete with ample evidence of Mamet's dry wit.

Things change; people don't.

So they say. David Mamet may just be the exception.

Just seven years ago, after his first screenplay (*The Postman Always
Rings Twice*), the tough-talking, poker-playing Chicagoan had this to
say about Hollywood: "It's like kindergarten out there. You have to
leave, because it's no way for a grown man to make a living."

Approximately ten plays, four screenplays, an Oscar nomination,
a Pulitzer Prize, two children, and two self-directed movies later,
Mamet sits behind Harrah's Casino swimming pool, eyes hidden behind sunglasses, a Spielbergian baseball cap pulled over his close-
cropped black hair, and says, "Who in his right mind would kick about
the fact that people are flying from all over to talk to me about my
work? It's great."

So, has Mamet changed? Columbia Pictures is giving a first-class
promotional treatment for *Things Change,* Mamet's latest effort as
writer-director, and Mamet calls the weekend "film camp."

This is what it's all about, he's saying. "I work with the best
people in the world, the finest people I ever met in my life, the
Filmhaus Production team. They trust me with anything. I trust them

with anything. It's a great feeling to be part of our little band of merry men and women."

This is *the* David Mamet?

Is this Mr. Nice Guy the same playwright whose coarse language in *Sexual Perversity in Chicago* and *American Buffalo* changed obscenity into poetry?

Is this careerist the same wiseguy who commented to the *Boston Globe* that "Frank Rich and John Simon are the syphilis and gonorrhea of the theater"—after both New York critics raved about his Pulitzer–winning *Glengarry Glen Ross?*

Could this sunny optimist be the same Hollywood assassin whose Broadway hit *Speed-the-Plow* portrays crass movie producers taking "creative venality" to new lows? The same moralist who once observed that "the inability to call things by their right name is a great sign of decadence"?

Say it ain't so, David.

But *Things Change,* which opens today, implies that Mamet's changed. The clues are on the screen: a gentle-sweet comedy about a self-destructive gangster (Joe Mantegna) luring an inexperienced shoeshine man (Don Ameche) to the gaming tables of South Lake Tahoe. There's only a glimmer of the sinister manipulation of his 1987 *House of Games.* Yet Mamet directed both, wrote both.

Maybe that explains it. Mamet cowrote the script of *Things Change* with Shel Silverstein.

"Yeah, my wife [actress Lindsay Crouse] says it's because Shel's a nicer guy than I am," Mamet happily agrees.

Mamet's essay "A Playwright in Hollywood" documents his first writing lesson from The Biz: "Working in the movies has taught me (for the moment anyway) to stick to the plot and not to cheat." Since that essay was published in his collection *Writing in Restaurants* [1986], what other changes has Mamet undergone?

"I'm learning all kinds of lessons from Hollywood all the time," he answers. "I just wrote a movie for [producer] Art Linson [*We're No Angels*], and the beginning was very languid. Linson tells me, 'You gotta start off with a big bang.' So I say to him, 'You whore,' as I usually do, that's my Jewish salutation, 'you don't know what you're talking about, you swine. I was making my living as a playwright, while you were just a tout at the racetrack.' But he kept harping that you have the audience's attention when the curtain goes up, why win them back?"

"So, I learned a real good lesson arguing with Linson," Mamet declares. "In the first ten seconds my script now has a whipping, an electrocution, a prison breakout."

Linson's behavior during the making of Mamet's screenplay for *The Untouchables* led to a notorious 1987 *American Film* article. There Mamet committed Hollywood's unspeakable sin: writing the ugly truth about back-lot politics.

Mamet shrugs in retrospect over the article. "I felt like saying it. You can't insult anyone in Hollywood, it's true. That's the bad part. The good part is I'm making movies, and to make movies is the reward. As we all know, the first rule of Hollywood is there is no net."

But mention that *Speed-the-Plow* is a scathing indictment of the way Hollywood does business, and Mamet just shrugs again. "I hope so. It's very dishy. A very, very inside Hollywood play."

"A lot of people have been spreading the ugly rumor that it's a play about my relationship with Art Linson, and I would like to squelch that rumor right now. So I should tell everybody in Hollywood that it has nothing to do with Art Linson. And that's exactly what my lawyers told me to say, as well as that it's absolutely not actionable that in an early draft the main character was called 'Art Linson.'"

All joking aside, doesn't Mamet worry that Hollywood might undermine him, as it has so many other idealists?

"I think no one can corrupt me except myself," he asserts. "There's all sorts of corruptions as one grows older. For example, there's a corruption that comes from facility. You get good at something; you do it with your left hand. A lot of times corruption doesn't come from evil. It comes from lack of watchfulness. So, as you grow older, I find, you have to learn new lessons all the time. That striving that one was doing at twenty is no longer appropriate. People who once said no to you now say yes. There is a different kind of striving that's appropriate at forty."

This brings him back to *Things Change* and the subject of people who won't succumb, no matter the temptations.

"I guess that's one thing the movie's really about, the guy who has such a strong sense of himself that he can't be swayed. No one can punch a button (in Don Ameche's shoeshine man) and command, 'You want to feel good about yourself? Do it for money, do it for this, do it for that.' The man says, 'No, I do feel good about myself; I prefer my own good opinion of myself.'"

So, *Things Change* subtly reveals Mamet's little secret about maintaining his integrity despite the lure of Hollywood. It's a simple formula: be yourself, do good work, and stay out of L.A.

Mamet does film business the old-fashioned way: theatrically. His movie making borrows from his play development experiences. . . . But his working preoccupations have changed. "I'm thinking a lot about myth lately. It's very important for this culture, the movement of popular media away from 'social concerns' and toward mythological concerns. As I get older and closer to death, my concerns become more spiritual."

"I'll continue to do both theater and film. My life in the movies and the theaters is a lot like the biathlon—cross-country skiing and rifle shooting. Now what are those two things doing in one event? But they all get harder as I get older. I used to write episodic plays that were pretty funny, Second Cityesque. The cumulative effect was not inconsiderable, but as I get more attached to more traditional forms they're harder to write."

At the end of *Things Change* there is a silent but eloquent sequence between Gino, the shoeshine man, and Mantegna's gangster, Jerry. What does their mysterious interplay mean to Mamet?

"Gino isn't really the one who changes," Mamet explains, "because he stood up for his values. But he found a friend. And what Jerry has found through Gino is that you may not be in the place you want to be, but no doubt you're in the place where you're supposed to be. And so they both find through each other an admixture of the desire to hope and the desire to accept. Hope accepts the aspect of acceptance; acceptance accepts the aspect of hope. And from that comes peace."

"That may be much, much, much too cerebral and probably is," Mamet sighs, "but that's what I think."

That may also be a metaphor for how Mamet succeeds in both theater and film. Whatever the explanation, as Mamet enters the casino to begins his weekend of "film camp," there's a touch of the shoeshine man's grace under pressure. He walks like a man who believes he can handle the Hollywood house of games because, the more things change, the more Mamet remains the same.

Hard and Fast

Brian Case

Brian Case sat down with Mamet in late 1989 to discuss his newest film, *Homicide,* and earlier works.

David Mamet was knee-deep in good and bad. He's writing his next movie, *Homicide,* based on William Caunitz's novel *Suspects* about a cop who is taken off a big investigation but finds the minor case he's working on doubles back. "The solution of this case is gonna define the nature of evil. If I can put it down. It's a difficult script."

He's wearing a workmanlike plaid flannel shirt and tie, cords, and habitual no-nonsense crew cut. You can picture him hunkered over a script in his cabin in Vermont, no electricity, glasses up on his forehead, cigar butt between his stubby fingers. "Traditionally, cop movies either picture them as stoics, which is to say as philosophers to whom nothing is more important in life than doing right—doing right as the utmost happiness—or give them some personal reason for doing their job like his partner gets killed or his family terrorized. I've used all of those routines shamelessly."

David Mamet made his reputation in the theater, as the poet of Chicago's lumpenproletariat—people Nelson Algren characterized as "the nobodies nobody knows, with faces cut from the same cloth as their caps, and the women whose eyes reflect nothing but pavement." In plays like *American Buffalo* or Pulitzer Prize–winning *Glengarry Glen Ross,* repetition, obscenity, and shopworn maxims fall thick and fast as his characters shake the bars of language in an attempt at lateral thought and reveal, instead, heart, soul, liver, and

From "Hard and Fast," *Time Out,* January 4–11, 1989, 29–30. Copyright © 1989 Time Out Magazine. Reprinted by permission.

lights. Self-awareness is not on the menu. His speeches play like a drumskin, recruiting actors of the clout of Al Pacino, Robert Duvall, Jim Belushi, F. Murray Abraham, and Kenneth McMillan. "Dead hard sound," he says affectionately of Chicago speech patterns. "It's a very harsh song." Chicago has always been a writer's town, and perhaps because there was no room for euphemism between the killing floors of Al Capone, Mayor Daley, and the stockyards, its literature has been traditionally tough, naturalistic, and populist. "Chicago audiences are difficult to fool. They like going to the theater and having their socks knocked off. Chicago has always been a town where people create things, where one can be a member of the community based on one's capacity to produce. Those are the people that were my models."

Mamet's screenplays include the third version of *The Postman Always Rings Twice,* the Oscar-nominated *The Verdict* and *The Untouchables;* lately he has turned to directing his own work. "The Untouchables" had been a highly successful TV series from 1959 to 1963, finally ousted from the screens by "Sing Along with Mitch," but the overfamiliarity of the material didn't present a problem to Mamet. Nor, as many critics pointed out, did abiding by the facts. "Biography makes rotten drama. People remember what was true and what was striking at the time. 'Wait a minute, I know Al Capone *actually* blah, blah, blah . . .' There really wasn't much of a mystery either. Everybody knows Prohibition was repealed and Al Capone went to prison for tax evasion. The dramatist's job is to create drama that proceeds from character and culminates in a surprising and inevitable conclusion."

He speaks very fast and low, turning his head aside from the listener, every so often tethering a point to an *a* or *b.* "There wasn't much of an issue about stamping out illegal liquor because everybody drinks now and drank then. The problem was, what *was* the issue? At the end of the movie I wrote a crawl sheet that was the correct end of the movie. They didn't include it in the finished film. The press say, 'Mr. Ness, Mr. Ness! What's gonna happen after Prohibition's over?' Then Ness says, 'I think I'll have a drink.' The crawl sheet comes up, and it says, 'In January, 1933 the Twentieth Amendment repealed Prohibition, but the organized crime and disrespect for the law that Prohibition spawned is with us to this day.' That was my summing up of my feelings about this. The story is *not* over. Obviously, liquor is not the point. What is the point? It's whether the law has been subverted, government has been corrupted, the police department's been corrupted, many people have been killed, and many injustices have been perpetrated."

Hardboiled thriller writer Loren Estelman had sounded off against Mamet's script, marveling that a writer lauded for being tuned to the American aphasia could write lines like "I have become what I beheld."

Mamet won't rise to comment on the King James Version cadences but hefts morality like a latterday Arthur Miller. Issues of power, corruption, and the commonweal are impossible to avoid in the Windy City—"Fellow hoodlums," Big Bill Thompson began his mayoral address to the citizenry—and Kevin Costner's straight-arrow federal agent, Eliot Ness, presents an unfashionable but convincing portrait of the moral citizen. This Ness looks like the sort of guy who got a briefcase for Christmas and was pleased. "Mr. Ness is brought in from the outside, a simple man in a corrupt time. He is a person who says, 'Other people might know better, but I don't. Because I don't know better, all I can do is enforce the law. Perhaps that will restore order.' The first speech he gives to the men—'You have sworn to uphold the law, and if you've sworn falsely, you've forsworn yourselves. Perhaps the difference between what you do and what you say you do is what's causing the disruption in the body politic.' I found Mr. Ness a sympathetic character. I feel they're all sympathetic characters."

Even Al Capone?

"I have a lotta sympathy for Capone. You can't create character without sympathy. I gave good speeches to Mr. Capone. He's a man who has also understood that order is necessary. When he beats that guy's head in with a baseball bat, he's trying to keep order." Capone's point of view, vehemently expressed in the confrontation with Ness on the staircase of the Lexington Hotel and finally in the courtroom, was certainly consistent. "Ya wanna do it now? You wanna go to the mat now? . . . If you wanna hurt me, do it in my face like a man, not this income tax evasion trial."

Mamet was shocked by De Palma's borrowing of the Odessa Steps sequence from *Battleship Potemkin*—"So what? So what?" said De Palma—for the Union Station shootout. "I was not impressed. Here was my name on the script, and here was a sequence that was written by someone else—ha! rather effectively!—seventy years previously."

The theme of embattled virtue, as well as the Mafia, surfaces again in *Things Change,* embodied in the character of the old immigrant shoeshine man, Gino. It seems quite a departure for the writer who is associated with the feeding frenzies of hustlers—"always be closing"—and the moral twilight. "It is true that different characters interest me now. I've just scripted a movie called *We're No Angels* about the very subject. Two convicts masquerade as priests."

Mamet's directorial debut, *House of Games,* probed the psychology of the confidence trickster and the piercing humiliation of the deceived. It's a walk on the wild side, a lexicon of the tell, the mark, the sting, and the biter bit. Sharks and gulls. Cheats and cousins. It's a world order that hasn't changed since Ben Jonson's time.

"The con man looms large in the history of Western civilization. Look at the prominence of confidence men in English literature— Smollett, Fielding, Defoe, constantly—there's a rage of them in literature. Oh sure, coney-catchers and all that stuff. They think of themselves as complete professionals and like magicians, take great pride in doing a trick and not showing you the trick. I met one real old-time big con man. I was really privileged to have met him, I think, because it's just not being done that much. The short con is being done all the time on the streets of New York—ten dollars, twenty dollars—but not the big con anymore. I was reporting a *Soldier of Fortune* convention at Las Vegas for *Esquire* magazine at the time. I spent several days with this British guy who represented himself as an Air Vice Marshal. I wrote the piece, and eventually a fact checker called me up and said, 'On your Air Vice Marshal—did you lend him any money? The guy's a con man, and he's taken a lotta guys for a lotta money.' Jesus Christ! I remembered he'd been talking about his investments in the Cayman Isles and dropping a lotta names. All of a sudden, all these things that were inexplicable at the time flashed back to me. We'd walked past this table of firearms, and he'd picked up a service pistol and said, 'Oh, look at that. I carried one of these in Aden'—but he didn't know how to cycle the action."

Nothing scalds as bad as being deceived. The fixed world flaps up, the stomach drops out, and the treadmill of retrospection begins. "Nothing's worse than that," nods the writer.

Trust was in short supply in the film business too. His play *Sexual Perversity in Chicago* had been filmed as *About Last Night* stripped of Mamet. He'd sold the rights for a pittance and promises, signed on as screenwriter, and been fired. "They fired me off it for reasons of greed. It happens. In revenge I didn't go and see it. I wouldn't give them my five bucks. I hear it was dreadful. I hope I'm right. No, one can certainly trust other people. Just not too many of them."

His Broadway hit *Speed-the-Plow,* it is rumored, based its cynical lackey Hollywood executives on Ned Tanen, head of production at

Paramount and producer Art Linson, both involved in *The Untouchables*. They see their job as to "make the thing everyone made last year" and the movie business as being like the beginning of a new love affair; "it's full of surprises, and you're constantly getting fucked." Faced with the prospect of making a concerned movie out of a novel about radiation, Mamet's producer says, "Hey, I believe in the Yellow Pages, but I don't want to film it." Small wonder that Mamet the movie director steered clear of "the sinkhole of venal depravity," grasped after autonomy, and surrounded himself with his own team. But Mamet can be paradoxical. Ethical debate may underpin his work, but it's the hustlers who get the zesty lines, and his condemnation of Hollywood packaging found room for Madonna on stage as the head of production's temp.

"No, she did not unbalance the play," he said tersely. "She unbalanced the press. In retrospect one can understand why. It *was* a tad daring of me."

Dream Sequence

Michael Billington

Michael Billington's interview with David Mamet in early February 1989 initially raises questions about *Things Change,* Mamet's second film as writer/director. Their conversation quickly turns to Mamet's view that film is best understood as a medium of "dream, myth, and fable."

In his new play, *Speed-the-Plow,* David Mamet implies that the typical modern American movie is a buddy-buddy picture with "action, blood, a social theme." Mamet's own second film as a director, *Things Change,* might be seen as a buddy-buddy flick in that it deals with a strange relationship between a Chicago shoeshine man and his Mafia minder.

But, in its quiet moralizing about the human capacity for change, it is closer to Frank Capra than to corpse-filled modern cinema.

How does Mamet do it? How does he manage to make films on his own terms and bite Hollywood's hand even as it feeds him? In a conversation shot through with street wisdom and academic reference ("I am by nature a pedant. I think it comes from my people having studied the Talmud for six thousand years") Mamet denies having any anti-Hollywood bias.

"The people I'm attacking in *Speed-the-Plow,*" he says, "are not the movie makers but the hucksters who manipulate them. Hollywood itself has been princely to me. People there won't take revenge on you unless you cost them money. I love the people who make movies: the crew, the actors, the producers."

"I often say it's like a cattle drive, where people get together for three months under arduous conditions. I read a book about a cattle drive, where a guy complained about loss of sleep. Another guy says, 'If you wanta sleep, you gotta sleep in the winter.' That's how movie making is."

"I've never had any interference. Orion Pictures, where we made *House of Games*, promised not to meddle. The one thing they said was, 'Please, please, please shoot us an establishing shot of Seattle because we don't have one.'"

"So, I got out a poster of Seattle and tacked it on a wall; we got a little toy boat and a piece of dental floss, hauled the boat across the picture of the bay, and had it fall into a watering can to make a splash. Orion said, "Ha-ha, now will you do us an establishing shot.' I thought it would be nice on my part if I complied, but, of course, we never used it."

Surprisingly, *Things Change* was cowritten with Shel Silverstein with no particular casting in mind. In fact, Don Ameche, who wound up giving an award-winning performance as the shoeshine man mistaken for a senior mafioso, was originally going to play a Mafia chief.

An Italian actor, unnamed, was penciled in for the role. When he backed down from the project, Mamet sent him a telegram saying, "Great chagrin and unhappiness at your decision, and I hope that your chagrin and unhappiness will be as great when you see the movie." His reply is not recorded.

Mamet bridles slightly only when I suggest that *Things Change* is an anti-Mafia satire, a film that suggests membership of the Brotherhood means you get treated like American Royalty.

"I didn't intend it as any kind of comment on the Mafia. Shel and I both come from Chicago, and the idea of organized crime is part of the Chicago myth. Very few people in the city have any contact with it, but we feel it is part of the myth to which we are entitled."

"The movie is a fable, and the setting is mythic. It is saying that, in a country far away, this could happen. There are films where realism is important, but this one is pure myth."

But surely, I counter, cinema is a literal and realistic medium.

"Absolutely the opposite," Mamet says. "It is the least literal medium. The great filmmakers are those who understand that it is the medium that most closely approximates the nature of a dream.

"Because anything can happen; because you can't perceive distance in a movie; because the light that falls on people is quite artificial. When movies were first made, they were seen as a novelty recording device: here's a train coming toward you; there's a guy kissing a girl in a park.

"But, as filmmakers became more acquainted with the nature of the camera, they discovered cutting and the juxtaposition of images the better to tell the story. They understood that, in the juxtaposition of the temporal and the plastic, they could conjoin things in a way that could only happen in one other place: dream. If you read Freud on *The Interpretation of Dreams*, it's as if he's writing about movie making.

"The great movie makers evolved at the time of Freud's thinking: [Sergei] Eisenstein, for instance, the vast power of whose films comes from the ability to juxtapose simple and uninflected images. Film is the least realistic of art forms."

What is extraordinary about Mamet is that he has made the move from playwright to movie writer and director with such ease. He himself sees his movie career as an exploration of different genres. The courtroom drama in *The Verdict*, the gangster genre in *The Untouchables* (both of which he scripted), and now the fairy tale in *Things Change*. But, for a writer, I wondered what the most seductive aspect of directing movies was. Power perhaps?

"Kurt Vonnegut once wrote that unanticipated invitations to travel are dancing lessons from God. That's how I feel about making movies. Writing is a lonely life. And, although I've worked in the theater all my life, I haven't the talent or the discipline to be an actor.

"I've always loved and envied actors, so directing a movie is a great chance to perform. There you are in front of a hundred people trying to do your job well and be funny. Having the illusion of power is not interesting. Having control over a medium in which I enjoy working is very gratifying."

Time and again Mamet returns to the notion of movies as dream, myth, and fable. But in his book *Writing in Restaurants* he says much the same about theater observing that, if a play poses questions that can be answered rationally, we feel diverted but not fulfilled.

I take up cudgels on behalf of the utilitarian aspect of art, citing *A Doll's House* as a powerful example of drama that is responsibly instructive. Mamet politely demurs.

"I'd love to find a first draft of that play in which Nora, having slammed the door, comes back half an hour later saying, 'Darling, I've been very foolish.' Again, *An Enemy of the People* is refreshing not because it offers a solution but because it corresponds to our own turmoil. The play also says that, although we are alone in our dark night of the soul, God has not forsaken us.

"Even in the most rational of plays, the element that has the power to move us is not the rational element or the polemic element but the mythic element. It is the unresolved, not the resolved, conflicts that matter. We see this in our everyday society and in the decay of disparate mechanisms: government, religion, theater. We have seen them decay into rational organizations, each of which thinks its purpose is the same: to determine by force of reason what is right and then do it. So, society ends up a fucking morass."

Mamet argues that the purpose of film and drama is the same as that of dream and that we do not seek from them answers that our conscious mind is capable of supplying. But then how does he explain his own ability, seen at its height in *Glengarry Glen Ross,* to set down realistic conversations with uncanny accuracy?

"I take that as a great compliment. But Oscar Wilde said that we did not have pea soup fogs until people started writing about them. What I would say is that perhaps you didn't hear salesmen talk until you saw *Glengarry Glen Ross.* My point is that my dialogue is not realism. It's a poetic restatement of my idea of how people talk."

When I asked Mamet, the spinner of dreams (who has two scripts being shot this year, one by Neil Jordan [*We're No Angels*], one by himself [*Homicide*]), if he is moving inexorably toward the cinema, he says, no—he's moving "exorably" toward it.

Mamet talks good, but everything he says is laced with a heavy-headed Chicagoan humor. He describes, for instance, sitting in his Vermont home watching a video of Charles Laughton in *The Private Life of Henry VIII* with his wife [Lindsay Crouse] and a friend who makes furniture.

Mamet and his wife were in tears over the beauty of Laughton's performance when his friend suddenly leapt up and cried, "My God, look at that chair." Which perhaps proves Mamet's point that what we all find in the movies is a fulfillment of private dreams.

David Mamet: The Art of Theatre XI

John Lahr

John Lahr interviewed David Mamet in the spring of 1994 in New York after the playwright responded to Lahr's astute review of *The Cryptogram* with a *Cryptogram* cast gift. Discussions ensued between them, and at the writer's suggestion Lahr conducted a formal interview for *Paris Review*'s series on modern playwrights. Mamet met the critic in his office at the *New Yorker*, and "the exercise in ducking and diving," in Lahr's words, continued over lunch, during which Lahr recalls attempting to persuade Mamet to reject "obfuscation" in favor of clarity. Their revealing conversation notably pins down the relationship between the man and his art.

LAHR: How was it that you were drawn to the theater?

MAMET: Freud believed that our dreams sometimes recapitulate a speech, a comment we've heard or something that we've read. I always had compositions in my dreams. They would be a joke, a piece of a novel, a witticism or a piece of dialogue from a play, and I would dream them. I would actually express them line by line in the dream. Sometimes after waking up I would remember a snatch or two and write them down. There's something in me that just wants to create dialogue.

LAHR: Can you put a date to this?

MAMET: It's always been going on. It's something my mother used to say when I was just a little kid: "David, why must you dramatize

---

From "David Mamet: The Art of Theatre XI." Copyright © 1997 by John Lahr. Originally appeared in *Paris Review* 39, no. 142 (Spring 1997): 53–74. Reprinted by permission of Georges Borchardt, Inc., for the author.

everything?" She said it to me as a criticism: why must you *dramatize* everything?

LAHR: And did you have an answer for her?

MAMET: No, but I found out (it took me forty years) that all rhetorical questions are accusations. They're very sneaky accusations because they masquerade as a request for information. If one is not aware of the anger they provoke, one can feel not only accused but inadequate for being unable to respond to the question.

LAHR: That happens in your plays a lot. There are a lot of rhetorical challenges.

MAMET: "Why must you always . . . ?"

LAHR: One of the things that interests me is how uncompromising you are, both with yourself and the audience. *The Cryptogram*, for example, forces the audience to solve this puzzle that also happens to be troubling the kid in the play. You, as the author, have put the audience and the kid in essentially the same place.

MAMET: Well, that, to me, is always the trick of dramaturgy: theoretically, perfectly, what one wants to do is put the protagonist and the audience in exactly the same position. The main question in drama, the way I was taught, is always: What does the protagonist want? That's what drama is. It comes down to that. It's not about theme, it's not about ideas, it's not about setting but what the protagonist wants. What gives rise to the drama, what is the precipitating event, and how, at the end of the play, do we see that event culminated? Do we see the protagonist's wishes fulfilled or absolutely frustrated? That's the structure of drama. You break it down into three acts.

LAHR: Does this explain why your plays have so little exposition?

MAMET: Yes. People only speak to get something. If I say, "Let me tell you a few things about myself," already your defenses go up; you go, "Look, I wonder what he wants from me," because no one ever speaks except to obtain an objective. That's the only reason anyone ever opens their mouth, on stage or off stage. They may use a language that *seems* revealing, but, if so, it's just coincidence, because what they're trying to do is accomplish an objective. "Well, well, if it isn't my younger brother, just returned from Australia . . . have a good break?" The question is, where does the *dramatist* have to lead you? Answer: the place where he or she thinks the audience needs to be led. But what does the *character* think? Does the character need to convey that information? If the answer is no, then you'd better cut it out, because you aren't putting the audience in the same position with the protagonist. You're saying, in effect, "Let's stop the play." That's what the narration is doing: stopping the play.

Now, there's a certain amount of *essential* information, without which the play does not make sense . . .

LAHR: And how do you fit that information in?

MAMET: As obliquely as possible. You want to give the people information before they know it's been given to them.

LAHR: So, to you a character is . . .

MAMET: It's action, as Aristotle said. That's all that it is: exactly what the person does. It's not what they "think," because we don't know what they think. It's not what they say. It's what they do, what they're physically trying to accomplish on the stage. Which is exactly the same way we understand a person's character in life: not by what they say but by what they do. Say someone came up to you and said, "I'm glad to be your neighbor because I'm a very honest man. That's my character. I'm honest, I like to do things, I'm forthright, I like to be clear about everything, I like to be concise." Well, you really don't know anything about that guy's character. Or the person is on stage, and the playwright has him or her make those same claims in several subtle or not-so-subtle ways; the audience will say, "Oh yes, I understand their character now; now I understand that they are a character." But, in fact, you don't understand anything. You just understand that they're jabbering to try to convince you of something.

LAHR: So, do you end up cutting a lot of material from your earlier drafts?

MAMET: Well, you know, Hemingway said it once: "To write the best story you can, take out all the good lines."

LAHR: But do you then sometimes find that the audience has a hard time keeping up with you? It seems to me that in this climate one of the playwright's problems is that the audience expects things to be explained.

MAMET: I never try to make it hard for the audience. I may not succeed, but . . . Vakhtangov, who was a disciple of Stanislavski, was asked at one point why his films were so successful, and he said, "Because I never for one moment forget about the audience." I try to adopt that as an absolute tenet. I mean, if I'm not writing for the audience, if I'm not writing to make it easier for *them,* then who the hell am I doing it for? And the way you make it easier is by following those tenets: cutting, building to a climax, leaving out exposition, and always progressing toward the single goal of the protagonist. They're very stringent rules, but they are, in my estimation and experience, what makes it easier for the audience.

LAHR: What else? Are there other rules?

MAMET: Get into the scene late, get out of the scene early.

LAHR: Why? So that something's already happened?

MAMET: Yes. That's how *Glengarry* got started. I was listening to conversations in the next booth, and I thought, My God, there's nothing more fascinating than the people in the next booth. You start in the middle of the conversation and wonder, What the hell are they talking about? And you listen heavily. So, I worked a bunch of these scenes with people using extremely arcane language—kind of the canting language of the real estate crowd, which I understood, having been involved with them—and I thought, Well, if it fascinates me, it will probably fascinate them too. If not, they can put me in jail.

LAHR: Going back to your roots in the theater, how did you get involved initially?

MAMET: I was a kid actor. I did amateur theatricals, television, and radio in Chicago. Always loved the theater.

LAHR: You loved it, but I wonder if your plays aren't in some sort of debate with its conventions and what it should be.

MAMET: Maybe, but I always understood that as one of its conventions. Like David Ogilvy said, you don't want to create an ad that says "advertisement." That you will not look at. Concerns of content, concerns of form, it's all the same to me. It's the theatrical event. As for thinking against the sort of conventional narrative formulas of the theater . . . well, I have the great benefit of never having learned anything in school, so a lot of this stuff . . .

LAHR: Were you a bad student?

MAMET: I was a nonstudent. No interest, just bored to flinders. I was like the professor in *Oleanna* who all his life had been told he was an idiot, so he behaved like an idiot. Later on I realized that I enjoy accomplishing tasks. I get a big kick out of it because I never did it as a kid. Somebody said that the reason that we all have a school dream—"I've forgotten to do my paper!" "I've forgotten to study!"— is that it's the first time that the child runs up against the expectations of the world. "The world has expectations of me, and I'm going to have to meet them or starve, meet them or die, and I'm unprepared."

LAHR: Do you ever feel unprepared?

MAMET: Much of the time. But the prescription for that is to do more, to work harder, to do more, to do it again.

LAHR: If you hadn't found the theater, what do you think you might have been?

MAMET: I think it's very likely I would have been a criminal. It seems to me to be another profession that subsumes outsiders or, perhaps more to the point, accepts people with a not-very-well-formed ego and rewards the ability to improvise.

LAHR: Is that why con men and tricksters appear so often in your plays?

MAMET: I've always been fascinated by the picaresque. That's part of the Chicago tradition: to love our gangsters and con men, the bunko artists and so forth.

It occurred to me while I was doing *House of Games* that the difficulty of making the movie was exactly the same difficulty the confidence man has. For the confidence man it is depriving the victim of her money; for me it is misleading the audience sufficiently so they feel pleased when they find out they've been misled, tricking them so that every step is logical, and at the end they've defeated themselves. So, the process of magic and the process of confidence games, and to a certain extent the process of drama, are all processes of autosuggestion. They cause the audience to autosuggest themselves in a way that seems perfectly logical but is actually false.

You know, also being a very proud son of a bitch, I always thought that the trick was to be able to do it on a bare stage, with nothing but one or two actors. If one could do it like that, then one has done something to keep the audience's attention, make it pay off over an hour and a half, on a bare stage with nothing but two people talking.

LAHR: Did you read a lot when you were a kid?

MAMET: I always read novels. To me that was "real" writing. I liked all the Midwesterners—Sinclair Lewis, Willa Cather, Sherwood Anderson.

LAHR: Was it just that the Midwest was familiar terrain or something in the tone?

MAMET: Both. I mean, I loved Dreiser—he talked about streets that I knew and types that I knew and the kinds of people and kinds of neighborhoods that I actually knew. But I also liked the Midwestern tone. It was very legato. Perhaps the rhythm of the Midwestern seasons—a long, impossibly cold winter and then a long, impossibly hot summer. It was a vast, impossibly big lake, a huge sea of wheat. It has that same rhythm, the same legato rhythm, moved on like that. Things were going to unfold in their own time, kind of like a French movie, except not quite that drawn out.

LAHR: You held a number of odd jobs while you were starting in the theater.

MAMET: Yes. After college I worked as an actor, a cab driver, a cook, a busboy—I did all of that. At one point, after I'd been running a theater for a couple years, this guy came up to me at a party and said, "I saw the whole play. I like it very much." I said, "Thank you." He said, "You want to come be an editor at *Oui* magazine?" I said, "Why did you ask me? I have no idea what the job entails, and, also, I'm sure I'm unqualified for it." And he said, "You know, I'm not sure what it entails either, but it will be a little bit of this, little bit of that, little bit of this. Make it up. And I'm sure you *are* qualified for it." And I said, "Well, I hate sitting in an office." He said, "Don't. Come in and do the work for however long it takes you and go home." And I said *hum, hum, hummer.* And he said, "I'll pay you twenty thousand dollars a year." This was 1975. Twenty thousand was a vast amount of money—about three times more than I'd made in my life. So, I said okay. I worked there for a while. Before that I was selling carpet over the telephone. Cold calling out of the blue book, absolutely cold.

LAHR: Do you remember your spiel?

MAMET: "Mrs. Jones, this is"—you always used a fake name—"Mrs. Jones, this is Dick Richards of Walton Carpets. I don't know what you've heard about our current two-for-one special—is your husband there with you now?" "A-buh-buh." "Will he be home this evening?" "A-wah-wah-wah-wah." "Fine, which would be a better time for us to send a representative over to talk to you, seven or nine o'clock?" Because what we wanted to do, it's the same idea as the Fuller Brush men: you get your foot in the door, you offer them something, keep talking, get them in the habit of saying yes, and then you've got them in the habit of accepting what you're giving them.

LAHR: Were you a good salesman?

MAMET: No. I was terrible. I kept identifying with the people on the other end, which is something you really can't do.

LAHR: You're much more ruthless as a playwright than you would be as a salesman.

MAMET: I'm a fairly gentle guy. When Greg Mosher directed *Glengarry,* we had a lot of salesmen come in to talk to the cast, guys who were making five million dollars a year selling airplanes or industrial equipment. These people were super-closers. There's a whole substratum of people who are *the* closer, like the Alec Baldwin character in the movie of *Glengarry.* But the most impressive salesman was a saleswoman, a Fuller Brush lady, who came in and showed us how to do the Fuller Brush spiel. It was great. The first thing they do is offer you a choice of two free gifts, and they make sure you take one in your hand. So it's not "Do you want one?" It's "Which would you rather have?" And, now that you've got one of their free gifts in your hand, how could you not answer their next question, which is also going to be answered—it's going to be yes, and the next question's going to be yes, and the next . . .

LAHR: Does this follow a rule of drama, too, for you?

MAMET: I don't know, but I was fascinated by it. And the idea was, you've absolutely got to stick to the pitch. Have to stick with it. There was a great book called *In Search of Myself* by Frederick Grove, a Canadian novelist, a great writer. Nobody's ever heard of him, but it's a great book. It's about the immigrant experience: coming here with nothing and what America does to that person. And one of the things he becomes is a book salesman who goes from door to door having to sell phony books. Heartbreaking, you know, that he has to do this. Heartbreaking.

LAHR: Going back to the odd jobs: did you see them as a means to getting your start in the theater, or were you just sort of rooting around?

MAMET: I knew I wanted to be in the theater, but I also knew I was a terrible actor. So, I started, by dribs and drabs, forming a theater company that I could direct, because I figured it was something I could do.

LAHR: When did you start writing plays?

MAMET: I didn't really start writing till I was in my twenties. And I started because the company, the St. Nicholas Theatre, couldn't pay any royalties—we didn't have any money. I was very fortunate, coming from Chicago, because we had that tradition there of writing as a legitimate day-to-day skill, like bricklaying. You know, you need to build a house but you can't afford it, or you need to build a garage but you can't afford a bricklayer. Well, hell, figure out how to lay bricks. You need a script, well, hell, figure out how to write one. There was a great tradition flourishing in Chicago in the early 1970s of the theater as an organic unit. The organic theater—in fact, the most important theater at the time was called the Organic Theater—but the organic (small *o*) theater consisted of a company of actors who also directed and also wrote and also designed. Everybody did everything. There was no mystery about it. One week one guy would be the director, the next week the woman would be the director and the guy would be acting, etc. So, that was the community and the tradition that I came back to in the 1970s in Chicago.

LAHR: Who were your dramatic influences?

MAMET: Well, primarily Pinter—*The Revue Sketches, A Night Out,* and *The Birthday Party.* He was my first encounter with modern drama. His work sounded real to me in a way that no drama ever had.

LAHR: What was a typical drama of the old school that struck you as dead or deadly?

MAMET: It was either a Shakespeare, which I wasn't hip enough to understand at that time in my youth, or bad translations of European plays, which were very bad translations, or American poetic realism, which just bored the bloomers off me. People talking too much—I didn't understand those people. They weren't like anybody I knew. The people I knew washed dishes or drove cabs.

LAHR: Were there advantages to starting in Chicago instead of New York?

MAMET: Being in Chicago was great. It was all happening, all the time, like jazz in New Orleans. We looked at New York as two things: one was, of course, the Big Apple, and the other was the world's biggest hick town. Because much of what we saw happening in New York was the equivalent of the Royal Nonesuch—you know, a bunch of people crawling around, barking and calling it theater. But the version in Chicago was people went to the theater just like they went to the ballgame: they wanted to see a show. If it was a drama, it had to be dramatic, and, if it was a comedy, it had to funny—period. And, if it was those things, they'd come back. If it wasn't those things, they wouldn't come back.

LAHR: How long were you there?

MAMET: I was in Chicago from like 1973 till 1976 or 1977. And then—whore that I am—I came to New York.

LAHR: *The Cryptogram,* can we talk a little about what that was trying to figure out?

MAMET: Well, it was trying to figure out itself, for one. It was trying to figure out what the hell the mechanism of the play was. And I had all this stuff about the kid not going to sleep, and it finally occurred to me, about the billionth draft, well, it's about why can't the kid sleep? It's not *that* the kid can't sleep but *why* can't the kid sleep? So, the kid can't sleep because he knows, subconsciously, that something's unbalanced in the household. But then why is nobody paying attention to him? I thought Aha! Well, this is perhaps the question of the play.

LAHR: So, you, as the writer inside *The Cryptogram,* you've sort of imagined my questions and led me gradually to revelation. You have certain designs on the audience's mind; you try to persuade them of certain psychological truths . .

MAMET: No, I'm not trying to persuade them of anything; it's much more basic than that; it's much more concrete. It has to do with those black lines on the white page. Finally, it comes down to— maybe this is going to sound coy—it just comes down to the writing of a play. Obviously, the point of the play is doing it for the audience—like the cook who wants to make that perfect soufflé, that perfect mousse, that perfect carbonara. Of course, he isn't going to do it if he doesn't think someone's going to eat it, but the point is to cook it perfectly, not to affect the eaters in a certain way. The thing exists of itself.

LAHR: Is there a moment in one of your plays that you really didn't know was there?

MAMET: Yes. I wrote this play called *Bobby Gould in Hell.* Greg Mosher did it on a double bill with a play by Shel Silverstein over at Lincoln Center. Bobby Gould is consigned to Hell, and he has to be interviewed to find out how long he's going to spend there. The Devil is called back from a fishing trip to interview Bobby Gould. And so the Devil is there, the Assistant Devil is there, and Bobby Gould. And the Devil finally says to Bobby Gould, "You're a very bad man." And Bobby Gould says, "Nothing's black and white." And the Devil says, "Nothing's black and white, nothing's black and white—what about a panda? What about a panda, you dumb fuck! What about a fucking panda!" And when Greg directed it he had the assistant hold up a picture of a panda, kind of pan it 180 degrees to the audience at the Vivian Beaumont Theater. That was the best moment I've ever seen in any of my plays.

LAHR: What sort of writing routine do you have? How do you operate?

MAMET: I don't know. I've actually been vehemently deluding myself, thinking that I have no set habits whatever. I know that I have very good habits of thought, and I'm trying to make them better. But, as for where I go, what I do and who's around when I work—those things are never important to me.

LAHR: Those habits of thought—how do they govern your writing?

MAMET: It's really not an intellectual process. I mean, as you see, I try to apply all sorts of mechanical norms to it, and they help me order my thoughts, but finally in playwriting you've got to be able to write dialogue. And if you write enough of it and let it flow enough, you'll probably come across something that will give you a key as to structure. I think the process of writing a play is working back and forth between the moment and the whole. The moment and the whole, the fluidity of the dialogue and the necessity of a strict construction. Letting one predominate for a while and coming back and fixing it so that eventually what you do, like a pastry chef, is frost your mistakes, if you can.

LAHR: Are you a computer man or a pad-and-pencil man?

MAMET: Pad and pencil. I want to see it, I want to see them all out in front of me, each one of the pencil adaptations, the pencil notations, and the pencil notations crossed out, and the pen on top of the pencil, and the pages . . .

LAHR: Do you look at all twelve drafts?

MAMET: If I have to. Theoretically, one should be able to keep the whole play in one's mind. The main thing is, I want to know that they're there. The idea of taking everything and cramming it into this little electronic box designed by some nineteen-year-old in Silicon Valley . . . I can't imagine it.

LAHR: In looking back at your work, are there plays that you feel were more successful than others?

MAMET: The most challenging dramatic form, for me, is the tragedy. I think I'm proudest of the craft in the tragedies I've written—*The Cryptogram, Oleanna, American Buffalo,* and *The Woods.* They are classically structured tragedies.

LAHR: How do you distinguish tragedy from drama?

MAMET: Circumstance. Drama has to do with circumstance; tragedy has to do with individual choice. The precipitating element of a drama can be a person's sexuality, their wealth, their disease . . . A tragedy can't be about any of those things. That's why we identify with a tragic hero more than with a dramatic hero: we understand the tragic hero to be ourselves. That's why it's easier for the audiences initially to form an affection for the drama rather than the tragedy. Although it seems that they're exercising a capacity for identification—"Oh, yes, I understand. So-and-so is in a shitload of difficulty, and I identify with them, and I see where the going's bad, and I see where the hero is good"—in effect they're distancing themselves, because they'll say, "Well, shit, I couldn't get into that situation because I'm not gay or because I am gay, because I'm not crippled or because I am crippled . . ." They're distanced. Because I can go on with drama. That's the difference between drama and tragedy. *Glengarry,* on the other hand, falls into a very specific American genre: the gang drama or the gang comedy. The prime proponent of it, the genius proponent of it—and maybe one of its coinventors—is Sidney Kingsley. Plays like *Detective Story, Men in White, Truckline Cafe,* to some extent *Waiting for Lefty.* These are slice-of-life plays investigating a milieu of society. A good example is *Lower Depths,* where the protagonist is elaborated into many parts. In a comedy of manners like *Don Quixote,* for example, we understand that the sidekick is just another aspect of the protagonist, just like everybody in our dreams is an aspect of us. A tragedy has to be the attempt of one specific person to obtain one specific goal, and, when he either gets it or doesn't get it, then we know the play is over, and we can go home and put out the babysitter.

LAHR: I'm interested to hear you say that you thought of *Oleanna,* which is more polemical than the other plays, as a tragedy.

MAMET: Classically, it's structured as a tragedy. The professor is the main character. He undergoes absolute reversal of situation, absolute recognition at the last moment of the play. He realizes that perhaps he is the cause of the plague on Thebes.

LAHR: Did it surprise you, the way the play took off?

MAMET: It stunned them.

LAHR: You were aiming for a nerve, and you hit it.

MAMET: No, I wasn't aiming for a nerve. I was just trying to write the play. After it was finished I thought, Jesus Christ, I can't put this play on! Especially at Harvard—people were going to throw rocks through the theater windows. I was frightened. And my wife [Rebecca Pidgeon] was playing the part—the part was written for her—and I was always frightened that someone was going to attack her, come over the footlights and attack her. One day we were doing some notes before the performance, and I was just looking out at the empty theater, and William Macy, who played the professor, came over and said, "Don't worry, Dave, they'll have to get through me first." I always felt they were going to put me in jail someday.

LAHR: Why?

MAMET: Well, for many reasons, not the least of which is, as a kid, I became so judgmental about the House Un-American Activities Committee. This person talked to the committee, that person talked to the committee—"How could you do that? How could you not do that? How could . . . ?" Later on I realized that everybody has their own reasons and that unless we've walked a mile in that man or woman's moccasins it's not for us to say, "Well, okay, here's what you're going to get for criticizing others' bravery as a writer or as a creative artist."

LAHR: I suppose all your plays, in one way or another, come very close to saying something unacceptable about society, something that's very hard for people to hear.

MAMET: Well, you know, we did *American Buffalo* here on Broadway, right around the corner, and I remember some businessmen—night after night one or two of them would come storming out, muttering to themselves furiously, "What the *fuck* does this play have to do with me?" and words to that effect.

LAHR: Where did the idea for *American Buffalo* come from?

MAMET: Macy and I were in Chicago one time, and he was living in this wretched hovel—we'd both become screamingly poor—and I came over to talk to him about something, some play equipment. I opened the refrigerator, and there was this big piece of cheese. I hadn't had anything to eat in a long time, so I picked it up, cut off a big chunk, and started eating. And Macy said, "Hey, *help yourself.*" I was really hurt. I went away and fumed about that for several days. Then I just started writing, and out of that came this scene, which was the start of the play: Ruthie [Teach] comes in furious because someone had just said to him, "Help yourself."

LAHR: What about when you were working on *The Village*? Did that change your routine?

MAMET: With a novel it's different. It's kind of exhilarating not to have to cut to the bone constantly. "Oh, well, I can go over here for a moment." I can say what I think the guy was thinking or what the day looked like or what the bird was doing. If you do that as a playwright, you're dead.

LAHR: Have you considered putting stage directions in your screenplays?

MAMET: No, because if you're writing a drama, to get involved in it is kind of nonsense. It's like, you read a screenplay, and it says, "BRENDA comes into the room. She's beautiful, she's sassy, she's smart, she's twenty-five, she's built like a brick shithouse: this is the kind of girl that you'll leave your wife for. When you see those deep blue eyes . . ." I mean, you're going to cast an actress, and she's going to look like something, right? Some idiot script reader from Yale is going to get a kick out of what you've thrown in, but it has nothing to do with making the movie, because you're going to cast an actress who will have qualities that are going to have nothing to do with what you made up. When you write stage directions: unless they're absolutely essential for the understanding of the action of the play ("He leaves," "She shoots him") something else is going to happen when the actors and directors get them on the stage.

LAHR: What led you to the movies? It seems to me that the demands of the truth that can be told in the theater are so much deeper and more intense than on the screen. If you could tell stories, in my view, the way you tell stories, why bother with the cinema?

MAMET: I like it. I think it's a fascinating medium. It's so similar to the theater in many ways and yet so very different. It's great: it takes place with a huge number of people, which is fine; it's very technical in ways that the theater isn't; it calls for a lot of different ways of thinking, purely mechanical ways of thinking, that I find fascinating. A lot of it, directing especially, is how many boxes are hidden in this drawing? That kind of thing. It's a fascinating medium to me.

LAHR: But I feel that, if you have a gift that's so enormous in a certain area, it would be very hard not to give yourself to that entirely. Is it simply a desire to make your life interesting or to change pace or . . . ?

MAMET: I think that's a large part of it.

LAHR: Where do you feel you have to work the hardest?

MAMET: That's a good question. I don't know the answer to it. I just feel like I have to work hard at all of it; it's not something that comes naturally to me. So, maybe that's why I like it: I get a great sense of accomplishment from being able to complete a project with a certain level of technical efficiency. Frankly, I don't feel I have a lot of talent for it, but I love doing it and have a certain amount of hard-won technical ability.

LAHR: Do you have a lot of unfinished work?

MAMET: I've got a lot of stuff I just shelved. Some of it I come back to, and some I don't.

LAHR: It tempts you.

MAMET: It challenges me, a lot of it, and it angers me.

LAHR: But are you prepared just to write and write and write, like pissing into a well or something?

MAMET: Sometimes.

LAHR: Not knowing where you're going, trying to see what the story is.

MAMET: I think it would be a lot easier to write to a formula, but it's just not fun to me. It's not challenging.

LAHR: I find it hard to understand how you can live with the tension of knowing something is unresolved, not knowing where it's going.

MAMET: But that's great. It's like Hemingway said: give yourself something to do tomorrow.

LAHR: So, you let go and wait till later for a resolution. That's very hard, isn't it, to live with that?

MAMET: Well, I think that's the difference between the Christian and the Jewish ethic. Judaism is not a religion or a culture built on faith. You don't have to have faith. You don't have to believe anything; you just have to do it.

LAHR: But what happens when you follow a character or a situation and it doesn't pan out?

MAMET: You do it again. Or, in some instances, stick it on the shelf, and either do or don't come back to it sometime.

LAHR: Do you try to put in five or six hours a day writing?

MAMET: I try to do as little writing as possible, as I look back on it. I like to talk on the telephone and, you know, read magazines.

LAHR: And sit in your office and forestall writing?

MAMET: Yes, and sometimes I like to do the opposite.

LAHR: Whatever happens, you get a lot out for somebody who doesn't write a lot or doesn't like to write.

MAMET: I never saw the point in not.

LAHR: But you just said you spend a lot of time trying not to write.

MAMET: That's true. But the actual point of being a writer and doing something every once in a while mechanically, I just don't see the point in it, and it wouldn't be good for me. I've got to do it, anyway. Like beavers, you know. They chop, they eat wood, because, if they don't, their teeth grow too long and they die. And they hate the sound of running water. Drives them crazy. So, if you put those two ideas together, *they are going to build dams.*

Working the Con

Geoffrey Norman and John Rezek

During the 1980s David Mamet had all but stopped granting interviews. In late summer 1994, however, Geoffrey Norman and *Playboy* magazine Assistant Managing Editor John
Rezek met with Mamet in Cambridge, Massachusetts, over
the course of three days. "At times," observe Norman and
Rezek, the writer spoke "with the crude wit of his best characters and at others with an informed, recondite precision."

PLAYBOY: Your film *Oleanna*—and the play—pushed the culture's hot
buttons, with a man and woman winding up, literally, each at the
other's throat. Why is there such tension between the sexes?

MAMET: This has always been a puritan country, and we've always
been terrified of sex. That terror takes different forms. Sometimes it
is overindulgence, and, of course, at other times it's the opposite.

PLAYBOY: Why should this be a time of repression?

MAMET: For one thing, there is economic scarcity. People tend to
get cranky when there aren't so many jobs to go around. Also, I think
our expectations are scrambled. Sexual drive is designed to make
sure the species will survive, as much as we fight the fact. But for
young people today it is very difficult to say, "Fine, either with you
this year or with someone else next year, I'm going to get married,
buy a house, get a job, settle down and raise kids." It's terrifying for
them to say that. They can't get married. There aren't any jobs. They
can't buy the house and have the dog named Randy. Our expectations have become greater than our ability to meet them.

PLAYBOY: So, the alternative is the kind of antagonism we see between the sexes?

MAMET: Alternatives are going to emerge. In the 1970s and 1980s there was the notion of continual romantic involvement. You said, "I don't want to get married; I just want to go out there and have a good time." That worked for a while, and then, suddenly, it didn't seem like such a good idea anymore. Back in the 1960s or 1970s *National Lampoon* published a story of a rumor about a new strain of the clap that guys brought back from Vietnam. If you got it, you died. Very funny.

So, now you can't become committed to somebody because you can't support a family, and recreational sex is out because AIDS might kill you. As a result, society is going to bring us to some sort of intermediary mechanism, something to keep people wary about getting involved with each other. Here it comes—sexual harassment. The culture has to supersede. Alternatives will emerge to take the problem off our shoulders.

"Gee, what does she want of me?" It's a rhetorical question. It means. "I don't understand—better back off." On the other hand, "I need him to be more sensitive to me." That's poetry. It doesn't mean anything. It means, "I'd better back off because of my fear."

PLAYBOY: Your timing with *Oleanna* was perfect. When the play was first performed, sexual harassment was probably the most incendiary issue around. Were you influenced by the Clarence Thomas [Senate] hearings?

MAMET: No. I didn't follow those hearings, actually. It was weird. I wrote the play before the hearings, and I stuck it in a drawer.

PLAYBOY: Why?

MAMET: Two reasons. First, I didn't have a last act. Second, when I wrote the play, it seemed a little farfetched to me. And then the Thomas hearings began, and I took the play out of the drawer and started working on it again. One of the first people to see the play was a headmaster at a very good school here in Cambridge. He said to me, "Eighteen months ago, I would have said this play was fantasy. But now, when all the headmasters get together at conferences, we whisper to one another, 'You know, all of us are only one dime away from the end of a career.'"

PLAYBOY: Was that a typical response?

MAMET: There was a great deal of controversy at a level I've never encountered in the theater. In the audience people got into shouting matches and fistfights. People stood up and screamed, "Oh bullshit," at the stage before they realized they'd done it. A couple of people got a little crazy and lost their composure.

PLAYBOY: So, it isn't a good date play?

MAMET: It is a terrible date play. But I never really saw it as a play about sexual harassment. I think the issue was, to a large extent, a flag of convenience for a play that's structured as a tragedy. Just like the issues of race relations and xenophobia are flags of convenience for *Othello*. It doesn't have anything to do with race. This play—and the film—is a tragedy about power. These are two people with a lot to say to each other, with legitimate affection for each other. But protecting their positions becomes more important than pursuing their own best interests. And that leads them down the slippery slope to a point where, at the end of the play, they tear each other's throat out. My plays are not political. They're dramatic. I don't believe that the theater is a good venue for political argument. Not because it is wrong but because it doesn't work very well.

PLAYBOY: Do you think you can understand and empathize with the female point of view in this hostile climate? Your critics would say your point of view is almost exclusively male. Cheap shot?

MAMET: Not cheap but inaccurate. Take *Oleanna*, for instance, the points she makes about power and privilege—I believe them all. If I didn't believe them, the play wouldn't work as well. It is a play about two people, and each person's point of view is correct. Yet they end up destroying each other.

PLAYBOY: So it is possible, then, that Anita Hill and Clarence Thomas were both telling the truth?

MAMET: Yeah, sure. You know the whole notion of American jurisprudence is that you can't determine who is telling the truth. That's not the job of the jury. The jury is supposed to decide which side has made the best case. Polls—which are replacing the judicial system as the way we settle disputes—are no better.

PLAYBOY: But they do provide clarity, which some critics find lacking in your work. They find your dialogue almost intentionally obscure. What do you say to them?

MAMET: First of all, I'd like to thank them for their interest in my work.

PLAYBOY: Then?

MAMET: Then, I suppose, I'd like them to think about *Oleanna*. They say the play is "unclear," and it occurs to me that what they mean is "provocative." That rather than sending the audience out whistling over the tidy moral of the play, it leaves them unsettled. I've

125

noticed over the past thirty years that a lot of what passes in the theater is not drama but, rather, a morality tale. "Go thou now and do likewise." That's very comforting to someone who is concerned or upset. When you leave the theater, and you say, "Oh, now I get it. Women are people, too." Or "Now I get it, handicapped people have rights," then you feel very soothed for the amount of time it takes you to get to your car. Then you forget about the play. If, on the other hand, you leave the theater upset, you might have seen a rotten play. Or you might be provoked because something was suggested that you could not have known when you came into the theater. Aristotle said we should see something at the end of tragedy that is surprising and inevitable.

PLAYBOY: But, while your structure is classical, the speech is entirely modern and urban, and, some critics have said, free of content. How do you get your characters to convey anything?

MAMET: There is always content in what's being said. That content is not necessarily carried by the context of the words. There has never been a conversation without content. If you're in a room where a lot of people are talking with one another and you can't hear a word of what's being said, you can still tell what the people are saying because their intent communicates itself.

One of the things I learned when I studied acting is that the content of what is being said is rarely carried by the connotation of the words. It is carried by the rhythm of the speech and the posture of the speaker and a lot of other things. All conversations have meaning.

PLAYBOY: Do men and women use speech differently?

MAMET: Probably. But men talk differently to other men under different circumstances. Conversations with their peers in a bar vary from conversations with strangers in a bar. No one ever talks except to accomplish an objective. This objective changes according to the sex of the person, the age of the person, the time of day. Everybody uses language for his or her own purpose to get what he or she wants. I think the notion that everyone can be everything to everybody at all times is a big fat bore. Men have always talked with one another. I find it interesting that in the past five or six years women have started talking with one another. It's called "consciousness-raising," whereas men talking with one another is called "bonding."

PLAYBOY: Is the rough, profane talk characteristic of your plays an exclusively male language?

MAMET: Anyone who would think that apparently hasn't met my sister [screenwriter Lynn Mamet Weisberg]. I have never found the issue of profanity to be very important. In the plays I was writing, that's how the people actually spoke. It would have been different if I had been writing bedroom farce. But I wasn't. I was writing about different kinds of people, people whom I knew something about.

PLAYBOY: Including con men.

MAMET: Absolutely.

PLAYBOY: The con game is one of the fixtures in your work. What's behind your fascination with the con?

MAMET: Well, I have spent some time around con men, and they are fascinating people. I've always been interested in the continuum that starts with charm and ends with psychopathy. Con artists deal in human nature, and what they do is all in the realm of suggestion. It is like hypnosis or, to a certain extent, like playwriting.

PLAYBOY: How?

MAMET: Part of the art of the play is to introduce information in such a way, and at such a time, that the people in the audience don't realize they have been given information. They accept it as a matter of course, but they aren't really aware of it so that, later on, the information pays off. It has been consciously planted by the author.

PLAYBOY: And he is working a con?

MAMET: Right. Now, in a bad play, the author will introduce the information frontally. You actually tell the audience that you are about to give them some information and that it is important to what happens later in the play. In a good play the information is delivered almost as an aside. The same mechanism holds true in the con game. If you're giving the mark information that he—or she, in the case of a film of mine called *House of Games*—is going to need in order to be taken advantage of and you don't want him to know that he has been given the information, then you would bring it in through the back door. Let's say my partner and I are taking you to the cleaners. The three of us are talking, and my partner and I get into an argument. We start saying things that you aren't supposed to hear. I say to you, "Excuse me for a second, I'm sorry about this, and blah, blah, blah." Then I take my partner aside, and we start screaming at each other, really out of control. You have not only been given information; you've been told to please look the other way. Well, that is going to put your mind on afterburner. Later you use that information, which you think you got accidentally, to put together what you think are the pieces.

PLAYBOY: A useful skill, then?

MAMET: Sure. The con game is what people do, most of the

time, with few exceptions. After we reach a certain economic level, we try to say that we're no longer trying to talk you out of your money. We're doing "investment banking," or we've got a film "in development."

PLAYBOY: Films in development is a world you know something about. You've written scripts and directed films.

MAMET: Yes.

PLAYBOY: And used Hollywood as material in your play *Speed-the-Plow*, which painted a pretty bleak picture of a world where the con is everything.

MAMET: Well, any business will eventually degenerate into a con game. The cause of the process is any kind of boom. If you get a boom, certain myths will crystallize around that success and cause eventual failure. If you get a boom in American virtue, like you did in World War II when the citizen-soldiers of this country flat out saved the world from Nazism, it is inevitable that you are going to have a military-industrial complex and wind up fighting a whole bunch of wars because you want to find a place to be virtuous again. Vietnam was the inevitable outcome of D–Day. We had the golden age of cinema and the consequences of it.

PLAYBOY: This sense of corruption was almost overwhelming in *Speed-the-Plow*. Because this is a world you know, was there some personal malice reflected in the play?

MAMET: Not nearly enough.

PLAYBOY: Is your work in movies a way to make money or a way to do interesting things?

MAMET: Well, both. I love making movies. I love writing them, and I love directing them.

PLAYBOY: At the end of the day, do you ever get a sense that you should go back to your room and to your real work, which is writing plays; that maybe movie making is a lesser form?

MAMET: I don't think it is a lesser form. I do, however, feel absolutely that the theater is my real work, and when I'm making movies I sometimes feel like I'm playing hooky. I'm like the pilot flying multimillion-dollar airplanes, landing them on aircraft carriers, and when he gets out of the cockpit he says, "And they pay me to do this, the fools."

PLAYBOY: Do you feel like you have to cultivate that part of your career fairly assiduously? Or can you stay in Vermont and write plays and go back to films when the spirit moves you?

MAMET: I think I am hanging on by my fingernails. But I also think most people feel the same way out there and don't show it. And I do spend a lot of time in Vermont.

PLAYBOY: In the theater—as a writer and a director—you worked with the same tight core group of actors. Has it been tougher in movies, with the kind of egos you find there?

MAMET: I've heard all the stories about big egos, but I have never encountered them myself. Maybe if I stay in the business long enough, I will. But I think it might be a bum rap. I've found on movie sets the most hardworking people I've ever seen. There is an ethic of help out, pitch in, get the job done, keep quiet about how hard it is to do. It is kind of the modern equivalent of a cattle drive. I'm sure there are bad apples. You'll find that in any business.

PLAYBOY: You like actors, then?

MAMET: They are absolutely the most interesting people I know. I loved hanging around them when I was young, and I still love having them for friends. I'm especially lucky that way.

PLAYBOY: You've written scripts that were altered and, when the movies were finally made, had other people's names on them. Do you resent that your own work wasn't accepted?

MAMET: Sure, of course. Like everybody else in the world, I would like everything to be exactly my way all the time. You know that old line about the scriptwriter who gives something to somebody to read. It's a first draft, and he's looking for a reaction. "Tell me," he says, "how much do you love it?"

PLAYBOY: Is there any story you especially want to do?

MAMET: Oh yeah. There's one project I want to do. A Hemingway novel—*Across the River and into the Trees*. I was talking with some of the people who have the rights, and I finally figured out a way to do the movie. It isn't one of Hemingway's better novels, but that could work in its favor. Somebody once told me that the better a play is, the worse the movie version will be. I think the same may be true of the novel.

PLAYBOY: Like a lot of other American writers, you have been compared to Hemingway.

MAMET: A heavy, impossible burden. You know, you can't play Stanley Kowalski without being compared to Marlon Brando—even by people who never saw Marlon Brando in the movie, let alone on stage. He revolutionized that role and the American notion of what it meant to act. The same is true of Hemingway and writing.

PLAYBOY: Any validity to the Hemingway comparisons?

MAMET: No, I don't think so.

PLAYBOY: The way you live? Your interest in hunting and guns?

MAMET: I have always felt that my private life is nobody's business except my own and, of course, that of the readers of this magazine.

PLAYBOY: What is the most curious description of yourself that you've read?

MAMET: I read only the good stuff. But, seriously, there is a kind of flawed thinking in the world today that has to do with celebrity, with the idea that there are special people who are somehow different from the rest of us, who lack the usual human weaknesses. So, inevitably, we revere them, and then, when we get closer, we are disappointed by them and turn on them. We're all the same. That's why I stopped doing the press. Until this interview.

In one of my last interviews I explained that I didn't like talking to the press because it made me feel stupid.

The interviewer said to me, "That is ridiculous."

I said, "See."

I stopped talking to the press because I just didn't know how to answer most of the questions. And my inability was seen as reluctance or coyness. I thought, Why should I subject myself to that? And so I quit.

PLAYBOY: Perhaps celebrities are no different from the rest of us. But don't people develop unique skills? Doesn't your gift for dialogue give you a better-than-average ability to size up people from what they say? To tell, for instance, when they are lying?

MAMET: I have a good sense of what people are like and when they are lying. Except when I'm emotionally involved. Then, like everyone else, I am hopeless.

PLAYBOY: How do you see through a lie—or a con?

MAMET: There are clues—they are called "tells," because they tell you something.

PLAYBOY: What are some examples between men and women?

MAMET: We see them all the time, but sometimes we choose not to because we're emotionally involved. It is in our interest to disregard the fact that someone was late, forgot a telephone number, got the wrong size, or forgot a birthday.

But these are things most of us know. Or, if we don't, you can't learn them from me. I think it's natural that when someone has a little notoriety we start to assign certain magical attributes to him that just aren't true. People say to me, "Can you tell us about the art of playwriting?" I say it isn't an art; it is a trick. There are no magic properties that go with a little publicity.

PLAYBOY: People nevertheless find fame to be irresistible.

MAMET: Absolutely. Let me tell you my favorite story about that. Gregory Mosher is flying from Chicago to New York because he's casting a play and he wants to see Rex Harrison. The plane is late, and he gets in the cab and says, "Forty-seventh and Broadway, I'm going to the theater."

So the cabdriver says, "What are you going to see?"

And Mosher tells him.

"Who's in it?" the cabdriver asks.

"Rex Harrison and Claudette Colbert." The driver stands on the brakes, pulls over to the side, turns around in the seat, and says, "Claudette Colbert? Claudette Colbert? I fucked her maid."

That is absolutely my favorite theatrical story.

PLAYBOY: If celebrity is a current American obsession, then violence is another. Do you think that we live in more violent times?

MAMET: More violent than what? The world is a very violent place. It always has been. Why is it a violent place? Because human beings are wired with a touchy survival mechanism that goes off very easily.

PLAYBOY: What is your personal response to actual flesh-and-blood violence? To a fistfight on the street, perhaps.

MAMET: Well, it's pretty shocking, isn't it? Not at all what we've been led to expect.

PLAYBOY: Are you attracted to violence? In prizefights, say? Or bullfighting?

MAMET: No. I've never been.

PLAYBOY: Do you consider your work to be violent?

MAMET: Violent? No.

PLAYBOY: As an artist, do you find it more challenging to deal with the evil and violent side of human nature? In your script for *The Untouchables* the Al Capone character—played by Robert De Niro—stole the movie from Kevin Costner's Eliot Ness.

MAMET: Drama can't be about nice things happening to nice people. Anyone who has ever been around gangsters knows that they are extremely charming. They speak colorfully; they're sentimental. Generous. They are interesting to write about, interesting to create.

PLAYBOY: In your work women are frequently the victims of violence, beginning with the violent seduction in *The Postman Always Rings Twice*—

MAMET: I should point out here that what I wrote for that scene was, "They kiss."

PLAYBOY: The tabletop scene—you didn't write that?

MAMET: "They kiss."

PLAYBOY: Okay. But there is a pattern in your work. Paul Newman decks Charlotte Rampling in *The Verdict* and now, in *Oleanna*—

MAMET: Look, you mention *Oleanna*. People might want to know why these two characters are at each other's throat. Well, you have a two-character drama. One person is a man, and one person is a woman. Two people in opposition. That's what drama means. I sincerely believe that my job as a dramatist is to explicate human interactions in such a way that an artistic—not mechanical but artistic—synthesis can happen.

It is just dead wrong to suggest that my work incites—or supports—violence. My job is exactly to the contrary. My job is to show human interactions in such a way that the synthesis an audience takes away will perhaps lead to a greater humanity, a greater understanding of human motives. I don't know how successful I am at it, but that absolutely is my job. If the net effect is otherwise, which I don't think that it is, then they should throw me in jail.

PLAYBOY: Are the best American characters people who get things done by violent means? Capone and the gangsters. Hoffa. Gunfighters in a western.

MAMET: Well, that's the American myth. See it and take it.

PLAYBOY: Going all the way back to *The Deerslayer* and other Cooper novels?

MAMET: It goes back as far as America. See it and take it. There's nobody there, boys, jump in and take what you want. Manifest Destiny. I mean, Lord have mercy, if it's Manifest Destiny to take over the country from the Atlantic to the Pacific, what is that except pillage, plunder, and steal?

PLAYBOY: Is there excessive violence in films and on television?

MAMET: Sure.

PLAYBOY: There are serious suggestions—from the attorney general [Janet Reno], among others—that society needs to control the depiction of violence. Could you live with that?

MAMET: The question, of course, becomes, What is violence, and who gets to say so? It is a serious question when the community standard gets so broad. Any law is going to be interpreted by community standards, because people aren't machines. Laws probably work as long as we have a community that understands them in more or less the same way or is willing to trust one another to interpret them ad hoc. When you don't have that community, it's like the blind men trying to describe an elephant.

PLAYBOY: What if the attorney general and her team could identify exceedingly and unacceptably violent content? Would it be helpful for them to eliminate it?

MAMET: Once you set up a czarship of any kind, rest assured that, however brilliant the original people are, those who come after will be swine. That's the way it works.

The problem is, who's going to decide, and what are his or her qualifications? There was a story in the papers recently about a fellow who calls himself a performance artist, and he very well may be. If I knew what performance art was, I'd be better qualified to say. Anyway, he is HIV-positive, and in his act he has an associate score his back with a scalpel and then press paper towels against the cuts to take blood impressions, which he hangs on a clothesline to dry. His performance is funded in small part by government money, and that has caused some controversy. Is it art? Hell, I don't know. And if I don't know, then Janet Reno sure doesn't know.

PLAYBOY: Okay. Then, if the government shouldn't be in the business of censoring expression, should it be in the business of supporting it? There is a lot of discussion about cutting off federal funding of the National Endowment for the Arts and the Public Broadcasting System. Do you think that this would be a disaster for the arts?

MAMET: Right. I'm going to say something heretical. My experience has been that literal, actual art flourishes better without government support. On the other hand, having come up the hard way as everybody does in show business, it would be nice if some people could be helped. I'm torn between wanting to see them helped and wondering if the government is the best way to do it. I mean, people object to the government's subsidizing—even a little—this fellow's performance art. Well, I object to a lot of the pablum that gets grant money. I think people who get that money would be better left to their own devices and eventually to lapse back into the real estate business.

PLAYBOY: Without public television, won't children be deprived of an alternative to repetitive violence, which some people say is the real threat? Doesn't the sheer number of killings they see on the screen eventually desensitize them?

MAMET: I don't buy it. The violence you see on television and the violence you see in real life have nothing to do with each other. Even kids know it. The reports of violence in the news, on the other hand, may desensitize them. Too much exposure to the O. J. Simpson case may desensitize them. The answer is, one does not have to watch television.

PLAYBOY: You're a father. Is it part of your role as a parent to censor what your kids watch on television?

MAMET: I don't think kids should watch television. Period.

PLAYBOY: Not even *Sesame Street?*

MAMET: Not even *Sesame Street.* And I love *Sesame Street.*

PLAYBOY: Then what's the problem with kids watching it?

MAMET: The problem isn't with *Sesame Street.* The problem is with television. If you aren't watching television, then you could be learning some other skill like carving wood or even reading. I was talking with a friend of mine, a guy who is something of a scholar of show business, and I said, "I don't get television. I believe I understand certain things about the essential nature of live performance and the central nature of radio and movies. But I don't understand television." He said, "Television is essentially a medicine show." And he was right. For *x* minutes of supposed entertainment television is going to have your attention for thirty seconds so it can sell you a bottle of snake oil. That is its essential nature. It's a sales tool.

PLAYBOY: Can't technology change that? With some cable channels, for instance, you have no ads.

MAMET: No. Not at all. It's possible to have television without ads, but that doesn't alter its essential nature. You can describe a painting—a Renaissance masterpiece—on the radio, and it might have a certain amount of value. But it is not the best way to do painting.

PLAYBOY: You've done some work for television. Didn't it change your opinion of the medium?

MAMET: What is television's agenda? It is a tool to sell you products. What are the tools it uses? Guilt. Shame. Envy. It tells you to be like Ozzie and Harriet. I grew up in the first television generation, and I spent a lot of time wondering why my life was so inferior to—and unlike—the lives I saw depicted on television.

PLAYBOY: Which brings to mind the British reviewer who called you "one of our chief critics of capitalism."

MAMET: I don't think I was ever a critic of capitalism. I'm a dramatist. The drama is not a prescriptive medium. Part of what the drama can offer—because it should work on the subconscious level—is the relief that comes with addressing a subject previously thought unaddressable. I'll give you an example.

On the day John F. Kennedy was shot, Lenny Bruce was performing in San Francisco. Everybody was waiting to hear what Lenny Bruce would say. He came out on stage, shook his head, and said nothing for five full minutes. Then he looked up at the audience and said, "Vaughn Meader." That was the comedian who'd made his career out of imitating one character—John Kennedy. Saying that—making that joke—was an incredible relief. Does that mean Lenny Bruce was insensitive to the terror and horror and tragedy inflicted on the country, on the Kennedy family? No. He was doing his job as a humorist, and he was doing it bravely.

Anything I might know about American capitalism is not going to be found in a play.

PLAYBOY: Just the same, your play—and film—*Glengarry Glen Ross* could be called an indictment of the kill-or-be-killed nature of business.

MAMET: Yeah. Well, Robert Service said it best. He said there isn't a law of God or man that goes north of ten thousand bucks. You know, money makes people cruel. Or has the capacity to do so. Human interactions—that's what I hope my plays are about. The rest of it is just a way to get somewhere.

PLAYBOY: How do you feel about money? Is it better to have money than not?

MAMET: I'd say so. But you can get carried away. There's a story about Herb Gardner, who wrote *A Thousand Clowns*. First a play, then a movie. He's hot, and his agent comes to him with a deal for a television show. Gardner thinks it's a dumb idea and says, "I don't want to do the show." The agent says, "Herb, listen, do this show, and you'll never have to write another word."

PLAYBOY: And?

MAMET: Well, you have to ask yourself if that's why you became a writer. So you'd never have to write another word?

There is another story. I was talking to a guy who'd been in the CIA and had an idea for a script. He said, "You know, you could probably make fifty million off this deal. For a half-hour's work."

I said, "Fifty million for half an hour's work, huh? That works out to four billion a week, if you don't put in any overtime. That comes to two hundred billion a year, if you take two weeks off for vacation."

"Listen," this guy said, "when you're making that kind of money, you can't afford to take a vacation."

PLAYBOY: Alright. Getting back to earth here, you mentioned Lenny Bruce, who made his reputation by saying what couldn't be said. Is there anything left that you can't say?

MAMET: You can't say Wayne Newton's head is too small. Or that Richard Simmons is too pudgy. Other than that, you can say anything. Or you can say anything you want so long as you don't mean it. If you mean it, you're in a lot of trouble.

PLAYBOY: Aren't we actually moving back, in a way, to a climate like the one that existed during Lenny Bruce's time? Isn't that what some aspects of the political correctness on American college campuses is all about, that there are some things you can't be allowed to say?

MAMET: Well, sure, but I think centralization will do away with free speech before PC [political correctness] does.

PLAYBOY: Centralization?

MAMET: Sure. One day three corporations will own all the means of disseminating public information. We'll have to get through their censors, who will make the PC kids look like mice.

There was a Russian dramatist who described working during the Stalin era. He had to sit down with this guy whose job was to censor plays for the Party. The guy would say, "You can't put this and that on stage," and the playwright would say, "Sit down, for Christ's sake. Have a cigar, have a drink, let me tell you what this play is about. Blah, blah, blah."

So, the censor listens and says, "Well, okay, but I got to check it out with my boss. Tell you what, when the guy says so and so, in act 3, take that out so I can tell my boss."

And the playwright says, "Fine. I can live with that."

And the censor says, "Good, can I have two tickets for Wednesday?" And he goes back to the building where he works. I would much rather deal with that guy than with some idiot who just got out of the Yale Drama School and works as a script reader at the XYZ studio in Hollywood. Those are the people who will eventually control publishing and movies.

PLAYBOY: You don't see a danger in fundamentalist groups that want to get J. D. Salinger out of the library? Or black groups that try to do the same with *Huckleberry Finn*?

MAMET: Of course. There is a vast danger. But, again, I say that's a minor threat. I noticed some black group wants to get *Uncle Tom's Cabin* out of the library somewhere. I wonder if they've even read the book. If there were ever a more beautifully written novel that was an indictment of slavery . . .

PLAYBOY: You know very well that people are sensitive about these questions. You wrote an article in the *Guardian* calling *Schindler's List* "emotional pornography" and "*Mandingo* for Jews." Can you elaborate on that?

MAMET: I don't think you can get more elaborate than "*Mandingo* for Jews."

PLAYBOY: Is anti-Semitism something you are especially worried about?

MAMET: As a Jew, I'm very concerned that we are falling back on the traditional answer of the Jewish intellectuals in the 1920s, which was to assimilate. To try to hide. You say, "I am an Austrian or a German or a German Jew, and I am such a part of the culture that I don't have this other identity."

I was talking to a survivor of the Holocaust, who had lost all his family. He said the worst fear of intellectuals was not in seeing their families killed and their possessions confiscated and their race destroyed. Their worst nightmare was in winding up naked in the field with a bunch of Jews.

But there is no ticket of admission. During the Holocaust all they cared about was if you were a Jew. They didn't care how much money you had or if you'd won the Iron Cross in World War I. To be Jewish meant to be dead.

PLAYBOY: Do you think this desire to assimilate is still a problem?

MAMET: Before I went to Israel I talked to my rabbi, and he said, "You are in for a shock." And I said, "Why? It is a Jewish country." He said, "No, that's easy. You are going to be in for a shock because what you will find is that there are rapists, murderers, litterbugs, and grumpy people in Israel, just like in any place in the world." He said that the lesson in Israel is that Jews are just like anybody else. That's what we've been fighting for three thousand years—to have a country just like anyone else.

But if you look at the depictions of Jews in the movies, it's the kindly little old lady, Molly Goldberg, or it's the Nobel physicist. People are bending over backward to say, "See, we're treating Jews with kid gloves."

I wrote another essay in which I said that you find few Jewish heroes in the movies. The Jewish answer has always been, "Well, that's okay. It's not important." Earlier you asked about things you cannot say—well, here are two: you cannot say you are a Jew first and then an American. And you cannot say that the movie business is a Jewish business. If there is anything wrong with that, I don't know what it is. Except that the Jewish moguls kept the Jews out of the movies. Where are the Jewish characters? When you find a Jew in the movies, it is probably something like the character in Spike Lee's *Mo' Better Blues,* which was a straight-up anti-Semitic portrait. It's not right. The end of it is murder.

PLAYBOY: Should Spike Lee have his wrist slapped?

MAMET: By whom? I sent him a letter.

PLAYBOY: Did he respond?

MAMET: No. It's not his job to respond. But it is my job to write a letter.

PLAYBOY: How do you respond when people challenge your characterizations?

MAMET: The first time we did *Oleanna* we had about fifteen young people from universities who came to see the play. Afterward I asked them, "Well, what do you think?" One young woman said, "Don't you think this is politically irresponsible?" I didn't know what it meant, and I still don't know.

PLAYBOY: Is this sort of thinking going to be with us for a while?

MAMET: I hope not, but I think so. Like I said earlier, young people are frightened. They wonder why they're in college, what they are going to do when they get out, what has happened to society. Nobody's looking out for them, and there's nothing for them to go into. It's no wonder they're trying to take things into their own hands.

PLAYBOY: Were your college years fearful, or did you find your vocation then?

MAMET: There was a light verse I heard once about Hamlet. It goes like this:

Young Hamlet was prince of Denmark
A country disrupted and sad,
His mother had married his uncle.
His uncle had murdered his dad.
But Hamlet could not make his mind up,
Whether to dance or to sing.
He got all frenetic
And walked round pathetic.
And did not do one fucking thing.

The last three lines sum up my college career. I spent a lot of time in the theater in college.

PLAYBOY: Was that the genesis of your interest in the theater?

MAMET: Actually, I grew up as something of a child actor in Chicago. My uncle was the head of broadcasting for the Chicago Board of Rabbis, and I used to do a radio show for Jewish children Sunday mornings. I was an amateur actor as a kid, then I got involved at Hull House in Chicago in the early 1960s.

PLAYBOY: And playwriting? Did you suddenly find your calling when you read *Death of a Salesman* at sixteen or something like that?

MAMET: None of it ever made any sense to me until I started reading Beckett and Pinter. That was my wake-up call.

PLAYBOY: When would that have been? College?

MAMET: I was fourteen.

PLAYBOY: That must have made you some kind of nerd.

MAMET: Not really. I hated school. But I was on the wrestling team, and I played football. I was sports editor for the school paper. And I read a lot. I used to hang out at the Oak Street Book Shop in Chicago. It was a magical place for me. In back they had a room full of books by playwrights, and I used to dream about what it would be like to have a book I had written on one of those shelves.

PLAYBOY: Did your feeling for drama sustain you through college?

MAMET: Yeah. That's all I did. Hung out at the theater.

PLAYBOY: When you were starting out professionally, back in Chicago, were you able to support yourself with your work in the theater?

MAMET: Lord, no. I had jobs. I worked as a real estate salesman and as a cabdriver.

PLAYBOY: How did you do as a real estate salesman?

MAMET: I never got out of the office. I was in charge of the leads, like the character in *Glengarry Glen Ross*.

PLAYBOY: Was that as unpleasant an experience as the play depicts?

MAMET: It was harsh. I also sold carpet over the phone. Cold calling. Anybody who has ever done it knows what I'm talking about.

PLAYBOY: How did you describe color over the phone?

MAMET: They had all these names that sounded like they could have been ice cream. Or horses.

PLAYBOY: If you learned business from handling real estate

leads, what about cabdriving? Did you get any material from conversations you overheard?

MAMET: No. But I always enjoyed driving a cab. For two reasons. You could start in the morning with no money, even to eat, and after a couple of fares you would have enough to buy breakfast. The other reason was those Checker cabs, which we all drove in those days. They had the best heaters in the world. It could be thirty below in Chicago, and you could drive all day in a T-shirt. It was so wonderfully warm. It was great.

PLAYBOY: Since *American Buffalo,* your breakthrough work that had you on Broadway when you were twenty-seven, you have been a prolific playwright. Do you have dry spells?

MAMET: Sure. You always have dry spells as a writer. What I usually do when I'm in a dry spell is write something else. I just like to write. And I reap all sorts of rewards from it. It supports me, and I've made a lot of friends doing it, and it gives me a feeling of accomplishment. If I can't do it one way, I'll do it another.

PLAYBOY: Do you pay much attention to the mechanics? Are you fussy about whether or not you are writing with number two pencils, that kind of thing?

MAMET: Oh, sure. If I've got nothing else to do, I'll bitch about that. For years I worked with the same manual typewriter. And I drank coffee. I'd sit down to write, take a sip of coffee, put the cup down on the right side of the typewriter, light a cigarette, and type the first line. Then I'd hit the carriage return, and it would hit the cup, and the coffee would go everywhere. I did that every day for twenty years. Then I quit drinking coffee.

PLAYBOY: And smoking cigarettes.

MAMET: That came first.

PLAYBOY: It has been reported that you like cigars.

MAMET: I gave them up, too.

PLAYBOY: Are you one of those writers who need a routine?

MAMET: Sure. I have all kinds of routines. But I like to describe myself as a free spirit–will-o'-the-wisp. So I keep myself blissfully ignorant of my routines.

PLAYBOY: Do you write every day?

MAMET: Sometimes.

PLAYBOY: What's the source of your feeling for speech?

MAMET: My family, I suppose. I had a grandfather who was a great talker and storyteller. His name was Naphtali. I was reading in the Bible the story of when Jacob is about to die and he is giving his sons his blessings. One of the sons, whose people became the tribe Naphtali, was given the blessing of speech, of being able to talk the birds out of the trees.

PLAYBOY: For all your success there have been some setbacks, such as *Lone Canoe* on stage and *We're No Angels* on film. How do you bounce back?

MAMET: Rudyard Kipling said, "If you can meet with triumph and disaster and treat those two impostors just the same." I'm getting to be middle-aged enough to see that there is more than superficial truth in his assertion that they are both impostors. It's nice to have people like your work. I also hope as a writer that I am my own best judge and worst critic.

When you're young, everything seems like it's the end of the world. Bad review? Okay, that's it. Oh my God, what's happened? You've just been excoriated in every newspaper in the country. How can you ever go on? Goddamn them all. I hope they all get the mumps.

Having spent too many years in show business, the one thing I see that succeeds is persistence. It's the person who just ain't gonna go home. I decided early on that I wasn't going to go home. This is what I'll be doing until they put me in jail or put me in a coffin.

Kids today say they are going to go to graduate school so they'll have something to fall back on. If you have something to fall back on, you're going to fall back on it. You learn how to take the criticism. You have to, or you get out. I was talking with a friend the other day about something I was working on that wasn't going right. I said, "I don't like it. It's a piece of shit."

He said, "Dave, never berate yourself. There are people who are paid to do that for you."

PLAYBOY: Any other advice for the young playwright?

MAMET: My best friend, Jonathan Katz, was for a number of years the kid Ping-Pong champion of New York State. And when he was twelve or thirteen he wandered into Marty Reisman's Ping-Pong parlor in New York City. Reisman was then the U.S. champion in table tennis and a genius, an absolute genius. Jonathan asked him, "What do I have to do to play table tennis like you?"

Reisman said, "First, drop out of school."

That would be my advice to aspiring playwrights.

PLAYBOY: And how did you break into movies?

MAMET: I got my first job in pictures through my ex-wife. She was going to audition for a part in *Postman*, and I told her to tell Bob

141

Rafelson, who was directing, that he was a fool if he didn't hire me to write the screenplay. I was kidding, but she did it. And, when it turned out he needed a writer, he called. When he asked why he should hire me, I told him, "Because I'll give you either a really good screenplay or a sincere apology."

PLAYBOY: One last question. Where do you get your titles?

MAMET: I don't know. But I thought of a good one the other day: *In These Our Clothes*. I think of titles, and I write to fit.

"The South Bank Show"

Melvyn Bragg

Melvyn Bragg met Mamet in Chumley's Bar, an old Greenwich Village speakeasy in New York, once the haunt of such writers as J. D. Salinger and John Steinbeck. Bragg, who had previously interviewed Mamet for "The South Bank Show" in 1984, met with the writer while Mamet was in New York editing *Oleanna*.

BRAGG: *The Postman Rings Twice, The Untouchables, The Verdict*—all tough films of the 1980s, all written by David Mamet. Mamet staked out his territory as a playwright bringing us the forked-tongued salesman of *Glengarry Glen Ross* and the macho dreams of petty criminals in *American Buffalo*.

But Mamet was in New York to finish his fourth film as a director, *Oleanna*, based on his controversial play. That's where we began.

[Extract of *Oleanna*, rough cut]

BRAGG: When the play opened in 1992, it immediately provoked sometimes strident arguments. . . . Were you surprised by the outrage it caused?

MAMET: I was flabbergasted. I was absolutely flabbergasted.

BRAGG: What do you think it hit there then?

MAMET: Well, perhaps it has something to do with the issues . . . that the, everybody in America at least, men and women, at least

From "The South Bank Show," London Weekend Television, London. This previously unpublished interview was taped and subsequently aired on October 16, 1994. The interview was conducted by Melvyn Bragg for London Weekend Television's "South Bank Show," copyright © LWT. Courtesy of Melvyn Bragg and London Weekend Television. Reprinted with permission.

middle-class white men and women, maybe who, who have . . . too much time on their hands, seem to be terrified of each other in . . . the main. What can one say? What can't one say? How does one behave correctly? And I think that, that the amount of anger and repression this causes in both men and women is, is enormous, and the play, perhaps the play got under their defenses.

BRAGG: And everyone came up with the idea of what it was about, not everybody but lots of people. What would you say it was about?

MAMET: If a play has any life past it being a *succès scandale,* it's, it's because it's provocative in a way larger than the issues. Not, not that it's about sexual harassment, which of course it is—that issue's going to fade at some point—but that it's about power.

[Extract from *Oleanna*]

BRAGG: Do you feel that because, as a man, you'd written a play about a man and a woman, that you felt sometimes accused of taking the man's side and giving the man too much favor in the play?

MAMET: Look, if, if you've got a play with two characters on stage and one is a man and one is a woman . . . they, they must be antagonists or else the play's no good. I don't believe that, I don't, I don't take, personally take the side of one rather than the other. I think they're absolutely both wrong, and they're absolutely both, both right. And that's to the extent that the play aspires to—or achieves—the status of . . . a tragedy. It's because of that. I think that what, what was responsible for the, the success of the play, was . . . legitimately controversial in that the controversy was one, one group of society would say, "He's absolutely, he's absolutely right, so you don't understand." They'd say, "You don't understand. I understand what controversy is. Controversy's all well and good, but you're wrong" and, the, the other person says that, "No, no, you're wrong." . . . And it wasn't necessarily split by sex. But in controversy one group would say to the other, "Yes, I understand, but you're mistaken."

[Extract from *Oleanna*]

I think something is provocative because it is artistic, not because it is realistic, that is, issue plays, issue movies, which we leave saying, "By God, now I understand!" by the next morning we've forgotten them because it's not real. As soon as you put something on the screen, it's an artistic experience, and to correctly fulfill an artistic experience it has to say something that, that is revelatory of an inner truth. That's something that's provocative. That's something, that's something we can apply to our daily life. The more something attempts to be documentary and realistic, the less useful it is.

BRAGG: So you think that the school of thought that says if you really want to know about mid-... early-nineteenth-century England, read Charles Dickens, don't read Mayhew, don't read, if you really want to know ...

MAMET: Absolutely.

BRAGG: You, you, you would go with reading Charles Dickens ...

MAMET: Well, I don't like Charles Dickens. I would read, I would read Anthony Trollope, personally, but that's ...

BRAGG: That's a matter of taste.

MAMET: ... or even Wilkie Collins.

BRAGG: Yes. ... Over the last few years you've done more work in films than you had the last time we talked, ten years ago. You'd just begun. ... Since then you've written more screenplays, and you've directed films. What has the further involvement with films, what effect has it had on your stage writing, do you think ... ?

MAMET: I think it's made it much better. I hope it has. The working on movies is, it's, it's fascinating for me. It's very demanding. It's all, it's just all plot; that's all it is. Take away everything else, take away the dialogue, you're left with the plot to make the audience wonder what happens next. And something I've been fortunate in, in getting an education on the job writing movies. I hope to take that back to writing plays, and I, I think it's, I think it's demonstrable. I think that ... the plots of my plays are, are getting—

BRAGG: Can you be more specific about that, David?

MAMET: Well, I wrote a lot when I was young. I wrote a lot of episodic plays, kind of discursive plays. One scene would follow into the next, and we'd follow the hero along, and, and I also wrote a couple of gang comedies, or gang tragedies. But the most difficult form to write is, is tragedy, where the hero or heroine is going to his ... Aristotle tells us, come to the end of the play and realize that he or she is the cause of their own problems and undergo[es] a change of the situation at the last moment of the play ... such that the audience will say, "Oh my God, now I understand. I've seen something that is both shocking and inevitable."

[Extract from *Oleanna*]

BRAGG: ... Now, somewhere or other you said, films, in a way, all films in a way, all good films, aspire to be silent films, that is, as you've just said, "It's the plot." You've also said that, if a play's a good play, you should be able to do it on the radio and it'll lose nothing.

MAMET: The best way to tell a story in a movie is with pictures without words. It's the best way. The best way to tell a story on stage is with words without plastic elements. You don't want car crashes, rain effects. If you've gotta put effects on the stage, you can't tell the story with words; you're doing something desperately wrong. Each medium has to move forward by, by, by plot. The plot is nothing other than the quest of the hero, or heroine, which achieve[s] his or her goal—specific goal—that goal specific to that play. . . . In a play on stage the best way, the only way, the only way really to move the plot forward is through dialogue. "Give, give me the five bucks you owe me, or I'll tell your employer" is moving the plot along . . . through dialogue. That same beat in a movie, you have. . . . The best way to move that along is through the picture.

BRAGG: How would you do a picture?

MAMET: I'm just thinking. That, that's, that's a little bit more difficult, but, but let me see if we can figure that out. Okay, the idea is I want, I want your money, or I'm going to tell your boss. Okay.

BRAGG: Right.

MAMET: Okay, we have a shot of the guy at the desk. You're sitting at the desk working, writing, writing, writing. You wave to me. Shot of me at the door. I come in the door, I look at my watch, I'm waiting, waiting, waiting, waiting, waiting. Shot of you at the, shot of you at the desk. You make a note; just a second, just a second. Shot of my—I take an insert out of my wallet—an IOU, says I owe you $2,700. Okay, you're still, shot of you, you're still waiting, shot of me, I look at my watch. I shrug. I walk over to the door, and it says "Supervisor." Knock, knock, knock—I knock on the door. You start to get up hurriedly. So that tells the same story in pictures. To tell stories in pictures is not better per se; it's just better in a movie.

BRAGG: So, let's, sort of, what sort of jam are you in now . . . ?

MAMET: Well, that's a very good question.

BRAGG: . . . between changing *Oleanna* from a play . . .

MAMET: That's a very good question.

BRAGG: . . . into a film.

MAMET: Here I am plagued by self-generated theories my whole life, in thrall and on the record as a devotee of Sergei Eisenstein and his theory of montage, stuck with a chatty piece of movie making . . .

BRAGG: So what do you do? Let's take the first . . . the beginning of it.

MAMET: Right.

BRAGG: And that would be wonderful, I think, on the radio, as it is on the stage. What are you going to do? What have you done on the film? . . .

MAMET: Well, I did two things . . .

BRAGG: How do your theories stand up?

MAMET: Good questions. I did two things, one of which was very, very, very intelligent, which was I hired a genius cinematographer [Andrzej Sekula], and the, the other one of which I kind of fell into on my own. And I found since that Alfred Hitchcock wrote that's the way you transfer a play to the screen. He said, what you do is have the hero open an envelope, pull back to show that he's in his, he's coming into his house, and he's just taken off his hat and loosened his tie, and he's poured himself a drink. He opens the envelope, crumples it up, puts it back in, throws down the drink, pulls off his tie, picks up his hat, runs out the door, gets into his car, drives away worriedly, screeches up in front of another building, fumbles for his key, lets himself in, goes into his office, opens, opens the door to his office where his partner is, and then you start the play [film]. Coincidentally, I think that the movie *Oleanna* works very, very well, but I don't know why.

BRAGG: Yeah. Are you quite pleased that you don't know why?

MAMET: No . . . I'm not, I'm not angry. I'm grateful. I'm a little bit perplexed, because it tends to blow a lot of my theories right out of the water.

BRAGG: When we talk about film, people tend to say . . . collaborative, collaborative, collaborative. What's your experience of that?

MAMET: Well, I don't know what *collaborat—*, *collaborative* means. I don't know what it means, but I don't like it. When I write something, that's my name on it for, for good or ill. If something, if something's wrong with it, it's my fault, and, if the script is good, I wrote it.

BRAGG: You said, we were talking about *Oleanna* earlier, you said, "Well, I made a genius of a decision. I hired a great cinematographer." So, how collaborative, how is that . . . collaborative, as it were?

MAMET: Well, here's what I think . . . The cinematog—, the cinematographer's going to do his or her job, and the director's going to do his or her job. Is this collaboration? Yes, well I suppose, if one wanted to mean collaborate meaning to work together—yes, we are working together. On the other hand, I think . . . as a director, I got the responsibility for the film. It's my responsibility to do, I feel, to do many things: to run a happy set, to, to, make sure that there's an atmosphere in which everyone can do his or her job, not only easily but happily; to help the actors understand what it is that I think is required of them. It's also my job to listen to everybody's opinion and then to decide. I've always felt that, that the term *collaboration* slights this process. It's a hierarchy, it's absolutely a hierarchy; it's no less a hierarchy than the military.

BRAGG: You said in one of your lectures almost no one in this country [the United States] knows how to write a movie script.

MAMET: Yeah, I think that's true.

BRAGG: Why is that? They've had a lot of practice.

MAMET: It's not that people can't write; it's being able to get a script in this country past the mercantile bureaucracy. One has to appeal to the script reader, who is, who is someone who, as far as I can see, has never had experience in movie making and has no interest in movie making . . . has, has an interest in movies. The person has an interest in, in their career. And who could blame them? Don't we all? The difference is that my career is making movies, and that person's career is getting ahead in the movie business, so we don't have a lot to say to each other. It's . . . very difficult for a lot of people to get what we would call a good script past that person. Now, maybe the movie business is not an art; maybe it's just a popcorn business. Who am I to say it's an art? One has to both be able to make a really great movie and to get ahead in that shithole.

BRAGG: When do the actors come into this, Dave, because, coming back to essays you've written about this, lectures you gave, I believe, to some—I don't believe I know—to some group of students, you've got strong views about actors. What do you think good acting in film is?

MAMET: Good acting in film is, I think, the same as good acting on stage. It's intention, absolute intention. What specifically does an actor want, and what is he or she willing to do to get it?

BRAGG: And it's always keeping it simple, is it?

MAMET: Sure. Well, . . . good intention is always keeping it simple. I mean, in real life, have you ever seen someone who, who really, who really said and meant, "I love you" or "I'm going to kill you" or "If you do that again, you'll wish you hadn't." The people who when they say that, we know they aren't kidding, do very little, don't they? It's the people who start supporting it by attempting to get us to believe that they mean it whom we doubt. As we should.

BRAGG: When you say, as you do often, "K-I-S-S—Keep It Simple, Stupid," what, why are you repeating that to your students . . . ?

MAMET: There are these schools of, of acting training, and these schools of actors say, "Okay, well, this line means that, and that line means this, and the next line means the next thing. Don't forget that it says you had lunch today early, so that you're probably a little bit hungry." You can't act all that stuff. All that . . . when one shows up on stage, that all goes out the window. One can only take on stage, "What do I want from the other person?" That's it—period; that's all one can take on stage.

BRAGG: So, all the business of going back to the roots of the character if you're playing a coal miner and going down a coal mine for a week and all, that's all nonsense, is it?

MAMET: Yes, it's absolute nonsense. It's not going to help anything. It's . . . it's like hanging garlic around your neck to save you from self-consciousness. Well, it's okay if you're self-conscious and act.

BRAGG: I mean Noel Coward said, "Don't forg—, remember the lines, and don't bump into the furniture."

MAMET: Absolutely.

BRAGG: . . . or words to that effect, and you'd go along with that.

MAMET: Yeah, I'm not even sure about the furniture.

BRAGG: So, you're sort of wiping away seventy years of this psychological, investigative, background Method method.

MAMET: I hope so. You know . . . this has been my, my life study and also my hobby and also my meal ticket for, for about thirty years now, working with actors. And, I studied the Stanislavski system, all that, the works of all those Russians when I was a kid, but it's not . . . it's just not necessary. What is necessary is intention—clarity and intention. And the rest is just, as I used to say to my students, the words are just gibberish. They really are. Not to the audience but to the actor.

[Extract from *Oleanna*]

BRAGG: Another thing your plays and books are full of are, are teachers and pupils. Mentors. Where does that come from? Why does it matter so much to you?

MAMET: Well, that's, that's the Jewish tradition. I mean, Christians used to call Jews "the People of the Book," and I think that the Jewish tradition prized learning above all things and that the . . . Ashkenazi tradition of the Eastern European Jews was vehement about that—that money was not important. That what was important was learning and that status was derived from scholarship.

BRAGG: What are you finding out about your own Jewishness, then? You've said again that you're finding out more about your own Jewishness, more attached to it, more . . .

MAMET: Well, sure, I think this is tradition, one getting older, to, to look back to one's roots. It's also terrific to belong.

BRAGG: But there's a sense of non-belonging that features in your work, too, like say *Homicide,* the film *Homicide,* where the hero, the Jewish . . .

MAMET: Detective.

BRAGG: . . . detective, yeah . . . who has turned his back on his Jewishness. It doesn't mean anything to him, certainly, but he's the generalized American, in a way that there seems to be a wish to be a generalized American. And when he hits the ethnic rock he . . . decides that, rather than flounder on it, he will try to build on it. But it messes up his Americanism.

MAMET: Uh-hmm. Aha!

BRAGG: Yeah.

MAMET: Yeah, well that's, that's . . . that's the question of the Diaspora, isn't it?

BRAGG: Yeah.

MAMET: . . . of being a . . . Jew and [living in the] Diaspora. Being an assimilated Jew is: What are you trying to do? What do you have to give up to get it? And is it worth it? Which is what *Homicide* is about. It's about a guy who wants to belong, but you have to belong to your group.

[Extract from *Homicide*]

BRAGG: As you become more interested in things Jewish, do you think you become more or less American, if that's meaningful at all?

MAMET: I don't know. See, that's a question that's been used to, that's been, that's been asked of Jews since there's been a Diaspora, so since [the destruction of] the Second Temple, a couple of thousand years ago: "Where do your loyalties lie?" And it occurs to me as I get older that, that a person can be held accountable under the law for his or her behavior, but, other than that, I don't know if it's a question that has an answer. But, on the other hand, I don't know if it's a question that is entitled . . .

[Extract from *The Cryptogram*]

BRAGG: Mamet's most recent play was *The Cryptogram,* set in the late 1950s, when his own parents divorced. It shows the emotional fallout of a disintegrating marriage.

[Extract from *The Cryptogram* and Bragg's lead-in]

MAMET: Well, *The Cryptogram* was a message in code. I guess my idea was that the, that memory is a message in code, like a dream is a message in code, and also a play is a message in code. And [as] one grows up, gets into middle-age, one can look back and try to decode the message of one's childhood, for example, as in the case of this play. I always thought, previous to that, that the domestic scene was best left to anyone else but me, that it wasn't a fit subject for drama. Then I realized as I looked back at plays like *American Buffalo*—really just a family play—is a play about a father and a mother and a, a little kid. And, as I started cruising into middle age, I thought, well, perhaps I would address that, that galaxy, as the psychologists say, a little bit more directly.

BRAGG: It's unusual to, to give a major part to quite a young boy. Was he the starting point of the play, the boy's imaginings?

MAMET: I, I don't think so, I don't think so. I think the, the play started off, and it was about the breakup of this marriage; it was about the woman and her friend, and over the course of a certain number of drafts it became clear to me that it was about the boy.

[Extract from *The Cryptogram*]

BRAGG: And this boy, who's plagued by, well, he can't sleep.

MAMET: No.

BRAGG: Terrifying when you're a child, and I think many people have been through that stage. Is there any sense you were drawing on your own background for that?

MAMET: I don't know. I, I seem to have had a childhood, but, like many of us . . . I don't know.

BRAGG: Because the essays that you write about your childhood, for instance with the difficulty with your stepfather, those essays and so on give an impression of a, not physically but emotionally violent childhood and a childhood that could legitimately be . . . leave deposits, great deposits of fear.

MAMET: Well, like everyone else, I had a lot of stuff happen to me in my life. Some of it affected me, and, I would hope, that that's the stuff that I write about. I'd hate, hate, hate to think that I found myself writing about stuff that didn't make any difference to me.

[Extract from *The Cryptogram*]

[I] don't think that there's a, at least I haven't found one, a code by which one can translate experience into, into drama. It's just, you gotta start. . . . My experience has been that one always starts like a complete idiot—at least I always do—saying I have no idea what this means. "It's, it's garbage, doesn't go anywhere, doesn't sound like a play to me. Oh hell, I've wasted one sheet of paper. I might as well waste another." And, I was talking to somebody last year, and I said I always knew that a, a good writer was one who threw out what most people kept, and I think that that's true. But then it occurred to me that a good writer is also one who keeps what most other people throw out and that to overcome the nausea and self-disgust dependent upon writing—"This is garbage," "I'm a fraud," "What can this mean?"—can sometimes have very important fruits.

BRAGG: You really mean nausea and disgust? You seriously feel those things when you're writing?

MAMET: Oh, yeah, sure. Or else what's the point?

BRAGG: What do you mean, "What the point?"

MAMET: I mean, I, I, like someone said about Jack Kerouac, "That's not writing, that's typing." You know, people in this country have gone kind of mad about computers, as if being able to type quicker could make one a better writer. . . . Everyone's always looked for a way around the difficulty of whatever, whatever he or she had to do, but in terms of writing, if the writing's going to be worthwhile, there really isn't one.

BRAGG: Your, if you have a rule at all . . . the rule is cut, cut, and cut again. . . . How did you know which bits to cut?

MAMET: Well, it helps to be rather schizophrenic. I seem to have a knack for writing dialogue that is independent of whatever skill I may or may not have in construction. I seem to have been born with a knack to write dialogue, which is being kind of schizophrenic. It's literally the ability to split oneself into two people. Now, all of us have the ability to a certain extent, because we do it all the time, except we don't call it writing dialogue. We call it talking to ourselves: "Oh, that son of a bitch, you know, you know what I should have said to him. I should have said, 'blah, blah, blah, blah, blah.' You know what he would have said? He would have said, 'dah, dah, dah, dah, dah,' and then I would have said—'" We do that all the time. I just do it professionally, so there's that, and then there's kind of a, a super-schizophrenia, which is to be able to abstract oneself yet again and become a member of the audience and say, while you're writing, something on the level of: "Is this interesting?" "Is this dramatic?" "Is this getting there?" To do that and not to do that effectively, I think one either has to have, to put it two different ways, either a knack or, as my countrymen say, to be crazy as a shithouse rat.

[Extract from *The Cryptogram*]

BRAGG: One of the things that I got out of *The Cryptogram*, which I think, as I've told you . . . I think highly of, was the discovery of deception—the boy discovers deception. He discovers he is being told lies. And a lot of your work has to do with deceptions through language and deceit. It's, it's terrible to ask a writer about, sort of, themes, but this does seem to me to feature an enormous amount in your work.

MAMET: Deception?

BRAGG: Hmmm.

MAMET: Well . . . as you were speaking, I was trying to remember what tragedy isn't based on deception. I think every tragedy's based on deception; that's the meaning of the, the tragic form . . . something has been hidden and can only be uncovered, uncovered at great expense. And when it is uncovered we say, "Oh my gosh, it was in front of me the whole time," whether that's *Death of a Salesman* or, or, or . . . any tragedy that it is in front of one the whole time. *Waiting for Godot*—he ain't coming.

BRAGG: Yeah.

MAMET: So that's what tragedy's about.

BRAGG: But there is a sense in which you take into an area of . . . I mean, *House of Games* is a con deception. You are also interested in playing poker, which has to do with bluff and counter-bluff, and *Glengarry Glen Ross* has to do with deception, too.

MAMET: Well, I was, as I say, I got interested in . . . the underworld, and the people who lived, in one way or another, lawless lives, because they seemed to me interesting, and also they gave me a nice milieu to set a bunch of dramas in. They seemed to be fairly upfront about the fact that they were living a, lives based on deception. I think that was an attempt on my part to escape from the bourgeoisie . . .

[Except from *The Cryptogram*]

I always wanted to be a writer, and to me a writer was somebody who wrote novels. That's what a writer was, and anything else was, was not a writer, so I figured well, hell with it, if you want to be one, why don't you try it. So . . .

BRAGG: How would you describe *The Village*?

MAMET: I'd say, I think I'd say a kind of laconic, stoic, Northern novel.

BRAGG: And not, not, I mean you might not like this comparison . . . and it's a completely different form, from *Our Town*.

MAMET: Well, I think that's very interesting that you say that. *Our Town* is always considered in this country kind of a joke in the professional theater, because it's the play everyone does in high school. Everyone does *Our Town*. But [it's] kind of a masterpiece. This is not kind of a masterpiece; it is a masterpiece.

BRAGG: I agree with you.

MAMET: Wilder had the sufficient genius to abstract, in the same way Chekhov did, an experience of the community into vignettes, in such a way that the abstracted experience gave the totality of, the emotional totality of, of a tragedy.

BRAGG: Are you, are you sort of finding values in *The Village* as a place and as a novel?

MAMET: Yes. I, I've been privileged to live in a little town in New England off and on for most of the last thirty years, and I'm always, I find people here extraordinarily generous and possessed of those Yankee values that are not a fiction.

BRAGG: Such as?

MAMET: Well, taciturnity, circumspection, self-respect, honesty, humor, patience.

[Extract from *The Village*]

BRAGG: The book is written in a way that anybody who knows your plays, and particularly has read your plays on the page, would recognize. I mean, it's very much pared down, pared back. What benefits do you get from that? One of the disadvantages could be that, in moving from section to section, it's quite hard beginning to sort out who the *he* is. What are the benefits that you see from the way you've done it?

MAMET: I don't think there are any. I just wrote it the best way I know how. I wrote one scene one day, and I took it back, as I take all of them, to show my wife [Rebecca Pidgeon], and I said, "What do you think?" and she said, "I like it very much." And I said, "I'm worried that it's too blatant," and she said, "Oh darling, no, no, don't worry, it's impenetrable." So . . .

BRAGG: Why does that please you?

MAMET: . . . then I could rest easy!

BRAGG: Why does it, why does it please you?

MAMET: Well, I wouldn't want anyone to beat me to the punchline. That's the worst thing that could happen. No, I didn't have any . . . theory to flog with that novel. I wrote it the best way I know how, and [I'm] working on another one. So I enjoyed writing it.

BRAGG: Now behind that again is another theory of yours, isn't there, that actually the more work the reader does, or the viewer does, the better it is for the work? Is that right?

MAMET: Well, I would put if differently. I, I, it's not my task to make the reader work harder. On the contrary . . . I've always felt it's my job to make everything as clear as possible. What I find in dramatic form is the best way to make things as clear as possible is to leave out the unessential.

BRAGG: Hmmm.

MAMET: *The Village* is . . . the more expansive form, you know. It's the epic, the epic form. Each person has his, his own interest, and the people are, in this novel, held together by a theme. I mean, obviously in some novels, notably the genre novels, you know they are held together by the plot. In this novel they're going to be held together by the theme, which is: How does one live in a harsh climate?

BRAGG: And the woods are very important to this book, aren't they?

MAMET: Sure.

BRAGG: What does the presence of them as a testing place and a place where a, where a man goes to meet nature, in a way. . . . Is that it?

MAMET: Well, yeah. Absolutely. I mean, it's hard to live in those hills; it's cold in the growing season, it's short, and transportation was difficult. People had to figure out a way to do it better, to make do or to do without. That tradition survives up there. How do, how do you get along in the woods, how do you get along in nature? I, I think I've learned a lot from those people. I know I have.

[Extract from *The Village*]

BRAGG: There's quite a bit in *The Village* about living for the moment. In fact, the passages I enjoyed particularly were where somebody was engaged in sitting, as often as not, and saying, "Well, this will do, this is life, this moment is good." And you, it almost seems to me, you almost seem to be risking telling us something there.

MAMET: Oh, heaven for fend!

BRAGG: I knew I would, it would be offensive before we were finished, but there is, there is a sense of that, isn't there, that this is what life is about—to understand and comprehend what is going on at the moment—and that's the hardest thing?

MAMET: Yes, that's the hardest thing, and I think, if you, if I look at American culture, that, that the idea of the moment. . . . Where are you going to find it if you spend half your life punching a computer, looking at a television screen? There's, there's nothing very interesting going on. The idea that you or humankind is creating everything that you watch, everything that you see during the day, there isn't a lot of rest in that.

BRAGG: I think another element in it is silence, which is rarer. I mean, that book's [*The Village*] full of people in locations, locations that are silent.

MAMET: Well, I . . . think that's the greatest luxury.

BRAGG: Hmmm. Seems to be now, doesn't it?

MAMET: Yeah. Indeed, it does.

BRAGG: And there's a sense of belonging there, and [you] seem to [have] found—

MAMET: Uh-huh. Yeah. The people are very, when you live [there], you know, people say, "What do you do there for enjoyment in the country?" Well, it's a very, very social place to live because people need each other—they need a ride here, then this person's born, that person died, so you need to help with something else, the other person needs help with something else. People are legitimately dependent on each other in a way we, in the cities, have forgotten. We're frightened of each other in the cities, at least in American cities. People compartmentalize their lives: this person is my lover, that person is my friend, this person is my boss, that person is my employee. I'll deal with each of them in their own circumscribed way . . .

BRAGG: You've said you're writing another novel [*The Old Religion*]. Do you, are you going to concentrate . . . more on films, novels, plays, or do you just take the next idea as it comes along and see where it leads you to?

MAMET: The second one. I don't have any, any plan other than to keep writing 'cause I enjoy it and, God willing, to keep paying the rent.

BRAGG: What's the place of the writer in America at the moment? Do you have, do writers have, importance? I mean, among other writers and among readers they do, but that's, they're a small, they're a very small minority.

MAMET: I don't know. I really don't know. I, I don't think that that's, as I said, I'm trying to do these two things [which] is to pass the time before dinner in such a way that I, that I won't think of myself as just drinking tea and napping and also to, to pay the rent. It's very easy to get, for me anyway, to get seduced by extraordinarily flattering exchanges, much like this one, into thinking that, that my work and the work of the profession has a, has some sort of importance. It beats me.

Someone Named Jack

Terry Gross

In the fall of 1994 Terry Gross met with David Mamet in New York City in a studio not far from the Neighborhood Playhouse, where Mamet had studied under Sanford Meisner in 1968. In the first of many conversations between Gross and Mamet that have aired on "Fresh Air" in the ensuing years, the playwright, apparently at ease with the interviewer, speaks extensively about his career in the theater, the responsibility of the director, and the place of rhythm in his plays.

GROSS: I love listening to dialogue written by David Mamet. It has the same effect on me as good music. I want to replay it over and over again. Mamet is one of America's most important playwrights and screenwriters. His film version of his play *Oleanna* opens next month. Also about to open is a film based on his adaptation of Chekhov's *Uncle Vanya*. Now David Mamet has written his first novel, called *The Village,* set in Vermont, where he lives part of each year. I asked Mamet if the dialogue he writes for actors is different from the dialogue on the page in his new novel.

MAMET: I think that what I'm concerned about is rhythm. And on a stage the actors communicate with each other, and the play's communicated to the audience, through the rhythm of their speech. But on a page I find it fascinating that the rhythm's very, very different. If you transpose the actual dialogue onto the page, the nature of

From "Fresh Air with Terry Gross," WHYY (Philadelphia). This previously unpublished interview was aired on October 17, 1994. "Fresh Air with Terry Gross" is broadcast on approximately 250 public radio stations each week and heard by 2.5 million listeners. Reprinted with permission of WHYY, Inc., producers of "Fresh Air with Terry Gross."

the medium is such that the rhythm is going to be changed by the interpolation of descriptions, "he said, she said, and then he picked up the coffee cup." And so that the most important rhythm, it seems to me, on the page is the rhythm of the written line, which contains both the dialogue and description, rather than the rhythm of the dialogue itself, which on the stage is all you have.

[Lead-in to scene from *Homicide* and scene itself]

GROSS: I think of you writing lines in a very musical way and them being performed, when performed well, in a musical way. And when I read your screenplays I can see that you italicize certain words for emphasis. Some words you put in parentheses so that they'll be read in a different way. If you want a pause, you'll write *beat* after the phrase is over. Do you think of yourself as "scoring" the dialogue?

MAMET: I suppose it's one way one could look at it. I just think of it as writing it. You know, you were describing the various things that I do writing dialogue, and I thought, "Oh, what a terrible way for a writer to behave."

GROSS: [*Laughs.*]

MAMET: And then I comforted myself by saying, "Oh, well, at least I don't write stage directions."

GROSS: [*Laughs.*] Well, are the actors bothered by the fact that you're telling them where the emphasis should fall and where the beat should fall?

MAMET: I don't think so. Well, first off, I tend to work with the same actors all the time.

GROSS: Like [Joe] Mantegna and [William H.] Macy.

MAMET: That's right. I mean, we go back about a quarter of a century together, the three of us. And one of the nice things about working with the same people over and over is that it's great to be trusted. It's great to be able to give an actor a script and know that he or she will trust that the line's going to work and read the line as it's written.

GROSS: Were the people in your family good talkers?

MAMET: Oh no, they were great talkers. Good wasn't even. . . . They were, and the surviving members continue to be, the best talkers that ever lived.

GROSS: What made them great?

MAMET: Well, many things. Our Ashkenazi Jewish heritage. The fact that my parents both grew up in the Depression in poverty. Perhaps a disrupted family life. And a six-thousand-year-old Jewish tradition of a love of argument.

GROSS: You started off as an actor, right?

MAMET: Yeah, that's right. I was actually a child actor in Chicago when I was . . . I was going to say, "when I was just a kid," but I guess that's when one would be a child actor.

GROSS: [*Laughs.*]

MAMET: Then, I got interested in community theater. And then I was very interested in acting in college, and, as I say, I studied for a while in New York. And I tried to support myself as an actor, and did marginally for a while, and realized that I was either going to need a personality transplant or I was going to starve. And, loathe to leave the theater, I did what countless millions have done before me: I found something else I could do inside of that society. And that happened to be directing.

GROSS: Why did you mention a personality transplant?

MAMET: I just didn't have the personality to be an actor. I think it's a great gift. I think acting is a skill that many people can learn a little bit of and that a few people can learn a lot of and that several people are born with a great talent for. And I think I didn't belong to any of those groups.

GROSS: So, you didn't think you were very good at it?

MAMET: No, I knew I wasn't any good at it.

GROSS: Did you have the ego for it?

MAMET: The ego? No, I think I had too much ego. I think that was the problem.

GROSS: Uh-huh.

MAMET: I think that . . .

GROSS: How does that get in the way? Too much ego?

MAMET: You know, Sandy [Sanford] Meisner was my teacher at the [Neighborhood] Playhouse. I seem to be talking about that a lot. I think it's because I'm in the studio which happens to be about four blocks from where the school was, and I seldom come back to this neighborhood. He used to say it took about twenty years to make an actor, and I often wondered what he meant. But now I've had the experience of working with actors, with the same actors, some of them for twenty years or more. And I have seen the great sacrifices, the great dedication, and the—and to use a perhaps overblown word—the cleansing process that one has to go through to become a great actor, to have the ego pared away and the preconceptions pared away and to have one's courage and character built up by years of striving. It's a magnificent process, and it's been a great privilege to watch it in the actors that I've worked with for those years.

GROSS: Was your ego so big that you'd be rewriting the lines you were given?

MAMET: Exactly so. I mean, perhaps I'm being too harsh on myself. Perhaps it wasn't a question of ego. Perhaps it was just a question of disposition. But that was my disposition—to want to rewrite the lines, to correct the director, etc.

GROSS: You've written that most acting training is based on shame and guilt. How did you experience that?

MAMET: Well, I went to a lot of acting classes and worked with a lot of directors, and I didn't see many of them that were capable of stating a direction or an instruction that was capable of being fulfilled. One heard a lot back in the 1960s and 1970s, and perhaps one still does today, things like, "Feel it more," "Be more yourself," "Relax," "Feel the space," "Use the space," "Listen to it with your body," "Reach out to the other person," "Talk like you mean it." These are the words that don't mean anything and that mask, on the part of the speaker, either an ignorance of their subject matter or the desire to defraud. And they confused the hell out of me as an actor.

GROSS: So, I imagine these are directions you try never to give actors who are working with you.

MAMET: That's right.

GROSS: What might you tell them instead?

MAMET: Well, what I try to do as a director is understand what the scene is about and communicate it to the actor in specific ways. Somebody wrote, "If the direction is more generalized or less actable than 'Go over there and open the window,' it's no good." And so that is the kind of direction to which I aspire. It calls for a lot of thought sometimes on the part of the director because there are many times when the director, like the actor, is under pressure. There's a tendency to think, "Oh my God, just do it better." But that sure don't help the actor, (a), and (b), the actor's trying to do it better. That's all the actor wants to do is do it better, for God's sake.

GROSS: From reading your essays I got the impression that you don't like it when somebody tries to put a lot of emotion into a scene and to put a lot of their personal expression into a scene. You write, the more an actor tries to make each physical action carry the meaning of the scene, the more the actor is ruining your movie.

MAMET: Well, they're also ruining their performance, sure.

GROSS: By putting in too much?

MAMET: Sure. I mean, all of us have had the experience, and we have it more the older we get, of having, of being in extraordinarily dramatic life situations: birth, death, loss, betrayal, enlightenment, danger, humiliation. And I've reflected, and I think that others perhaps have a similar experience, that in these situations we and those around us tend to act in a rather undramatic manner because our task and our difficulty are so vast that we have no energy left over to describe them to ourselves or to communicate them to others. We have only energy left over to do them as simply as possible because our life depends on it. And that to me is what great acting is. It's doing the most extraordinary things in the simplest possible manner.

GROSS: You grew up in a middle-class family in Chicago, but you write that you used to think that the middle-class was unfit for literature. Why did you think that, and what, if anything, changed you?

MAMET: Well, I wanted to get out of the house. I was a nice Jewish boy, and I think I probably am a nice Jewish boy, and I wanted to be anything but a nice Jewish boy. I wanted to be Jack Kerouac. Or Jack London. Or someone named Jack.

GROSS: [*Laughs.*]

MAMET: So, the one thing I didn't want to do was write to about that day-to-day bourgeois existence. Now I turn around thirty years later and see much of the stuff I wrote under the guise of the picaresque was nothing other than a domestic play. *American Buffalo* is finally a play about a family constellation.

GROSS: Well, did not wanting to write about your own middle-class life have anything to do with writing about con men and cops?

MAMET: Sure. That was another part of the escape. Yeah, I wanted to get out of the birth family. And perhaps, like a lot of people who go into a hermetic world, I wanted to escape into another family.

GROSS: Well, it seems to me you ended up hanging out at pool halls and having your poker games and meeting people from a different world. How did you meet them?

MAMET: I got out of the house. I had to make a living. I was out there working at many, many different kinds of jobs and meeting very interesting people. I loved it.

GROSS: What kinds of jobs?

MAMET: I worked in a truck factory. I drove a cab. I worked for a while one summer on the ore boats. I worked in a canning factory. I sold land over the telephone. I cleaned offices. I worked in a book shop. I did a lot of food work, busing and short-order cooking and waiting on tables.

GROSS: One of your early plays is called *A Life in the Theatre,* and you've written that you were taught, and that you believe, that the purpose of the play is to bring to the stage the life of the human soul. Now the actors in your play *A Life in the Theatre* say they believe that, too, but all the plays they act in are the worst clichés: the lifeboat scene—

MAMET: . . . Right.

GROSS: . . . the battle scene when a young soldier's tour of duty is up in two hours, but he's about to be shot down in a battle.

MAMET: . . . Right.

GROSS: I wonder, in your life in the theater when you were an actor, if you were up against that, too. Having all these deeply felt aesthetic ideas of what a life in the theater is, but you found yourself acting things you, in fact, felt were quite clichéd.

MAMET: Oh, sure. That quote, by the way, is from Stanislavski. I do believe that—that the task of theater is to bring to the stage the life of the human soul. But that's a quote from Konstantin Stanislavski.

I was once at Sardi's Restaurant here, and they'd just refurbished it. And I was giving a speech for something or other. I can't remember what it was. And I looked out and said, "It's so nice to be back here at Sardi's and look out at all these beautiful tables, and I know that there has never been a conversation at any of these tables that did not contain the phrase, 'And do you know what that son of a bitch did?'"

GROSS: [*Laughs.*]

MAMET: So, you talk about . . . dealing with clichés in the theater at one point. Well, all of us in the theater, on day 1 and on day 20 and thirty years later and fifty years later and eighty years later, still get together every night and one could say (a) with a sense of wonder at the world around us, or one could say equally (b) bitching at the very interesting and the very exacting life we've chosen.

On Theater, Politics, and Tragedy

Charlie Rose

Mamet's first live televised interview on the "Charlie Rose Show," hosted by the New York–based cultural commentator, was a rare television appearance and the first of many interviews with Rose. Their wide-ranging discussion of Mamet's life in the theater and his provocative plays, *Oleanna* in particular, was conducted shortly after work on the film version of *Oleanna* was completed and the playwright's first novel, *The Village,* was released.

ROSE: Why did you write *Oleanna?*

MAMET: I don't know. . . . I was living in Cambridge and, and Boston, and I used to hear these stories about sexual harassment. This was five years ago. So and so had a brother who got fired because he said, "blah, blah, blah"; or So and so had a niece and the professor came on to her, and she had to "blah, blah, blah." And I began to hear a lot of these stories and—

So, I sat down and started making up a fantasy about an interchange between a young woman who wants her grade changed and a professor who wants to get her out of the office so he can go home to see his wife, and one thing led to another, and the story kind of evolved and became this story about the power struggle between the two.

From the "Charlie Rose Show," WNET-TV (Channel 13), New York. This previously unpublished interview was aired on November 11, 1994, before an audience of approximately three million viewers of the Public Broadcasting Service in the United States and Canada. Copyright © Rose Productions, Inc. Courtesy of Charlie Rose Show / Rose Communications, PBS.

ROSE: And did it offend you when people . . . I assume the controversy and how men and women reacted to it pleased you because you had written a play that produced a reaction.

MAMET: Yeah. It first frightened me because I'd never imagined that kind of reaction to this play. People used to get into literally fistfights with each other in, in the lobby, and screaming matches and going home . . .

ROSE: Primarily couples?

MAMET: Primarily couples, that's right. Yeah.

ROSE: And it also . . . they began to label you, or it somehow reinforced this notion of David Mamet as misogynist.

MAMET: Well, perhaps some people did.

ROSE: But, I mean, I would assume—and everybody that knows you says that's simply not—that's an unfair labeling—but it seemed to, for some, to cause them to strike out again.

MAMET: I don't know if the label—labeling's unfair. I mean, I'm fairly sure it's inaccurate . . .

ROSE: Yeah. Well, *inaccurate* is a better word.

MAMET: The, there are two characters. There's a man and a woman in the play, and each of them has a very firm point of view, both of which I believe in. And I think the way—the, the reason that the movie succeeds, if it does, and I think it does, is because each person, the man and the woman, is saying something absolutely true at every moment and absolutely constructive at most moments in the play, and yet at the end of the play they're tearing each other's throats out.

ROSE: But you know what they said. I mean, they felt like that, that this was clearly a cir—, a circumstance in which it wasn't. I think the argument has been made by many people when they, when they began to criticize it or to be so—it became so controversial, is that they thought that, that the debate was one-sided because of the way you'd structured the relationship between the two of them.

. MAMET: No, that's not what I heard. What, what I . . .

ROSE: Well, tell me what you heard.

MAMET: Well, I heard from most people, many people thought that the, the balance of power or the balance of rectitude, if you will—

ROSE: Right.

MAMET: —between the two protagonists was lopsided. But they didn't always think that the same person was on top. A lot of people thought that the, the man was right and the woman was wrong and that I'd slanted it that way, and a lot of people thought the opposite.

And that's why the people were slapping each other around in the lobby because they each, the audience each thought, or the members of the audience vehemently believed, that their hero in the play was correct and that the person's hero was wrong.

ROSE: . . . This is a clip, and you know what we're going to see. Maybe you can set it up for me. This is "Should All Kids Go to College?"

MAMET: The, the young woman, a young student, Carol, played by Debra Eisenstadt, has been trying to get the professor to change her grade, and he's been trying to deal with her problems, at the same time he is trying to get out of the office so he can go home and have a private life. It's at the end of the interview, and he's trying to get her out of the office—

ROSE: Right.

MAMET: —trying to give her a few thoughts to live by, and, and please go home, now we've had our nice little chat. And . . . she's not ready to go home.

[Extract of *Oleanna*]

ROSE: And so that becomes the incident?

MAMET: Well, yeah, that becomes the first incident.

ROSE: You wanted to say what in *Oleanna?*

MAMET: I didn't want to say anything. I wanted to write the, I wanted to write the play. I know lots of people find it hard to think that it's that, that because something seems to contain a message that it's not the, that it's not the playwright's intention to send out—

ROSE: Right.

MAMET: —to send that message. But I'm trying to write a, write a story, to try to follow a provocative grouping of individuals to its logical conclusion to see where that goes.

ROSE: . . . but you're laying it on the groundwork of one of the hottest sort of social issues of our, of, of the time. You wrote this, what 1980? 19–? What?

MAMET: This?

ROSE: Yeah. Oh, in 1990, 1989?

MAMET: Somewhere around there—1990.

ROSE: Okay . . . 1980s, early 1990s. You laid it on the groundwork, on the, on the basis, on the foundation of the subject matter of intense—sort of a time sexual harassment was under great discussion and debate—

MAMET: Right.

165

ROSE: —on campus, in the country.

MAMET: Right.

ROSE: Second, it was a time of political correctness and all of those issues.

MAMET: Right.

ROSE: You didn't want to say something about those issues in terms of how you had your characters engage in the kind of dialogue they engage in?

MAMET: Well, the thing—I mean, those issues terrify me. They, I was rather frightened to even take up my, my pen about them.

ROSE: Why?

MAMET: Well, bec— well, I think because even a fish wouldn't get in trouble if he kept his mouth shut, you know, as us, as us fishermen.

ROSE: Yes, that's what they say. Yes.

MAMET: But I think for that, perhaps for that reason, among others, I thought that I'd, it might be a good idea to, to, write to open that can of worms. But basically what I wanted to do and I, I think mainly what I usually want to do is just to simply tell a story. That something is an important topic in our daily newspaper or in our breakfast table discussion does not necessarily mean it's going to make a, make a good play.

ROSE: What makes a good play is the creation of interesting— well, what does make a . . . you're the best person to tell me that. What makes a good play?

MAMET: Well, I think what makes a good play is a protagonist who wants something vehemently and is going to set out to get it, whether that's Hamlet finding out who killed his father or Oedipus finding out what, what's the cause of the plague on Thebes, you know, or, or, or Nora in *A Doll's House* finding how she can live as an oppressed woman in a man's world, or Anna Christie finding out what she can do to get her father to take her back. That's what makes us want to come out, see the next, hear the next line on stage, or see the next cut in the movie: What happens next? When we really understand what the character wants, and we understand what they're going through to get it, that's what keeps us in our seat.

ROSE: Let me take you back in your life. The thing that people notice best about you from the beginning, I think, was dialogue—

MAMET: Yeah.

ROSE: —and was the, the silence, that you were able to use silence well, and it was the clipped dialogue that you captured among the subjects and how you drew on your own experiences. Did that come from home? Did that come from a family where there was an emphasis on semantics and dialogue and expression?

MAMET: Oh yeah, yeah. My, my family have, have been Jewish for about four thousand years, I mean, fi—fifty-seven hundred years, and my people tend to place a great deal of emphasis on the ability to express oneself well and to, and to parse a book or a sentence or a thought or interchange into oblivion. So that's, that's the tradition that I'm very happy to have grown up in.

ROSE: Well, your sister—I think Lynn—says that at, at your home, your father was very strict about semantics. He was a labor lawyer.

MAMET: Yeah.

ROSE: In Chicago?

MAMET: Yeah.

ROSE: And very strict about it and would insist that all of you kids spoke with clear expression and dramati—and, and grammatically correct.

MAMET: Yeah. He was pretty great.

ROSE: Yeah. He was great?

MAMET: Yeah.

ROSE: When you look at what, what you have become, I mean, can you trace it back? Do you see some linkage to your father?

MAMET: Every day.

ROSE: In what way?

MAMET: Well, I wrote that movie, *Hoffa*—

ROSE: Yeah.

MAMET: —for Danny DeVito and—

ROSE: Right.

MAMET: Jack Nicholson. My dad was a, a labor lawyer, a one-man labor lawyer, and it was really a movie about him. I didn't know Hoffa, but it was about my dad and the way he spoke and the way he comported himself. And he always, he always believed in working harder. You know, he would come home from work at eight o'clock at night and wolf down his dinner and be at the dining room table still working at one, one o'clock in the morning. And he believed that, he believed there was no problem to which he couldn't surmount in the interest of his client by working harder, thinking harder, and being more inventive. And he used to say, for example, any time something terrible would happen, he would say, "Okay, let's, let's stand this on our—on its head—and see how it's really to our advantage."

167

ROSE: But that's what they say about you, too, that you view writing as a craft—

MAMET: Uh-huh.

ROSE: —that you view writing as something you do in the morning. If you're in Vermont, I guess you go out to a cabin—

MAMET: Mm-hm.

ROSE: —and you write in longhand in a cold cabin, that you see it as going to work, and you see it almost in a blue-collar way.

MAMET: Mm-hm.

ROSE: Do you?

MAMET: Well, I, I hope that that's true, and, if it is, I think it's true because of my, my home life, and also because that's, that's the Chicago tradition that, at least in the theater, which is the only art I know anything about, the only world I know anything about. We had the, the blue-collar tradition. It was something that you did. You know, you got together. You had your theater company—the Organic or the St. Nicholas or the—

ROSE: Yeah. St. Nicholas, which—

MAMET: —Steppenwolf.

ROSE: —you created.

MAMET: Yeah. I was one of the people who did—

ROSE: Yeah.

MAMET: —or Joey Mantegna was with the Organic, and you know, Meshach Taylor and—

ROSE: Greg Mosher and others.

MAMET: —Greg Mosher at the Goodman Theatre. And you had your company and you went to work, and it was your job to please the audience. That was your job. If it was a drama, the drama had to be interesting, and, if it was a comedy, it had to be funny, period.

ROSE: Take you back a little before that, though. So you, you were—your parents were divorced.

MAMET: Yeah.

ROSE: Impact on you.

MAMET: You'll have to ask me when I get over it.

ROSE: You still . . .

MAMET: Well, I, yeah, it still affects me. It was a very traumatic time. You know, it was the, they got divorced in the 1950s, and I didn't know anybody who knew anybody who'd been divorced, you know, let alone have it happen to my family. So, there was a lot of trauma in my childhood.

ROSE: You went to live with your mother.

MAMET: Yeah, I went to live with my ma. I lived with my dad later on for a couple of years.

ROSE: Yeah. And then went to college thinking you would do what?

MAMET: I went to college thinking I'd get out of the house, and that was, that was enough for me.

ROSE: Yes, why did you want to get out of the house?

MAMET: Well, it was, well, it wasn't a very happy house.

ROSE: Because of the divorce or—

MAMET: I think. And also, I really wanted to . . . I didn't know anything about the middle-class life, except that I'd had enough of it. And so I went to college, and a lot of the, the verbiage in the play in both characters—

ROSE: Yeah.

MAMET: —is my working out of the idea of what, what constitutes worth. The student says, "I've been told all my life I'm stupid, I'm stupid, I can't learn, I'm stupid, I'm stupid." And the professor says, "No, you aren't. You're rather smart, as a matter of fact. You're just angry. I think if I can get you past that point, you'll see there's a lot of enjoyment in life that you've heretofore missed." Now—so it—I'm—to a certain extent, I'm being the professor comforting myself as the student. And the other thing is, is true, too. I'm being the student saying to the professor, "You can be clearer. You have a responsibility to me. I'm lost. I need your help. Paternalism's not going to help. Charisma is not going to help. Telling me to go and do my homework is not going to help. I need someone to explain to me what's required of me." So, there, again, I'm casting myself, the writer, as the student demanding that of figures in authority. . . . It was, I always said nobody with a happy childhood ever went into show business—

ROSE: Yeah.

MAMET: —and I think that's pretty true. That's the nice thing about being a, a writer is you get to work a lot of things out.

ROSE: When you went to college, though, you wanted to be an actor.

MAMET: Yeah, I'd spent some time as a, a kid actor, in Chicago and doing a little bit of television and a little bit of radio and a little bit of stage work. And it seemed like a lot of fun. It didn't seem like work.

ROSE: What happened?

MAMET: I found that I couldn't act.

ROSE: That'll do it every time, won't it?

MAMET: Yeah. I was going to say that.

ROSE: Well, no. It doesn't always do it. Some people never learn.

MAMET: Yeah. I was going to say that I'd, I'd be the first one to tell you I couldn't act, but Billy Macy would actually be the first one to tell you I couldn't act.

ROSE: Billy Macy is the star in *Oleanna*. He knew you at Goddard, did he?

MAMET: I was his teacher. I went back, I went to Goddard College as a student, and I came back a couple of years later and taught. And he was my student in the, I guess, the late 1960s and early 1970s.

ROSE: How did the playwriting begin?

MAMET: I started a little theater company among my students at Goddard College and eventually moved to Chicago with them. And we didn't have any money to pay royalties. We just, we had no money.

ROSE: Right.

MAMET: And there were, there were some plays written, which were suitable for a small, young company, but you had to pay royalties on them, and there were many plays written that were suitable that you didn't have to pay royalties on but that were suitable for a twenty-four-character company of middle-aged people. We couldn't do those, so there was nothing to do. So, in our ignorance we started writing plays for each other. Billy used to write plays, and I, I wrote plays, and we would direct each other and act them. We all did everything.

ROSE: . . . you said, I think, at some point earlier when you went back to Chicago, "We discovered that we were, I discovered that I was a mediocre actor and a part-time playwright."

MAMET: Yeah. That's right. So, I became a director of the company and, and a playwright, and—

ROSE: And at twenty-seven you wrote *American Buffalo*.

MAMET: Yeah.

ROSE: And you thought it was going to win a Pulitzer Prize.

MAMET: Well, hey.

ROSE: But the story is that you told, you bet, what, five thousand? You put five thousand dollars in the bank, or was it five hundred dollars? Which was it? I've read two accounts.

MAMET: Oh, I can't remember.

ROSE: You know, it was either five hundred or five—and you said to Greg Mosher, "I'm go—, I'm going to put this here, and, and I'll give it to you if I don't win the Pulitzer Prize."

MAMET: I think, I think—

ROSE: Right?

MAMET: —I probably did. You know, five hundred or five thousand, looking back was equally—an equally fantastical amount to me at that—

ROSE: Yeah.

MAMET: —time.

ROSE: But did he get the money or not?

MAMET: No, but Greg did the play. I mean, he's—you know, those instances of, of intercession are, are so precious. You know, you're a young struggling kid, and everybody reads your stuff and says, "No, it's no good," or "Yes, it's good, but I don't want to do it."

ROSE: Yeah.

MAMET: And Greg was then the second in command at the Goodman Theatre in Chicago, and I brought him the play, and I, I said something like that, or else, "Please do my play. I, I think it's not without merit." And he read it and said, "Okay." And he did it, and that's been his attitude ever since for my work, both in Chicago at the Goodman and then when he was running Lincoln Center.

ROSE: Yeah. Did that give you some stability to know that there was someone there that, who you'd worked . . . ?

MAMET: Oh, yeah. I mean, for an artist, it's, it's, it's marvelous. It's the best thing in the world, someone to say, "I believe in you," and back it up by staking his reputation on your own.

ROSE: And then seven or eight years later you came with *Glengarry Glen Ross,* which won a Pulitzer Prize.

MAMET: Right.

ROSE: Yeah. You were, what? So, you were not more than, what, thirty-four or thirty-five when you did that.

MAMET: I think so. Yeah.

ROSE: What was your persona at the time? How did you see yourself?

MAMET: Oh, I don't know.

ROSE: You know why I ask that? Because—

MAMET: No.

ROSE: —so many people write, well, you do know. Come on. So many people write about you. Every time I read something about you, you know, they talk about the Mamet persona and the, this sense of the, the . . . in the beginning they talked about no female characters. Clearly, you later wrote female characters and . . .

MAMET: Yeah. No, that's not true, by the way. I always wrote for female characters.

ROSE: But they wrote about that. They said that. Now, come on.

171

MAMET: Yeah.

ROSE: Yes?

MAMET: Many people did, yeah.

ROSE: Yeah. And they said that, and they also made comparisons between you and Hemingway—

MAMET: Uh-huh.

ROSE: —in terms of the kinds of male things that you love to do and, and some sense of gun col—, knife collecting and loving guns and loving poker, and a kind of—do you reject that? Or, when you read those things, do you think that they have no meaning or are irrelevant or off-base or none of the above?

MAMET: Well, I don't know. I always loved Hemingway. I mean, he came from Oak Park, which is—

ROSE: Yeah, right.

MAMET: —al—, almost Chicago. And I loved, to say it again, I loved escaping from the middle class. Of course, I wasn't escaping from the middle class because we all, you know, we all have to be what—

ROSE: Yeah, I know. I know.

MAMET: —we are.

ROSE: I know.

MAMET: I turned out to be a, a nice Jewish boy, that's what, which I always was. But, I hope, but it pleased me to think that I was putting something over in myself, you know, and living in Vermont and doing things that it seemed were not acceptable behavior for a nice Jewish boy whose family has always had the gene for liberalism— spending a lot of time gambling, hunting, fishing, etc. And, I spent a lot of time in pool rooms, and I enjoyed the life there.

ROSE: Someone said to me, even today, they said that, that you, that they believed that recently you have, in a sense, rediscovered your Jewishness. Do you think that's . . .

MAMET: Oh, I think that's absolutely true.

ROSE: Yeah. What happened?

MAMET: Sure. Well, I went to my niece's bat mitzvah and I realized that I hadn't been inside a, a synagogue in 30 years, and I started wondering why; and that I was chagrined and shocked to find that it had something to do with a sense of, not only assimilationism, but perhaps self-hatred that was nobody's fault but my own. And that I thought perhaps I could remedy that.

ROSE: You don't do a lot of television . . . , I don't think; I haven't seen you on a lot.

MAMET: No, I don't.

ROSE: And, and everybody, when they knew that you were going to come here, was curious and had ideas, and they wanted to talk to you, and one of the things they said is, "Ask him why he continues to write for the theater," because . . . . they thought, you know, a lot of people who write for the theater go on to write screenplays and leave the theater, but you, they have a sense, will always come back to the theater and will continue to write for the theater.

MAMET: Because, because I love it. I mean, it's the . . .

ROSE: Because that's what you . . .

MAMET: Yeah, that's what I do best, and I just adore it. I mean, it's—. It's very hard to be happier than, than, than sitting, you know, working with my friends, working with my family, working on a play.

ROSE: Let me talk about friends and people that you have a relationship with. Harold Pinter.

MAMET: Mm-hm.

ROSE: What's the relationship? What's the sort of friendship?

MAMET: Well, Harold Pinter was very close at one time, and I think is close again with Sir Peter Hall, and Sir Peter Hall wrote a diary in which he—

ROSE: I know. I read that.

MAMET: —mentioned Harold Pinter.

ROSE: Yeah, right.

MAMET: In fact, very favorably. And Harold Pinter didn't talk to him for five or six years. So if you think I'm going to say anything about Harold Pinter, you're crazy.

ROSE: Is that right? Peter Hall didn't, he didn't talk to Peter Hall after?

MAMET: Yeah.

ROSE: He wrote that diary for five years?

MAMET: Yeah.

ROSE: But there is something about, I would think, about Harold Pinter that appeals to you. He's your kind of character.

MAMET: Well, he's Harold.

ROSE: Other than being a brilliant playwright and, and also a, a director.

MAMET: Harold Pinter. Well, when I was just a kid, Harold Pinter and, and Samuel Beckett were the playwrights of the . . .

ROSE: Yeah.

MAMET: I, I, I still think so. He was always a, a hero of mine and really was responsible to a large extent for me starting to write. And then he was very, was very helpful and, and generous to me—and still is—at many points in my career, in promoting my work and directing my work.

ROSE: Did he direct? What's he directed in London of yours?

MAMET: He directed *Oleanna,* the play.

ROSE: When it was in London.

MAMET: In London, yeah.

ROSE: . . . Alan Dershowitz.

MAMET: Yeah.

ROSE: You live in Cambridge. He's a friend.

MAMET: Yeah. He's great. I mean, he's, he's, and he was so very helpful with the, again, with the play *Oleanna,* because there is a lot of legalism involved in the play.

ROSE: Yeah.

MAMET: And I asked him to come over from the law school [Harvard Law School] over to where we were rehearsing about a block away, and he would sit in on rehearsals and give us ideas about the legality of what the woman was saying and the legality of the man's position. He was very very supportive. In fact, we put him in the trailer for the movie.

ROSE: When you, when you look at where you are now and all that you have accomplished, is there satisfaction? Is there a sense of . . . how do you sort of sum up where you are at, say, midlife? I mean, you're about, you're approaching fifty, yes? In about three years. You're forty-seven.

MAMET: I'm supposed to be forty-seven, God willing, in about five more shopping weeks.

ROSE: Yes.

MAMET: So—

ROSE: So you're—how do you feel about, about where you are and, and the body of work that you . . . is it what you set out to do? Does it surprise you that you've been able to do so much and that, that you've been able to express yourself in so many different ways?

MAMET: Yeah. It, it kind of shocks me. I didn't set out to do so much. You know, I set out to get one play done, and then, and then do another one. And I think I was always frightened of failure and always, always frightened by the specter of poverty. And I think I got that very much from my dad, who grew up very very poor and had to get out, and he just had his wits to earn a living for himself and his family. And the same was true of me. You know, I got out of college, I didn't have . . .

ROSE: Then if somebody came to you and said—you go to some faraway land, and someone says—"Mr. Mamet, I hear you're a famous writer," or "I hear that you're a very good writer. Send me something you've written." What would you send them?

MAMET: I would send them nothing! Are you kidding me?

ROSE: Why? Because you wouldn't want to, wouldn't want to lower their expectations, or you'd be afraid they . . .

MAMET: Well listen. Have they paid for it first?

ROSE: No, they haven't paid for it.

MAMET: Oh, no, no, no, no. I would—

ROSE: No, no. They'd have—

MAMET: —I would dir—

ROSE: —to pay.

MAMET: —I would direct them to a bookstore.

ROSE: The other thing that's interesting about what you write is so much of it is, is taken from your own experiences. I mean, you worked in a real estate firm.

MAMET: Yeah.

ROSE: *Sexual Perversity in Chicago*—you had been there.

MAMET: Yeah.

ROSE: You know. I mean, *Oleanna,* you were a college professor. And in fact, you said that almost every young professor you knew at the time that you were there— you were quoted, at least as saying— was having a relationship with some young student.

MAMET: Yeah, that's right.

ROSE: And that's why it was explosive or frightening for you to deal with the, the subject matter?

MAMET: No, no. Not at all. It just seemed, there seemed to be such vehemence—

ROSE: The change of attitude.

MAMET: —surrounding the, the issue of, of, of sexual harassment that I—part of me really didn't want to raise my head up above the foxhole and say, "What's going on here?"

ROSE: But just, I, to come back to this point. Are you surpri—, were you surprised by the controversy it ignited and at the conflicts that erupted over it?

MAMET: Oh, yeah. I, I was, I was, I was shocked. As I say, I had never seen reactions like that in a theater before.

ROSE: And why do you think it was true?

MAMET: Because, night after night and couple by couple, the people would split down the middle, and it wouldn't always be by sex, and it wouldn't always be by age. But one or the other would say, "I think he's right," "I think she's right."

ROSE: You see, my impression is that most men thought he was right, and most women thought the men didn't understand it. And that's not, in your judgment, the way—

MAMET: It wasn't; no, it wasn't.

ROSE: —it was.

MAMET: That wasn't my experience.

ROSE: Yeah. Your experience was it varied from night to night.

MAMET: That's right.

ROSE: Sex to sex.

MAMET: That's right. That's right. Because I think, I, I, think that the play got un—, and I think that the movie, too, gets under a lot of people's skins.

ROSE: Because?

MAMET: Because it's well, it's like, like Shakespeare said, you know, "the play's the thing in which we'll catch the conscience of the king." People suspend their disbelief for a second. They say, "Okay, I'm going to watch a, a funny little story, and everything will be under my control."

ROSE: Yeah.

MAMET: And then it, because the, because, because of the structure of the piece, because it, it moved so fast—

ROSE: Right.

MAMET: —and it's so clear what each one wants next, and you get two-thirds of the way through the play, and you think you know what's going on. And all of the sudden it takes a turn that you don't want, and you find you've identified with one of the two—or the other protagonist—and you start feeling like, "Wait, wait a second."

ROSE: Yeah.

MAMET: "Ah, ah, ah, ah." It gets under people's skins not because of the issues, I think, but because of the drama involved in the two protagonists.

ROSE: —You once said an interesting thing that, that the, that you could sum up what you knew about male-female relationships, at least in the following, that this was the key for a man: Be direct, was first; second was the men had to realize that women were smarter and that they therefore valued courtesy and kindness.

176

MAMET: Mm-hm.

ROSE: Third was—do you remember any of this?

MAMET: No, I like it—

ROSE: You don't.

MAMET: —though.

ROSE: You like it so far?

MAMET: I, I believe it so far, too.

ROSE: Third was . . . I don't remember what third was; and fourth was, when it came to the question of who got out of the elevator first, you were on your own. You had no idea—

MAMET: Yeah.

ROSE: —what the rules were. This leads to this question. Where do you think, because you have in one way or another dealt with relationships, and whether it's between men in a competition in *Glengarry Glen Ross* or among men for a Cadillac and in *Sexual Perversity,* you were dealing with some of these kinds of dynamics. . . . There has always been the element of, of, of the Mamet image, which I talked about earlier, that you don't reflect on. . . . You don't seem to have any sense of when you say, "Mamet," what that means to people in terms of image, other than just a very skilled playwright, essayist, now novelist.

MAMET: Well, I try not to think about it. You know, I, I think it's—

ROSE: Don't you really think about it? I mean, you have no sense of self, of, of, who you are in terms of how you are perceived by others?

MAMET: I, I suppose I might at any given moment.

ROSE: Yeah.

MAMET: You know, like anybody I know, the guy's in the elevator. One time he's going to think of himself as Galahad, the other he's going to think of himself as Jean Valjean.

ROSE: Here is what's interesting about it because a lot of your friends have commented on it.

MAMET: Yeah.

ROSE: And that's why I'm trying to bring it out of you, and, and I am generally not doing so well—

MAMET: Well, I'm sure Harold—

ROSE: —at.

MAMET: Harold Pinter's not going to talk to them either.

ROSE: But there is some sense of, of this notion of this maleness and how you see that and, and all of that. Now, maybe that's because people read what you write, and they want to somehow look, look at a persona and say, "Well, therefore I understand it." It's the Hemingway comparison. It is, in a sense, the fact that for a while people did not see female characters that they thought were very strong female characters. Now you tend to want to debunk all of that, yes?

MAMET: I guess. I mean, you know, see, it's . . .

ROSE: Mr. Mamet, do you plead guilty or not guilty?

MAMET: See, finally, it's the worst idea in the world for me to be doing—for any, as Virginia Woolf says . . .

ROSE: To be doing what?

MAMET: Publicity.

ROSE: Right.

MAMET: Because, as Virginia Woolf and many other writers—

ROSE: Yeah.

MAMET: —because the last thing in the world that a writer wants—

ROSE: Should ever—

MAMET: —wants to do—

ROSE: Is?

MAMET: —is to get involved in his or her own self, self-promotion.

ROSE: Okay. Fair enough. You're right. Okay. Then I leave it.

ROSE: Is it easy for you, writing?

MAMET: To write? Sometimes it is; sometimes it's, it's—

ROSE: What's easiest? I mean, plays, essays, screenplays, now a novel?

MAMET: It's . . .

ROSE: It's all part of the same.

MAMET: Well, you know, some, some aspects. It's like what's easier: to build a skiff or to build a boat in a bottle? Certain aspects are similar.

ROSE: To build a skiff, I think. I can't imagine it would be easy to build a boat in a bottle.

MAMET: Yeah. Well, on the other hand, you don't got to put, you don't got to put the skiff in, into the glass thing and pull up the mast.

ROSE: How do you see this relationship between men and women today? You've talked about it in *Sexual Perversity* in, in *Oleanna*. You've just made a film that has to do with the dynamics of the time.

MAMET: I think men and women need each other. I think men and women love each other. And I think these are very frustrating times. I think that . . . again, a mention of Virginia Woolf. As she tells us, women have been oppressed for a great deal of history, and for them to, to claim rights rather than to live in a society where they're being awarded rights is very upsetting to the society as a whole, as it should be. And it's a period that we're all going to have to live through, and we will.

ROSE: Do you believe feminism went too far in, in . . .

MAMET: Well, it depends on what you mean by feminism. You know, I'm not a woman. It's not for me to say that any woman has gone, has gone too far in the struggle for, for women's rights.

ROSE: But, but clearly, you have thought about these issues because they are reflected in what you write.

MAMET: Well, Sidney Kingsley wrote a play called *Detective Story*.

ROSE: Yeah.

MAMET: Great play.

ROSE: Right.

MAMET: Because that happens to be a great play about cops and robbers doesn't mean you're going to go to Sidney Kingsley and ask him what he thinks about crime control.

MAMET: Now, it's a very, it's a very, very equal exchange, by the way, and I'm very grateful for you for having me here. It's absolutely an equal exchange. I'm, I get the opportunity to indulge in self-promotion, and you get the absolute right to ask me these questions.

ROSE: Yeah.

MAMET: But it's, it's a terrible idea for me.

ROSE: But, but you, it's a terrible idea for you because what? . . . Tell me why it's a terrible idea—

MAMET: Well, somebody said . . .

ROSE: —to, to, to elaborate on the question, because it's done in print about you all the time. So it's a natural thing for me to do, but you think—I'll grant you that, but it's not for me, as David Mamet, natural to answer these questions.

MAMET: Well, I don't know the answers to a lot of them.

ROSE: Right.

MAMET: But, also, somebody once said another very important thing to me about writing. They said—

ROSE: Yeah.

MAMET: —steal from anybody but yourself. So if the, if I start stealing from myself or imitating myself or thinking about what does that mean, rather than looking at the problems on the page, then I, I feel . . .

ROSE: And, and if we—

MAMET: [*unintelligible*]

ROSE: And if we look at the whole list of things that you wrote—that whole list. I mean, it's an extraordinary body of work. I mean, you write constantly, don't you?

MAMET: Yeah.

ROSE: I mean, you, why do you feel the urge to write all the time? Because you have some . . . ?

MAMET: Because it beats thinking.

ROSE: Beats thinking.

MAMET: Yeah. It's so, it's so much, it's so much gentler than thinking.

ROSE: That's true.

MAMET: You know, he's just telling a story. And the same thing with me and this . . . and *Oleanna*.

ROSE: Yeah.

MAMET: I'm just telling a story.

ROSE: Are you a dreamer?

MAMET: Oh, sure. You?

ROSE: You bet. Yeah. Wouldn't, wouldn't have it any other way, I don't think. I mean, if you can't, if you lose dreams, then, don't you?

MAMET: Oh, yeah.

ROSE: I mean, that's sort of the beginning of the end, when you lose the capacity or, or you no longer dream. What do you think of this obsession with O. J. Simpson?

MAMET: Well, it's, it's terrifying. You know, gossip, I always felt, is the, is the need to define social norms. We need to discover what's correct for the community, and so we gossip. And, also, we need to identify ourselves as the good people. I think we all, we all—Jewish tradition calls it *leshon harad*, evil tongue, and says it's a great, great, great crime. And, in fact, the Orthodox Jews won't talk, won't say anything about anyone else. They just won't talk about third parties for fear of engaging in, in *leshon harad*, evil tongue. It's probably a very good idea. Each—the idea that anybody could be a, a victim, and the idea that anybody could be a murderer is a, it's a terrifying idea. You know, people whom we have elected to have a mythic status, the heroes, that they, that they might be either one of those things is, is very upsetting, don't you think?

ROSE: I do think that, but I—and, and that's why we're obsessed by it. . . . You know, it, it is the incomprehensibility of thinking that our, our mythic heroes could be—

MAMET: Could be human, which of course, they are.

ROSE: —could be human.

MAMET: Because if they're human, what that means is that we're human. Don't you think?

ROSE: I do, but don— Do you think that's a play here? I mean.

MAMET: Oh, yeah. Sure.

ROSE: I mean, we have had so much come out about this particular case, and, and at first, the first reaction—not among friends of Mrs. Simpson, the deceased Mrs. Simpson—but the first reaction of friends, fellow players, was that it's incomprehensible—

MAMET: Mm-hm.

ROSE: —that this man could have done that crime.

MAMET: Mm-hm.

ROSE: Yet, on the other hand, I also think that . . . God, I mean, there is a part of me also that believes that, I mean, when we have seen so much evil in this world that, that nothing would surprise us in terms of the capacity of evil. You?

MAMET: Well, I think that's what tragedy is about. That's the, that's why tragedy is cleansing because it confronts us with, with our humanity, with our capacity for evil. And, having been confronted by that capacity to have bad done to us and to do bad ourselves, we leave feeling chastened and, and cleansed, as Aristotle would say, rather than incorrectly buoyed by being reassured, as melodrama does, or as . . . that we, that we are not the bad guy. Melodrama completely differentiates between the good guy and the bad guy and says, "You have a choice: the, the evil guy in the black hat, who is a swine or the angel in the white hat, who, who's a saint. Which would you rather choose?" We say, "I think I'll identify with the angel in the white hat," and then you leave at the end of the melodrama and say, "Well, boy, I'm so glad that the angel in the white hat won. I feel great!"

ROSE: Yeah.

MAMET: But that feeling lasts until you get out of the door of the theater, whereas tragedy says, "Choose which one you want to be. Whichever one you choose, you're going to be wrong, and, P.S., you never had a choice to begin with. You're just human." And we leave shaken and perhaps better for the experience.

A Great Longing to Belong

Charlie Rose

In their second televised conversation Charlie Rose and David Mamet take up the issues of self-hatred, race hatred, and Jewish identity, which Mamet addresses in *The Old Religion*. In this powerful second novel Mamet imagines the mind-set of Leo Frank, a man accused of rape and murder, as he questions the nature of justice, the definition of a good man, and the charges against him.

ROSE: David Mamet has been very busy lately. The Pulitzer Prize–winning playwright has several new projects: a novel, a Broadway play, a guide for actors and several film projects in various stages of production. He is known for plays like *Glengarry Glen Ross* and also *Speed-the-Plow* and also screenplays like *The Verdict* and *The Untouchables*. I'm pleased to have him here to talk about drama and cinema, the craft of writing, and a lot of other things. It is also good to have him at this table for the second time. I'm especially pleased. Welcome back sir.

MAMET: Thank you very much.

ROSE: Before we start talking about *The Old Religion* and also *The Old Neighborhood*, tell me about your quest and your engagement with this idea of being Jewish. I said to you going in that I sometimes am jealous of Jews—and *envious* is a better word—because there's always this sense of what it means to be Jewish and a constant questioning of what it means and how I can be better.

From the "Charlie Rose Show," WNET-TV (Channel 13), New York. The previously unpublished interview was aired on November 11, 1997, and was viewed by approximately three million of the Public Broadcasting Service viewers in the United States and Canada. Copyright © Rose Productions, Inc. Courtesy of Charlie Rose Show / Rose Communications, PBS.

MAMET: Right. And I said to you, "Say it on the air" because that's been my experience—

ROSE: Right.

MAMET: —that that's an extraordinary statement.

ROSE: Because?

MAMET: Well, it's a very important statement because I think that everyone likes to belong and that we Jews, especially assimilated Jews, have a great longing to belong, and I think that it's been documented that a vastly disproportionate number of the people in cults are Jews—that is, people who feel that they, people who have been deracinated because the Jew—

I mean, you can't get a longer heritage than, than the Jewish heritage. Passover's supposedly the longest continuously celebrated ceremony in the world. And to cut oneself off from one's identity is a terrible, terrible thing, and I think that there are other groups in this country today, notably African Americans, Hispanic Americans, and gay Americans, who are saying, "You must be who you are. You have no choice," that the anomie, which is the down side, has to be faced and whatever your fears are about embracing yourself, your tradition, your heritage, your sexuality, your religion, it's not going to be as bad as not doing it.

ROSE: Where did this notion of "self-hating Jew" come from?

MAMET: Well, I think it came. . . . There's, there's two aspects to it, I believe. One is that people who have—whether that's Jews or gays or African Americans or whomever—a famous sports figure said, "I'm not black, I'm O.J.," for example.

To deny what you are, to deny who you are, to deny what you want, to live a life of hypocrisy, has got to have an ongoing effect of self-loathing. Bruno Bettelheim said something rather extraordinarily brilliant, I thought, about the Nazi salute. He said that the Nazis were very, very smart. They made people give this stupid salute.

Five hundred times a day, a thousand times a day, they had to raise their arms and give this stupid salute. And if they didn't feel like doing it, after a while, every time they gave the salute they had to say to themselves, "I'm giving the salute, but I don't mean it." And so they subsequently said to themselves, "Therefore I am either a coward because I don't stop giving the salute, or I am a hypocrite." So, eventually, the struggle was too great and they simply forgot about it and started giving a salute, and, as soon as they started giving the salute, their soul was gone.

ROSE: Yes.

MAMET: And so, if you start giving the salute to something that you aren't, eventually you have to stop fighting and lose something that you are.

ROSE: Let me move to some of the things that you've been writing. *The Old Religion*—Leo Frank—a novel—

MAMET: Right.

ROSE: —not a play.

MAMET: That's right.

ROSE: In fact, somebody—Alfred Uhrie's going to write a play, evidently—

MAMET: [*unintelligible*] I heard.

ROSE: —based on the Leo Frank story.

MAMET: That's right.

ROSE: Tell me, who was Leo Frank—

MAMET: Leo—

ROSE: —and, second, why you decided to make this exploration in this novel.

MAMET: Well, Leo Frank was a Jewish fellow, a young Jewish fellow around thirty who was the manager of a pencil factory, came down from up North, went down to Atlanta, Georgia, to manage a pencil factory that was largely staffed by young Southern women who'd been drawn from the farms. And they were very low-paid, and the work probably wasn't very pleasant. And, like most of us in jobs like that, nobody liked the boss.

A young woman was raped and murdered, and Leo Frank was accused, on no evidence whatever, of the crime, and there was a huge show trial. It galvanized Atlanta. Newspapers sprang up, and fortunes were made in anti-Semitic journalism. And Atlanta was galvanized, as the South was, to protect the rights of Southern womanhood by murdering Leo Frank, which eventually happened. Frank was convicted of the crime, sentenced to death, and the sentence was commuted to life in prison, and he was taken from the prison and lynched.

And at the time it was called "the American Dreyfus" case. It was a fabulously celebrated case. There was outcry from all over the world to spare Frank's life. It was the, I believe, the beginning of the ACLU [American Civil Liberties Union]. And I think it's very good that the case is coming back to public consciousness now.

ROSE: And why did it appeal to you as the subject of an exploration of him and his thoughts in a novel?

MAMET: Well, it's, it's, the book is very, very much an interior monologue. It's, it's a fellow, it's an imagined piece. It's a fellow who's put in a position where he's done nothing wrong, and in an attempt to find out, therefore, why he's being punished, he has to begin examining the nature of the world.

What does it mean? What is justice? What is God? What is reason? What can a good man reasonably expect? Is he a good man? What is the definition of a good man? And he has—one of the paths that he takes is to toy with and subsequently embrace his own invented brand of Judaism.

ROSE: And you want to come away with what—the reader?

MAMET: I, I don't, I—

ROSE: As a writer do you write hoping the reader will come away with an experience, with, with that?

MAMET: Well, I try to make it. . . . That's a good question to which I don't know the answer. All that I know is that what the reader . . . I try to write the story the best way I know how.

ROSE: And the story you're writing here is what you just said—I mean, this interior monologue. And the subject attracts you because?

MAMET: Well, the subject attracts me because I'm a Jew. The subject attracts me because, as I grow older, I've become more and more interested in what the hell is going on here anyway.

ROSE: Right.

MAMET: And that's why the subject, the subject of racial hatred, the older I get, the more it baffles me. So to get back to your question about self, self-hating—

ROSE: Right.

MAMET: Assimilated. . . . People who are assimilated, I think, can feel lonely. And, if there are pangs to rejoin or to rediscover or to embrace that from which one came, perhaps it's easier to—to still those pangs by scoffing at them, which has got to make them, got to create a certain bit of self, of self-hatred. I think. "I don't need that."

I mean, one hears, if you listen and you're a Jew, you're going to hear it five thousand times in a year, "My parents are Jewish. I'm a Jew, but I don't practice. I'm a Jew, but I don't"—blah, blah, blah. Well, why this confession?

ROSE: Why?

MAMET: Because, because it comes out of a sense of longing, and it comes out of a sense of loss, and it also comes, to a certain extent, out of a sense of shame.

ROSE: Are you coming to these questions now, or have they been a part of your own interior monologue for a long time?

MAMET: Well, I don't know. I mean—

ROSE: You don't know?

MAMET: I don't know. My earliest play is called *The Duck Variations*—

ROSE: Right.

MAMET: —and it was about two Jewish guys sitting on a bench. I wrote that thirty years ago.

ROSE: This is when you were in Chicago or—

MAMET: In Chicago. I actually wrote it in Vermont about 1968 or 1969. And I've written about being Jewish throughout. I mean, one of my movies is called *Homicide*, a movie about a Jewish detective.

ROSE: Right.

MAMET: Part of my play on Broadway now is called, the play is called *The Old Neighborhood*, and one of the sections is called "The Disappearance of the Jews," about two Jewish buddies getting back together.

ROSE: Right.

MAMET: It's something that, that, that fascinates me.

ROSE: Yeah. What interests me is, why do people create what they do? What is it that drives them to create, whether they . . . what brings it to the forefront? I mean—and is, in fact, what your work here, and these two examples, the novel and the play, and the other instances you just referred to, in a sense, an ongoing dialogue in your personal life, and is that dialogue—what permutations does it take, you know, and where are you? Is this just an academic exercise, or is this a parallel . . . ?

MAMET: No, it's not an academic exercise. I mean, the question, the "go to work in the morning, have a couple eggs, go and sit and you stare at your typewriter" question is, finally, "Who am I, and what's going on here?"

ROSE: Exactly.

MAMET: If the day is going to be any fun.

ROSE: And is this the most central and substantive and important inquiry for you?

MAMET: At that time.

ROSE: At that time.

MAMET: That's absolutely right.

ROSE: And at this time, then, because this is just coming out.

MAMET: That's right.

ROSE: You know? Let me touch on some other bases, too, because I want to just get a—you haven't been here in a while, and I want to—in the time I've got—this is instructions to an actor. Why did you do this?

186

MAMET: Well, I don't know if it's instructions so much . . .

ROSE: Okay, it's *True and False*.

MAMET: It might be, but it's philosophy of acting. It's a book about how to think; it's a book about how to think about acting.

ROSE: Right.

MAMET: And it's a book, I believe, for actors and primarily for young actors.

ROSE: And how they relate to a playwright.

MAMET: How they relate to a playwright—

ROSE: Among other things.

MAMET: —and how they relate to each other—

ROSE: Right.

MAMET: —how they relate to their craft because young actors are, in my experience, another deracinated group. They're a group that's been told, "You're no good. Try harder," when, in effect, they aren't—they aren't no good. They're quite good. I think it's a great art, and I think it's a great mystery and . . .

ROSE: A mystery?

MAMET: Yeah.

ROSE: In terms of how to do it.

MAMET: Well, to a certain extent how to do it, and also the difference between good acting, which is extraordinarily enjoyable, and great acting, which is rare and breathtaking is, it's a gift, it's a gift. It's a gift from God to be able to act.

ROSE: You think so?

MAMET: Yes. I think that, like—

ROSE: You're born with this combination of genes and chromosomes that make it possible for you to do it.

MAMET: Well, I think anybody can learn to throw a baseball. Some people can learn to throw a baseball accurately, and it takes a great genius to throw it accurately at ninety-five miles an hour. And I think the same is true with acting, that most people can learn certain rudiments of acting, and then it takes a lot of hard work and a certain gift to be able to do them well, and then it takes an extraordinary, very, very rare gift to be able to do it surpassingly.

ROSE: But then did you, I mean, I, this flows out of what you just said. Do you, do you value higher the capacity to excel at a brilliant level, like Michael Jordan in professional basketball in comparison to whoever, whatever actor you put at that level in acting, whoever it might be, whether it's Brando or Pacino or De Niro or, or Olivier?

MAMET: Well, I think the job of the actor is to tell the truth.

That's the job of the actor, that, that takes great courage and that the different levels of truths that one may, may tell are going to vary from actor to actor, from performance to performance, and also over the vast range of people in the profession.

ROSE: Yeah. Can you compare it to the craft or the skill or the given gift of writing?

MAMET: Maybe. I think so. I think that's probably a gift, too, that—

ROSE: Writing is a gift, too?

MAMET: I think, I think that, that there are certain rudiments of expression that, that most people can learn and that some can excel at them to a greater level and that once in a while someone comes along who's just so good, like a Mark Twain, you know, or a Virginia Woolf. All of a sudden, you say, "Oh, my God. Where did that come from?" It's just words.

ROSE: It's—you can't fathom how they got that good.

MAMET: No. I mean, all the words are all in the dictionary. Anybody can use them.

ROSE: Yeah. How does an actor determine whether he or she has it?

MAMET: Well, I don't think that that's their job.

ROSE: Someone else will tell them.

MAMET: Yeah. I think that what they pay off on is sticking with it. I mean, that's the one thing that society pays off on in show business is courage and—

ROSE: Perseverance.

MAMET: Yes. The person doesn't go home. And over the course of years that person may blossom into a great artist, the person may blossom into a competent artist and/or that person may have themselves a career and a good time. But, if you don't go home, you are home.

ROSE: Where do you put yourself, in your own mind, as a writer?

MAMET: That's not my job.

ROSE: Again, not your job.

MAMET: No.

ROSE: When did you know you had something, some time ago?

MAMET: I started writing when I was about twenty.

ROSE: I know.

MAMET: I just sat down and just started writing, and I liked it very, very much, and it looked acceptable to me, so I just kept doing it.

ROSE: You liked what about it?

MAMET: It was a way of, it's a way of, I mean, it beats thinking, let me tell you. It's a way, it's a way—

ROSE: Does it?

MAMET: Well, yeah. It's a wonderful; it's a way of expressing one-self. I did it with a certain amount of fluidity, and I, it diverted me, and, I mean, the rabbis say whoever rises, who rises from their prayers refreshed, their prayers have been answered. And that's kind of how I always felt about writing.

ROSE: You arose from writing refreshed?

MAMET: Yeah.

ROSE: Feeling like, a sense of accomplishment, feeling a sense of energy, feeling a sense of what?

MAMET: That's right. That's exactly right, yeah.

ROSE: Why do you write in so many different mediums—screen-plays, novels, plays?

MAMET: Well, because as I get older, I have less and less of a ca-pacity to take a nap.

ROSE: Really?

MAMET: Yeah.

ROSE: Less and less capacity to take a nap?

MAMET: Yeah. Also, I have no powers of concentration, so, when I finish one thing for that day, I'll go to something else.

ROSE: Maybe you have no powers of leisure.

MAMET: Maybe. I don't know. Maybe. Anthony Trollope used to get up every morning; he paid a guy to wake him up at five o'clock. He'd write twenty-five hundred words, and, if he finished a novel at two thousand words, he'd write five hundred words on his, on his next novel. Pretty good writer.

ROSE: Yeah. Who's influenced you most?

MAMET: Oh, as a playwright, I think it's Beckett and Pinter and lately Terence Rattigan wrote some—

ROSE: Yeah.

MAMET: —magnificently structured plays. Tennessee Williams, of course, and Arthur Miller.

ROSE: But Pinter struck me when you went through your list.

MAMET: Well, he's a—

ROSE: Because he's a contemporary.

MAMET: Well, yeah, he's a touch older than I am.

ROSE: I know—[Cross-talk]

MAMET: —much closer to Beckett.

ROSE: Yeah.

MAMET: And he really blew the top off it for me. I mean, Beckett was, was, and is, kind of a demigod to me.

ROSE: Because he was an angry young man or because he—

MAMET: No, no, no, no, because the son of a gun could write.

ROSE: The themes of what he wrote about or what?

MAMET: The son of a gun could just write!

ROSE: Write! Yeah.

MAMET: And he would write about a—[*Cross-talk*]

ROSE: He could create dialogue.

MAMET: Yeah, and he wrote about an interchange on a bus and two people talking about what stop they get off of and that was—it didn't have to be about Mary, Queen of Scots. He said that the small interchanges between people carry all the drama of the bombastic, of Shakespeare's histories or of—

ROSE: Yeah.

MAMET: —or of the "problem plays" of the 1930s.

ROSE: So, you don't need historic figures mouthing words to create the drama of conflict that is insightful.

MAMET: That's right.

ROSE: You said also once that you don't necessarily go out and—if you're going to create two characters on a bus—I think it was on a bus you talked about this—and write and take notes of what they say or listen for dialogue because, in fact, the job of the writer is to create something better than—

MAMET: Yeah.

ROSE: —what the conversation that'll take place between two people on a bus.

MAMET: Well, or more dedicated to the point, the point being the plot.

ROSE: Yeah.

MAMET: Somerset Maugham said writing wasn't an art; it was a trick. And it is an art, but what he meant was that the trick is being able to make the interchange in any moment extraordinarily interesting and still absolutely tend toward the plot: Who wants what from whom?

ROSE: When have you felt that you used your skills and your talent to the maximum?

MAMET: I don't know, but most of the time I did that, looking back on it, it probably wasn't my best work.

ROSE: Really?

MAMET: Sure, because, as I said—

ROSE: You say, "Sure"?

MAMET: Well, I mean, it's not—because, because it's not, it's really not my. . . . I don't think it's the artist's job to, to, to judge him or herself. That's, that's the, I was maligning myself one day. You know Billy Macy, William H. Macy?

ROSE: Yeah. Sure. Right. Good actor.

MAMET: Wonderful actor. [*Cross-talk*]

ROSE: *Fargo* and a lot of other things.

MAMET: And I was maligning myself one day. I said, "You know, this just isn't any good," blah, blah, blah. He says, "Dave. Dave. Never speak badly of yourself. There are people who are paid to do that. They're called critics." So—

ROSE: Good. That's a nice note to end on. I should mention David Mamet, *The Old Religion, The Old Neighborhood* at the Booth Theatre in a couple of weeks, which is one of your favorite theaters, yes?

MAMET: I think it's, I think it's the best theater in America.

ROSE: Really?

MAMET: Yeah.

ROSE: So, when they called—they called and said, "You got something for us?" Is that basically what happened?

MAMET: Yeah. Jerry Schoenfeld of the Schuberts—

ROSE: Right. I know.

MAMET: He'd heard I did this show, and he said, "Want to come and put it on in the Booth Theatre?" I said yes, so God bless him.

ROSE: Yeah. *True and False* is about—is that *True and False: Heresy and Common Sense for the Actor?* I've just mentioned in passing *The Edge* was written by you.

MAMET: Yeah.

ROSE: Some wonder why you're out writing screenplays of action-adventure stories, but that's your business.

MAMET: I enjoy it.

ROSE: You enjoy it. That's good. And *Wag the Dog* is—

MAMET: Yeah, *Wag the Dog* is a movie for—Barry Levinson did [it] with Robert De Niro and Dustin Hoffman. It's going to come out in December.

Mountebanks and Misfits

Barbara Shulgasser

Barbara Shulgasser, film critic for the *San Francisco Examiner*, interviewed Mamet at the Herbst Theatre in San Francisco. Their conversation was part of a yearly series produced by City Arts & Lectures. The occasion was the publication of two new books, Mamet's second novel, *The Old Religion*, and nonfiction essays entitled *True and False: Heresy and Common Sense for the Actor*. *The Old Neighborhood*, produced by San Francisco producer Carole Shorenstein Hays, had just opened on Broadway the night before. This discussion was being recorded for a future broadcast by KQED-FM in the San Francisco Bay area.

SHULGASSER: You're turning fifty in ten days, so Happy Birthday, first of all.

MAMET: Thank you.

SHULGASSER: Only fifty.

MAMET: Not yet. [*Laughter.*]

SHULGASSER: Not yet, right. And, given your prodigious output, I'm just wondering when you eat and sleep. What's your work schedule like? How do you get all that out?

MAMET: Well, that's what I do. That's all I do. And I've been doing it professionally for about thirty years, and what else is there to do? [*Laughter.*]

SHULGASSER: What else is there to do? Well, that's one way of

From City Arts & Lectures, Inc., Herbst Theatre, San Francisco, on November 20, 1997. This previously unpublished interview took place before a standing room only crowd of two thousand. Reprinted by permission.

looking at it. [*Laughs.*] You've said that, if you hadn't found the theater, you probably would have become a criminal.

MAMET: Yeah, I think that that's probably true. I knew a lot of criminals. I used to live with criminals.

SHULGASSER: How do you mean? Literally in a house with criminals?

MAMET: No, no I used to spend all day playing poker with them.

SHULGASSER: Uh-huh.

MAMET: And then I sold nonexistent real estate for a while with people who [*laughter*] were basically criminals.

SHULGASSER: Preparation for *Glengarry* [*Glen Ross*]?

MAMET: Yeah, well, that's what it turned into. And I was one of those kids who was always told that he probably possessed a great intelligence, but why must he act so stupidly? And so I never did very well at anything. So, I figured I was going to end up in prison somewhere.

SHULGASSER: Uh-huh. What was your response when people asked you why you must act so stupidly?

MAMET: Well, it took me thirty years to find out that every rhetorical question is an attack. [*Laughter.*]

SHULGASSER: Yes. [*Laughs.*] I won't ask any.

MAMET: Oh, good. Hey, listen, was this a legitimate theater? [*Audience members respond in affirmative.*]

MAMET: Was it? Well, then, they should be able to hear us without a microphone. Let's try that. [*To audience.*] Can you hear me when I talk like that? [*Audience members respond in negative.*] What are you, deaf? [*Laughter.*]

SHULGASSER: No, but the radio recording won't work. [*Laughs.*]

MAMET: Okay. [*Laughter.*] Well, then, how did you know what I said? [*Laughter.*] I've got you there, you must admit. Okay.

SHULGASSER: Um. [*Laughs.*] Hollywood. Have you had to fight a lot of idiocy in your work in Hollywood?

MAMET: Only my own.

SHULGASSER: Your own?

MAMET: Sure.

SHULGASSER: Well, that's very modest of you, but I'm sure that's not true.

MAMET: Well, it says in the Bible, "What is he who conquers a city compared with him who overcomes his own nature?" So the thing about Hollywood is: There it is. I mean there's nothing hidden about Hollywood. It's what it is. And—

SHULGASSER: Well, I think a lot of people go there with that attitude and hope that they can overcome but find that it's just an avalanche of one form of moron telling you how much they love your work when they buy it and then how much it has to change in order to be made into a movie.

MAMET: Yeah, but to try to change Hollywood is like someone who goes out to work for the Ford Motor Company and says, "You know, we should really invest in public transportation because it makes a lot more sense." [*Laughter.*]

SHULGASSER: [*Laughs.*] I see your point. Let's talk a little about your early screenplays. I love *The Verdict.* How did you get that job?

MAMET: I got the job for *The Verdict.* . . . . I was hired by [Richard D.] Zanuck and [David] Brown to write a movie based on a book by Barry Reed [III], a lawyer in Boston, Mass. And it's based on an actual case. They had me write the movie, and they didn't like it. They were very polite about it. They paid me. They said, "We just don't like it, and, if you'd like to write it again, we'll pay you again." [*Laughter.*] They did. I said, "That's very flattering, but I couldn't write anything differently."

And so the project went on, and they hired several other well-known writers, and I became morose and sent a copy to Sidney Lumet, whom I knew in passing, just to get someone else's opinion, hoping he would praise it. And the good fairy descended. The director, who was going to be, I believe, Robert Redford, dropped out of the project when they were committed to making the movie, and they sent the scripts that they had commissioned—not mine—to Sidney Lumet. They never sent him my script. And, coincidentally, that same week I'd sent him my script, and he called them back and said, "I'd love to do the movie. I'm just going to do Dave's screenplay." And, lo and behold, the day was saved.

SHULGASSER: Wow. [*Laughs.*]

MAMET: You know, one time in thirty years, what the hell? [*Laughter.*]

SHULGASSER: [*Laughs.*] Well, the difference between movies and theater, as far as writers are concerned, is the difference between a medium that values the writer and one that kind of undervalues the writer. I'm wondering, since there has to be some kind of adjustment for a playwright who gets to write the way he wants to when he goes to Hollywood, how that changes the writing.

MAMET: Well, it's a completely different medium. One of the fascinating things about writing is that, when you write for radio, radio is different from stage, and stage is different from television, television is different from movies. They're all different. And it's like the poker player who says, "I sat down at this game, and they were playing deuces wild. And you had to trade in a one-eyed Jack on another card. I can't play that game." Well, if you can't play the game, you shouldn't play the game.

The point for the poker player is to understand the rules of the game and for the writer to understand the essential nature of the medium—if he or she can—because each is very, very different. Writing movies and writing plays are extraordinarily different endeavors. Application and study would probably help anybody understand them a bit, but to say, "I don't know why they don't like my plays when I wrote movies well," is like saying, "I don't know why I'm not winning at Indian poker when I can play five-card stud." You got to understand the rules of the game.

SHULGASSER: I thought after I saw *The Postman Always Rings Twice* and *The Verdict*—I lived in Chicago and saw quite a lot of your work— that in your writing movies and having to fulfill the dictates of a much more market-oriented medium, which Hollywood turns out, there would be more plot, there would be more structure, and that it might change your plays as well. And I thought it did. Did you?

MAMET: I think it absolutely did. Thank you. When you write a movie, when one writes a movie, that's all a movie is, is plot. All that you and I care about when we watch a movie is what happens next. And it's told with pictures. And the pictures go by at twenty-four frames a second. And we get the idea pretty damned quickly. There's nobody here who can't come into a movie or television show at any point and understand in a tenth of a second what's happening. And so what moves a movie along is plot. What happens next. "Oh, yes," the audience says. "Oh my God, now he or she has gotten into an even worse scrape. Let me sit here a little longer and figure out what happens next." So, when I started writing movies, I had to really feverishly apply myself to understanding, to learning, how to write a plot. And I think it very much affected my plays for the better.

SHULGASSER: Tell me. Was there an enlightening moment when you first realized that the theater had some power, had something that you wanted to be a part of?

MAMET: I think that moment was the moment I first realized that it wasn't work and that people could go there and never work. [*Laughs.*] I figured out that I had found the circus, and I just wasn't going home. And I found it very young. My Uncle Henry, who lived out here for a while—and his wife, my Aunt Esther, still lives out here with that part of the family—was a producer of radio and television in Chicago for the Chicago Board of Rabbis. And he gave me jobs as a kid and my sister jobs as a kid, portraying Jewish children on television and radio. And through him I got into community theater in Chicago.

SHULGASSER: It was a stretch—

MAMET: What?

SHULGASSER: [*Laughs.*]—portraying Jewish children.

MAMET: That's right. It was a great stretch. And I always loved it. It seemed like a great idea.

SHULGASSER: So, you started by wanting to be an actor?

MAMET: That's right.

SHULGASSER: Isaac Bashevis Singer was once asked if he believed in free will and he said, "Yes, I have no choice" [*laughter*], which sounds like something from one of your movies. You seem to believe in fate. No matter what your characters do, they seem bound up in a fate that's decided already by their class and by what neighborhood they're from and their childhoods. I'm wondering if you think very much in those terms when you're writing these characters.

MAMET: No, I never think about fate because, as we all know, "Fate is the fool's word for chance." Right? No?

SHULGASSER: And why wouldn't that enter into your writing?

MAMET: Nobody saw that movie? Oh my God, where are you people from? [*Laughter.* One audience member shouts out, "*The Gay Divorcée.*"] Yeah, *The Gay Divorcée.* Eric Blore. Fred Astaire. "Fate is the fool's word for chance." Oh my God, where am I? [*Laughter.*] No, Aristotle used to say [*Laughter.*]

SHULGASSER: You used to hear him say this?

MAMET: That's right. Aristotle used to say, until someone would tell him to shut up, he used to say that character is fate. So tragedy is about character, which is about the capacity for the human being to make choices. And Don Marquis, who wrote *Archy and Mehitabel,* said—and I think Isaac Bashevis Singer may have been cribbing from him—that the ultimate reconciliation of the doctrine of free will and predestination is we're free to do whatever we want and whatever we choose is going to be wrong. [*Laughter.*] And that's what tragedy is about.

SHULGASSER: Well, religion seems to be another circumscribing factor for your characters. In *The Old Religion,* Leo Frank. And in *Homicide,* the movie that you wrote and directed, Joe Mantegna plays a police officer who's kind of forced to face his Judaism, something he's apparently denied or ignored. You've recently returned, or stopped—

MAMET: —Yeah, I think that's a fairly accurate description, sure.

SHULGASSER: And how did that change things for you?

MAMET: Well, it made me happier.

SHULGASSER: Really?

MAMET: Sure.

SHULGASSER: How?

MAMET: Well, in very many ways. It's a great thing to be able to put down the intolerable burdens of, if one happens to be me, of arrogance, egoism, and self-absorption for a while. [*Laughter.*]

SHULGASSER: All that from Judaism?

MAMET: Sure. I have this great rabbi—his name is Larry Kushner—who has this magnificent congregation [Temple Beth El] in Sudbury, Massachusetts. And on Yom Kippur he said, "The bad news is you're going to be here all day. The good news is you've got no place to go." [*Laughter.*]

SHULGASSER: [*Laughs.*] So, he's a comedian. But how does this help you overcome arrogance and those other burdens?

MAMET: Well, there's two answers to that question. A-ha, right?

SHULGASSER: [*Laughs.*]

MAMET: And one of them is that the rabbis would say, "Whoever rises refreshed from his prayers, his prayers have been answered." And the other equally nonresponsive answer is that the rabbis would say, "Put on *teffilin,* put on *tallis,* hold a prayerbook in your hand. Now, sin." [*Laughter.*]

SHULGASSER: [*Laughs.*] It's better that way. So, that's what you've been doing?

MAMET: Yeah, sure.

SHULGASSER: Well, good. [*Laughs.*] Was it a surprise to your children?

MAMET: I don't think so. No. After growing up with me, I think very little surprises them.

SHULGASSER: Oh, I see. In *Homicide* the Bobby Gold / Joe Mantegna character says, "There's so much anti-Semitism the last four thousand years. We must be doing something." Did you feel that way?

MAMET: No, certainly not. But I heard people say that one. I heard Jews make a similar comment. The book I wrote, *The Old Religion,* is about the Leo Frank case. Leo Frank was lynched in 1915. He was falsely accused of a crime that was fairly evident he didn't commit.

The city of Atlanta and the state of Georgia and much of the South imploded in a one-man pogrom and identified Frank as this demon and decided he was a demon because he was a Jew.

And it was the rebirth of the Ku Klux Klan, which had died out after Reconstruction, and also the birth of the Anti-Defamation League. It was a show trial, and one of the many "Crimes of the Century." It was called the "American Dreyfus" case. And I wrote a book about my imagined interior monologue in the persona of Leo Frank, a man who goes to work one day and comes home to find out he's a monster that the world wants to kill and the process he goes through trying to find out why that is true. It's a book about race hatred. And one of the things that he experiments with in an attempt to explain to himself a world gone mad is that, perhaps, there is some rectitude in the libels of his accusers. I think that that's [something] many abused people—children, for example—adopt to deal with intolerable injustice. So, no, that's not something that I feel.

SHULGASSER: I'm wondering how aware of your Judaism you were as a child growing up. Because it's another kind of outsider, and you ended up becoming a writer.

MAMET: Well, I was pretty aware of it. As I said, my Uncle Henry worked for the Board of Rabbis. My grandparents all came from the Old Country, from Russian Poland. We were fairly Episcopal Reform as far as religious practice went. And the kids from the other side of the tracks used to come over once in a while and hit us on the head, call us all sorts of derogatory terms. But I didn't see a lot of upside in the proposition until I got older.

SHULGASSER: [*Laughs.*] I wanted to talk a little bit about your book about acting, *True and False.*

MAMET: Sure.

SHULGASSER: The most staggering thing to me that you say in the book is this tip to the actor: If the audience enjoyed the play, you have done a good job. That just sounds like pandering to me. Does this mean that *The Bridges of Madison County* is a good book?

MAMET: That very well may be. I haven't read it.

SHULGASSER: Trust me on this. [*Laughs.*]

MAMET: If the audience enjoys the play, the actor has done their job, because the audience pays to come to enjoy the play. See, actors, as another maligned subspecies of humanity [*laughter*] love to flagellate themselves, because it takes free-floating anxiety and transforms it into a yummy little phobia: that it's not that the world is bad, it's not that my teachers are worthless, that the critics are mannerless swine, it's not that the plays are no good, but, rather, that I am insufficiently prepared. And, if I just try harder, everything will come out well, and there will be no tears before bedtime.

SHULGASSER: You don't know actors that use those other excuses, too?

MAMET: What other excuses?

SHULGASSER: Those ones that you said that it's not.

MAMET: I'm saying that most actors use those excuses. I've very seldom met an actor—and I've worked with the greatest actors in the world and am greatly privileged to do so—who didn't say, at one time or another, when you said, "Jeez, you were great," "Naw, I wasn't very good tonight." It's a terrible thing to say. It's an insult to the person who's paying the compliment, and, more important, it's an insult to yourself. The audience comes to hear the play. If they had a good time, you did your job. If you know how to do something better, do it better tomorrow night.

SHULGASSER: But isn't it possible for people to enjoy something that really isn't any good?

MAMET: Sure, I do. Don't you? [*Laughter, some clapping.*]

SHULGASSER: Yes, but we're talking about what a good actor is.

MAMET: If the audience enjoyed the play, the actor did their job because the job of the actor is to communicate the play to the audience. The job of the actor is not to obtain some magical, mystical state of perfection in him- or herself. It's nothing but self-consciousness. It's heresy. And it's the heresy of people who've been exposed to just a little too much education and haven't had enough time trying to earn their living by it. [*Laughter and applause.*]

SHULGASSER: Well, you talk about a formal education not only being useless to an actor but harmful. You say that it generally ruins a young actor.

MAMET: That's right. That's absolutely right. For several reasons. The first is, show business smiles on early entry. That the things you can do when you're sixteen and seventeen and eighteen because you have a lot of time on your hands; you don't need a lot to live; you can't do when you're twenty-eight and twenty-nine and thirty. You should be out there getting your teeth kicked in and learning something and meeting some people and working hard.

Scott Zigler, a great, great director, directed my play *The Old Neighborhood* that Carole Hays produced, which just opened on Broadway last night [*applause*], and he also teaches at Harvard. He's a great, great teacher. He says to the kids, "Get out there. And if you go to work for nothing in the movie business, if you do two movies for nothing" (he's talking about on the technical end), "you can be gainfully employed for the rest of your life." And it's true. The movie business particularly smiles on people who are reliable, dedicated, and hard working.

SHULGASSER: But not necessarily good.

MAMET: Well, why should they be good? Why should anybody be good when they're sixteen, seventeen, and eighteen? You gotta get out there and be bad.

SHULGASSER: Yeah, but sometimes they don't get better.

MAMET: Well.

SHULGASSER: Isn't that possible?

MAMET: Yes. But they're not going to get better in school, and here's the reason why. Acting is something that's done for a paying public. It's not something that's done for school administrators and for teachers. The skills needed to please an acting teacher, a casting agent, a school administrator, are those that are completely opposite from the skills needed to please an audience. The audience—just like you and me—comes to the theater to be delighted, to be surprised, and to give everyone the benefit of the doubt because they want to have a good time. The teacher, the administrator, and the casting agent come to the session as if to greet a thief who's going to be underprepared and rob them of their time. [*Laughter.*]

An audience isn't judgmental. That's why they come. That's why I come. That's why you come. There's nothing one is going to learn in school except to pander to authority. And the learning to pander to authority not only wastes the individual's time but ill equips the individual to deal with the authority of the greater world that is going to continue to exploit him or her. The casting agent, the fraudulent teachers, the people who take the headshots, the unskilled teachers of voice who are going to say, "Sit still and stay in class for the next million years, and I will tell you when you're any good." It's an absolute fraud.

SHULGASSER: But that pandering to authority, isn't that to the detriment of anybody who wants to do anything, not necessarily just an actor?

MAMET: Not if they want to be a teacher. [*Laughter.*]

SHULGASSER: [*Laughs.*] There's one.

MAMET: I've got some very good friends who are home schoolers, and they say the benefit of spending enough time in an institution is that eventually you get to be one of the guards.

SHULGASSER: Another thing you say about actors, you tell them not to interpret. You say that to create the illusion the actor has to undergo nothing at all.

MAMET: That's right.

SHULGASSER: What if you're a shy person trying to play a bore? Is there some kind of mock transformation that you have to go through in order to muster up whatever?

MAMET: No, you have to say the words.

SHULGASSER: And that's it?

MAMET: That's it.

SHULGASSER: From this point of view, how can you tell a good actor from a bad actor?

MAMET: A good actor is one whose performance you enjoy. I mean, if you want to get more technical, I would say a good actor to me is one whose performance I enjoy because I find it truthful. Which is to say, I enjoy the performance. [*Laughter.*]

SHULGASSER: Well, that's not necessarily the most truthful performance, though. That's just the one you enjoyed.

MAMET: It's the most truthful performance to me. To whom else am I going to refer it? If you're making love to someone, you say, "Jeez, I feel great." They say, "Yeah, I'm going to do better next time." [*Laughter.*]

SHULGASSER: Well, if you're playing to an audience of sadists and you really screw up in front of them, they'll enjoy that.

MAMET: The objections that you're raising, they're moot points. You can't argue them. But at the end of the day the theater is a profession of mountebanks and misfits, much like myself, who've come in through the back door because no one else would have them and learned to find a place in society by getting up on a stage and doing plays that people need to hear and doing them well in an interesting, provocative, and unusual manner. Who haven't had the life bred out of them.

I've been teaching off and on since I was a kid, in many, many institutions, in the English departments and the drama departments, and all that I can tell you is—only I alone am escaped to tell thee— it's a big shock. You want to learn to act, go act. Go start a theater company. Go apprentice yourself. Go carry coffee. Go take voice lessons. And get up on the stage. You're going to be bad for the first *x* years anyway. You might as well be bad from sixteen to twenty rather than from twenty-eight to thirty-five.

SHULGASSER: You also talk about how you're very much against interpretation of the text. In another book I was reading, you refer to a rabbi who points out that as one studies the Torah, the same portions at the same time of the year, year after year, that one sees in them a change. But, as they do not change, it must be you who is changing. And that made me think that, isn't that another way of saying that the text has a depth that reveals itself through study and interpretation?

MAMET: If one is studying the text. On the other hand, for an actor, the text reveals itself to the audience through the juxtaposition of the uninflected words, which the author wrote, and the moment-to-moment truthfulness of the actor. I don't want to hear some actor's good ideas. I and you and everyone here has the capacity to go to a library and understand what the author meant. What the actor can contribute, which is a great contribution, is the immediacy of the moment, is the organic moment-to-moment, back and forth, the Ping-Pong game of the unforeseen.

What does it mean of somebody of whom we say they have a great technique? Of a chef of whom we say they have a great technique? It means you didn't enjoy that dinner.

SHULGASSER: Why? [*Laughter.*]

MAMET: Why? Whoever said that of a dinner they enjoyed? What we say of a dinner we enjoyed is "Yum." [*Laughter.*] And what we say of a performance we enjoyed is, "Gol-ly!" We don't say, "What technique." We say, "What technique," when we have been defrauded of anything more enjoyable. So, we appreciate our own ability to appreciate. [*Laughter, some clapping.*]

SHULGASSER: So, you would call a performance by Meryl Streep doing one of her accents or Dustin Hoffman in *Rain Man* or De Niro doing *Awakenings*—

MAMET: First of all, I'm not going to name names because it's not my job, and my taste is not the point. Everyone has his or her taste, and they're entitled to it. That's what you're entitled to when you buy a ticket. You're there to see the show. You get to make up your own mind. Let me ask you a question. What is the line, "I never want to see you again." What does that line mean?

SHULGASSER: It depends.

MAMET: Exactly. That's exactly correct.

SHULGASSER: Thank you. [*Laughs.*]

MAMET: It depends on what's happening in the moment. It can mean any number of a million things. And, just so, when the line is spoken on stage, it can mean any number of a million things. As I say in the book, for any actor to prepare what he or she thinks the "character is going through" and then bring that onto the stage is an error of the same magnitude for the basketball team to say, "We're going to go out, and we're going to perform these plays irrespective of what the other team is doing." [*Laughter.*]

SHULGASSER: Well, how about Horowitz interpreting Chopin? Is that any different from an actor interpreting Mamet?

MAMET: Well, it depends. It's a very good example. There are some pianists whose technique is so good they just bore you to death. One would rather hear a twelve-year-old who wanted to play the music. And I would, too, of the actors. I would rather hear somebody who wanted to get on stage and mix it up a little bit than someone who's going to share with me his or her good ideas about the text.

It's not the actor's job to be interesting. It's the author's job to be interesting. It's the actor's job to be extraordinarily brave and forthright. And, when I was a kid growing up, we used to say the best thing you could say about an actor was that he or she was "dangerous." That's what people want in the theater. You know, we look at early performances of [Marlon] Brando. You look at something Joey Mantegna did. You look at Patti LuPone in this play [*The Old Neighborhood*] on Broadway. You say, "Gee, where the hell did they come from? Man, I never could have thought of that." Exactly. You know, you see Whoopi Goldberg when she was doing her comedy on stage—

SHULGASSER: I never could have thought of what?

MAMET: Whatever the actor—

SHULGASSER: The way they were doing it?

MAMET: Yeah. And neither could they.

SHULGASSER: Well, isn't that their interpretation?

MAMET: No, it's their performance.

SHULGASSER: Could you elaborate on that?

MAMET: Yes, Stanislavski said there are three kinds of actors. There's the actor who's gonna be the hack actor and give you his or her version of what they think an actor would do in this role. They're gonna interpret other actors. And then there's the mechanical actor, who gives you their version of what they think their character would be like. They're gonna think it up. They're gonna practice it in front of the mirror, and they're gonna bring it in. And then there's the organic actor, who's simply going to determine what is needed in the scene and then go on and do whatever they can to get that from the other person.

Now, a good example of this organic behavior is a child who

doesn't want to go to bed. A lover who wants a second chance. A man or woman who wants a job. Somebody who wants to get laid. There's nothing that these people won't do. [*Laughter.*] And that's called having an objective. Having an objective is just a fancy word for wanting something real, real bad. And when all of us—or any of us—are in these situations, there's nothing we won't do. All of our attention's on the other person. And we'll change horses in the middle of the stream to do anything to get them to give us what we want. Now, when you see that in an actor on stage it's awfully damned compelling. Because what the great actor's doing on stage is changing his or her tactics to get what they need from the other person on stage, rather than performing what they dreamed up at home.

SHULGASSER: Isn't that technique, though?

MAMET: No. [*Laughter.*]

SHULGASSER: It seems to me that it is for this reason: if you're trained, part of your training is to be constantly aware of all your opportunities on stage, and one of them means, "I must change tactics when called for." Rather than going out there every time without any understanding of what may happen, you have that understanding already, and you're ready for it and can do it.

MAMET: One doesn't have to be constantly trained to be aware of all the opportunities on stage any more than one has to be constantly trained to be aware of all the opportunities in trying to talk a cop out of a traffic ticket. We're born with this capacity.

SHULGASSER: Some people are better at it than others, though.

MAMET: Exactly so. And some people are better actors than others. But it's an innate capacity to be imaginative. And what's needed in the actor is not these dull whips of authority with which we flagellate ourselves of concentration and discipline and technique. Who cares? What's needed is bravery and intelligence and imagination. And all of us have all of that that we need.

SHULGASSER: But, as you say, the addition of emotion and all that kind of stuff is not something you want to see in your actors.

MAMET: It's false. It's lying. There's nothing anyone can do to control his or her emotions. If there were, we wouldn't need psychiatrists. [*Laughter.*]

SHULGASSER: I wonder. I don't really agree with that. If—

MAMET: Did anyone ever tell you, "Cheer up"? [*Laughter and applause.*]

SHULGASSER: [*Laughs.*] Yes.

MAMET: What was your reaction?

SHULGASSER: Let me ask you this. [*Laughter.*] What if you, right now, were suicidally sad, but you decided for the hour and a half it would take you to promote your book on this tour that you could set that aside? And then, when you knew it was going to be over, you go back to your room and cry or shoot yourself or whatever. I think that—

MAMET: —That's not manipulating emotions. That's having an objective. [*Laughter and applause.*] The two things are very, very, very different. [*More applause.*]

SHULGASSER: Well, that's semantics.

MAMET: What?

SHULGASSER: Certainly, it's manipulating your emotions. I think that the theory that one can control one's emotions and urges for short periods of time is the basis of the philosophy of teaching children good manners.

MAMET: No, what the child controls is not what he or she feels. What they control, if they can—

SHULGASSER: —is behavior. That can look like emotions.

MAMET: Well, it might look like emotions to you, but there's nothing a human being can do to control their emotions. Cults function by suggesting to a human being that this control is possible and then shaming them when they find that it's not. That's how a cult functions. And, when psychiatry becomes a cult, as it can, that's how it functions. When a self-help group becomes a cult, as it can, or a religion, as it can, that's how it functions. Or an acting class or any kind of class.

To say to the individual, "I've asked you to do something. Now why can't you do it?" The individual gets the idea that he or she is bad, and the only cure for their inherent badness is to work harder, to, in fact, enslave themselves to, in the case of acting schools, to the teacher. And I've seen it for thirty years, and it's a vast imposition on the acting student. And, it's a fraud. There's nothing that the human being can do, there's nothing that the acting student can do, to control their feelings, to control their emotions. And it may be practiced unwittingly, and it may be practiced for the best of all possible reasons, but it, nonetheless, is a fraud perpetrated on the student.

SHULGASSER: You wrote your first movie, *The Postman Always Rings Twice,* and you were asked by Bob Rafelson to do that.

MAMET: Sure.

SHULGASSER: Did you know him when he did that?

MAMET: Yeah, he called me up once. He saw a play of mine, *Sexual Perversity in Chicago,* and called me up to tell me he liked it. So, when he told me he was doing the film, I suggested to him that it would be a good idea to hire me, and he agreed.

SHULGASSER: [*Laughs with audience.*]

MAMET: God bless him. He's a great, great fellow and a great friend. And loved—and loves—to take a chance on talent, and he took a chance on me.

SHULGASSER: Did you look at the first version?

MAMET: Sure.

SHULGASSER: And did you work from the novel as well?

MAMET: I worked from the novel exclusively. The first [film] is an interesting movie, and everybody loved it, but nobody remembers it. They remember Lana Turner wore a white dress. The thing was so bowdlerized, as it had to be to be, according to the interpretation of the production code at that time, that there really wasn't a lot of the novel left in it, I thought. A pretty good writer wrote it—a San Franciscan, Niven Busch, wrote it—but he had to deal with the strictures of his time, and I had to deal with the strictures of twenty-five or thirty years later.

SHULGASSER: Your first film that you wrote and directed was *House of Games*. And that was from an idea you had in college?

MAMET: Anybody ever see *Dr. Katz: Professional Therapist*? [*Audience members respond.*]

SHULGASSER: [*Laughter.*] Yes.

MAMET: Great, great show. And that show stars—and is largely written by and is the brainchild of—my best friend, Jonathan Katz. And I used to hang around with him playing poker, shooting pool. And he was a Ping-Pong champion of New York State as a kid. And he would hustle guys at the Ping-Pong games, so I got to hang around with him at very, very interesting places around the country. Guys would play Monopoly for money. [*Laughter.*] Jonny Katz would play sitting in an armchair, and he'd say, "I'll give you eighteen points, and I'll sit in the chair. You play with the Ping-Pong bat; I'll use an ashtray." [*Laughter.*] And I got to meet some very interesting people, and we sat down one day, and we started writing a treatment based on those people. And it eventually became the movie *House of Games*.

SHULGASSER: Were you happy with the way that came out?

MAMET: Oh yeah.

SHULGASSER: When you're not the director on one of your films, do you have much input during the shoot?

MAMET: Oh no. No, no. Generally, the writer gets shepherded

until the camera starts rolling, and then no one will take his or her calls. [*Laughter.*]

SHULGASSER: Do you find that bothersome?

MAMET: No, I don't because I figured out if you're writing a movie for somebody else it's like being an interior decorator. You do the best you can, and then you start fuming because they moved the couch after they move in, you know? [*Laughter.*]

SHULGASSER: [*Laughs.*] But aren't you sure that the couch looked better where you first put it?

MAMET: Yeah, sure, but as a sometime movie director myself, when the clock starts ticking you got a lot of things on your mind. My mentor, the great producer Mike Hausman, said, "All mistakes are made in preproduction." And that's true. It's like Sisyphus putting the rock at the top of the hill, and then, when you start making the movie, it becomes an athletic event. You're going to be out there fourteen hours a day, and you gotta get the shots in the can the best way you know how.

SHULGASSER: Your sister said in the *New York Times* that she read the section of the play [*The Old Neighborhood*] that just opened in New York called *Jolly,* which is the name of the sister in the play. And she said that it seemed like a transcription of telephone conversations she had had with you on some pretty emotional subjects. Do you ever feel any qualms about using material that isn't entirely yours? For example, conversations that you've had with others?

MAMET: Well, first off, I'd like to point out that she's not my real sister. [*Shulgasser and audience laughs.*] Reliable medical evidence has surfaced. She was a switched baby. [*Laughter.*]

SHULGASSER: [*Laughs.*] Does this woman know you at all?

MAMET: Hmm?

SHULGASSER: Does she know you at all, this person?

MAMET: You know, you meet a lot of people. I can't be expected to remember everybody. [*Laughter.*]

SHULGASSER: Uh, where were we? Oh, the other thing that this woman said about you was that she felt you were the angriest person who was ever born.

MAMET: Well, that burns my butt. [*Laughter and applause.*] No, when we were growing up, my mother, Rest in Peace, used to say to both my putative sister Lynn and myself, "Why must you dramatize everything?" [*Laughter.*] And so I'm glad to know both she and I are still doing it.

SHULGASSER: She's a writer, too.

207

MAMET: Oh yeah.

SHULGASSER: [*Laughs.*] That section of the play—well, the entire play—would you call it autobiographical, if pressed?

MAMET: Well, I don't know. I suppose. But not necessarily about myself. [*Laughter.*] Okay, let's get serious now.

SHULGASSER: Another "auto"?

MAMET: Okay. I have to give you a profound *maybe* on that one.

SHULGASSER: And *The Cryptogram?*

MAMET: You know, I gotta tell you, I've been working on this movie a while. I hope to shoot it in a while. It's called *State and Main.* It's a movie about a movie company. At one point the actress is having a breakdown, and she's sobbing and the director's comforting her. You know, it's a fairly stock scene in real life, too, for that matter. She's sobbing, and she says, "I never had a childhood." And the director says, "I had one. It's no big deal." [*Laughter.*] So, I suspect that having had a childhood is a little bit like going to college: that it doesn't mean anything, but, for it to not mean anything, you have to have experienced it. [*Laughter.*]

Well, I hope each and every person here will go see that play and determine for him- or herself how autobiographical it might be.

SHULGASSER: I see. Well, what I'm trying to get to is the possibility that you're writing more autobiographically the older you get. Is that a possibility?

MAMET: Maybe. I don't know. I mean, the last play I wrote was called *The Cryptogram.* It played in New York, and that might have been a little bit autobiographical, too.

SHULGASSER: In your book *The Cabin,* a collection of essays—I better ask you this—are most of them nonfiction?

MAMET: Oh, in the essays they're all nonfiction.

SHULGASSER: Oh. One, "The Rake," was a pretty ghastly account of a horrific, violent childhood. That was yours? Sometimes it seems to me that the violence of the language in even your earlier plays may have been a way of dissipating that kind of sense of violence without actually being violent or describing violence in the plays.

MAMET: Uh, maybe. It occurred to me, and I wrote in the book that nobody with a happy childhood ever went into show business. And I think that that's absolutely true.

SHULGASSER: Why would you say that?

MAMET: Well, it's been my observation. And if you look at theater, especially tragedy, which many people feel to be the highest form the theater can aspire to. . . . I don't know if it is or not. Joseph Campbell actually thought comedy was.

SHULGASSER: Stand-up?

MAMET: [*Laughs.*] No, no. But that tragedy is about horrific things. It's about bringing the hidden to light so that one can grieve. And that's why tragedy, in the perfect form, is cleansing, because it enables us to deal with repression. It enables us to take the repressed and investigate it. And, as Freud would have said, instead of living a happy life, be more capable to live a life of ordinary misery. Whereas a feel-good melodrama, we say, "Gosh, that's great. I knew the villain was bad because they were wearing a black hat. I wonder why those other people in the play didn't see it till the third act." But it's not very cleansing. We come to the theater to cleanse ourselves. And even fairy tales—Bruno Bettelheim wrote extensively about this—enable the child to deal symbolically with unresolvable feelings, feelings that are unresolvable through the use of the intellect. And that's what a great play does, too.

SHULGASSER: Did you have that cleansing feeling from writing something like "The Rake"?

MAMET: I don't remember. Perhaps. I like to write. It makes me feel good. It's what I do for a living. It's what I do for enjoyment. And I also do it out of habit.

SHULGASSER: You've gotten a reputation for being a misogynist. What do you think about that?

MAMET: I think that it's a loathsome libel. And it's not pertinent by any possible definition that I know. I think that it's malicious gossip. I think that it began because the first play that I did professionally was very well received. It was called *Sexual Perversity in Chicago*. It's a play about misogyny and, specifically, about a misogynist. And it's quite evidently an indictment of the same.

But part of being, to a certain extent, in the public eye is that one has to—in return for the ability to publicize one's work, to improve one's currency, to attempt to improve the reception of one's work—one opens oneself up to gossip, and that, as a reader myself of the newspapers and as an occasional watcher of television, I engage in it, too. I form opinions about people about whom I know nothing. And I'm encouraged to think and am pleased to think and am diverted to think terrible things about them and call it news. That being the case, it's probably not unjust that I should be subject of the same. [*Laughter.*]

SHULGASSER: I actually think that your female characters are extraordinarily strong and written by, I don't know, a feminist . . . in a way. You've recently had a long article in the *New Yorker* written about you. Did that feel odd, to have yourself [profiled]?

MAMET: Sure.

SHULGASSER: What was that like to read that or to even be interviewed for it?

MAMET: Well, it was written by John Lahr, who's not only a terrific writer but, I think, has written some of the best theatrical biographies I've ever read. He wrote *Prick Up Your Ears* about Joe Orton. Wrote a wonderful book about Noel Coward. And he wrote a superb book about his father [Burt Lahr] called *Notes on a Cowardly Lion.* Terrific writer. The terrible thing about the article is I thought it was very perceptive. [*Laughter.*]

SHULGASSER: That is terrible.

MAMET: Yeah.

SHULGASSER: Any surprises there?

MAMET: Maybe—

SHULGASSER: —Did he know something you didn't?

MAMET: Maybe. Maybe he did; I don't know.

SHULGASSER: You don't want to go into it?

MAMET: Yeah.

SHULGASSER: Oh. What about the [*New York*] *Times* and your so-called sister?

MAMET: Well, Bruce Weber wrote that article, and [he] bicycled across the United States from the Santa Monica Pier to Amagansett, Long Island. And anybody who does that is okay in my book. [*Laughter.*]

"Face to Face"

Jeremy Isaacs

Sir Jeremy Isaacs's conversation with David Mamet took place in February 1998. It stands as one of the most comprehensive and forthcoming of Mamet's discussions about his life in the theater. Although the impetus for this conversation was Mamet's promotion of *True and False: Heresy and Common Sense for the Actor,* their far-reaching discussion provides insights into those issues that continue to animate his writing.

ISAACS: David Mamet, you're one of the great American playwrights: *American Buffalo, Glengarry Glen Ross, Oleanna.* You write screenplays for the cinema: *The Untouchables.* You direct movies yourself. There's a novel coming out and a new book of essays on acting. What is it that gets you to work in the morning?

MAMET: Oh, well, I've been doing it for a long time, and, when I first started out, I started writing because it interested me, and I was good at it. And it occurred to me that, being a ne'er-do-well, if I was good at it and it interested me and it had the prospect of being able to support me, if I didn't work rather hard at it, then I was a complete fool. And so I think there is still some aspect of all those things motivating me. And, after a great number of years, also there's habit.

ISAACS: Do you sit down at the typewriter everyday of your life?

MAMET: Oh, I think more or less. And I always have a notebook with me if I'm not in my office. Or I'll write on the plane, or I'll write on the bus.

From "Face to Face," BBC 2. This previously unpublished interview was broadcast on February 23, 1998. Courtesy of British Broadcasting Corporation. Reprinted by permission.

ISAACS: The new book of essays on acting, *True and False,* what does it tell the actor? What should an actor do?

MAMET: Well, I've been working with actors all of my life. I was a child actor and was acting in community theater, so it's been many, many years. And I encountered a lot of very bad acting teachers and very bad directors, a few good ones. And the book is called *True and False: Heresy and Common Sense for the Actor,* and it's really directed toward the young actor and suggests that he and she use their common sense. And if the teachers and directors with whom they're working aren't capable of describing what they require in simple English, then those teachers and directors don't know what they're talking about.

So, to a large extent, the book is a riposte to bad teaching of what's generally called the Stanislavski system, which suggests that the actor and actress create in themselves an emotional state and then go out and perpetrate it on the audience. It's a bunch of nonsense. It doesn't make for good acting; it doesn't make a happy audience; and it makes for extraordinarily unhappy actors.

ISAACS: What should they do, instead?

MAMET: What they should do is they should learn the lines, understand very, very simply what the character in the script is doing, and try to find a congruent action for themselves, which is physically capable of being done. The laws of human consciousness aren't suspended just because an actor steps foot on stage. Whether on or off stage, no human being is going to do anything well that doesn't interest him. So, what's required of the actor is not concentration, which is a bugaboo.

We used to beat young actors over the head who weren't concentrating enough: "Concentrate on your emotional memory," "Concentrate on your sense memory," "Concentrate on your character." That's nonsense. Concentration is like water; it seeks its own level. That's how magic works. We're drawn to that thing that's most interesting. And, while we're drawn to that thing that's most interesting, the magician's putting the rabbit in the hat.

Just so, on stage we're drawn to that thing that is most interesting. To most people that's their performance. And whether they say to themselves, "How am I doing? I want to do a good job," or they say to themselves, "How am I doing? I want to make sure I understand how I felt when my kitten died"—those two are exactly the same: concentrating on one's own performance. The way you make a performance interesting is the way you make anything in life interesting: by taking your attention off yourself and putting it on something that you're doing.

ISAACS: What does the director do?

MAMET: Well, the director most often gets in the way of the actors. That's their office. What a director can do is to help the audience understand the play through the medium of the actor and also through the medium of the plastic elements of the production.

ISAACS: What's the rights of the author? What's the role of the author once a play is in production?

MAMET: Well, the role of the author—Stanislavski said something really great. He said that once a play has opened it's the author's job, especially in the last few dress rehearsals, to pace up and down in the back of the theater muttering to himself, "Well, they've ruined it."

But I think the writer's job is to—everybody's job is the same in the theater—communicate the play to the audience. That's what they're there for. They aren't there to undergo something. They aren't there to perfect their self-knowledge. They aren't going to become the character. It's a bunch of bushwa. People pay to hear the play. And it's the job of the writer, the director, the actors, and the scenic people to make the play clear and as enjoyable as possible. So, the author should be cutting where cutting is needed if the scene, the play, the sentence, is too long, clarifying where clarification is needed if the action is not clear and learning—it takes a long time—to hold his or her piece if the issue's in doubt.

ISAACS: Have you beaten time? Do you want people to keep a tempo? Do you set a pace?

MAMET: Well, I hope that the line is doing that. The line is written in a certain rhythm, and it's probably easier to speak it in that rhythm.

ISAACS: In the theater it's words that carry the story. Words are the story.

MAMET: Right.

ISAACS: In movies it's pictures that carry the story. How do you set about facing that very different task?

MAMET: Well, it's two different tasks. It's the same as building a model boat or framing out a house. There are different aspects of carpentry in them. You do have to keep your attention on what the end product is. As you say, the end product of the screenplay is pictures because, when we see a picture, we understand the story immediately. The perfect screenplay shouldn't have any dialogue in it. So, that's something to strive for.

ISAACS: And should the perfect stage play have no [stage] business in it?

MAMET: Well, it shouldn't have any business in it. It should have surely those stage directions without which the play is incomprehensible. For example, "He shoots her" or "She shoots him" or "Everyone dies of the plague," etc.

ISAACS: When you write for the stage, do you hear the words in your head?

MAMET: I think so.

ISAACS: Do you say them out loud to yourself as you type?

MAMET: I think so.

ISAACS: Have you captured a language that characterizes much of your work, or have you invented a language?

MAMET: Well, that's a good question. I mean, I don't know. It was somebody—it was Matisse, I think, [who] was nearsighted and—it's a famous story—at the end of his life he got eyeglasses, and for the first time he could see. He said, "Oh my God, I see like Bouguereau." You know? Was it a defect or a gift?

ISAACS: Where did you hear the rhythms of American speech that you give us?

MAMET: Well, people talk them. I mean, that's what people say on the street.

ISAACS: Do they say them on the streets in Chicago or across the States? Is this a Chicago language?

MAMET: I think so. I grew up in Chicago, and the patterns of speech around the country, even in spite of television, are different.

ISAACS: Is it a Jewish language?

MAMET: I don't think so. I always thought that New York was at bottom a fairly Jewish town, and people used to say that Chicago was at bottom a fairly Polish town, a fairly Irish town. In any case it was a working-class town.

ISAACS: So, the language is captured in the territory. It's bringing a demotic American onto the stage.

MAMET: I think so. I mean, in Apollonian plays or in Dionysian plays, rather, I tried to write them in something approaching that poetry.

ISAACS: Your writing has mostly described, when it's writing a stage play, an active present. People talking because they're doing something. Now, at the age of fifty, you've given us *The Old Neighborhood*, which begins to be a play, doesn't it, about memory? You've started to look back to your childhood.

MAMET: Well, yeah. *The Old Neighborhood* is kind of a companion piece to the play I did before called *The Cryptogram*, both of which deal with a situation, a domestic situation. *Cryptogram* deals with it in the present, forty years ago. And *The Old Neighborhood* deals with it retrospectively. And *The Old Neighborhood* is very much in the American tradition of what used to be called the "kitchen play." It's people sitting around in the kitchen, probably in their T-shirts, kvetching about something that happened some time ago.

ISAACS: But not the "kitchen sink"?

MAMET: No. I hope not.

ISAACS: When did your family come to this country?

MAMET: My grandparents came here on my mother's side just before World War I. And on my father's side in 1921.

ISAACS: Where did they come from?

MAMET: My mother's people came from Warsaw. And my father's side came from a little village on the Bugg River. I think it was Hrubieszów but on the Russian-Polish border.

ISAACS: Have you ever been back to have a look?

MAMET: No.

ISAACS: Did you know your grandparents?

MAMET: Oh, sure. I knew them well.

ISAACS: Tell me about your grandfather. What sort of man was he?

MAMET: My mother's father was a traveling salesman. He was a real Willy Loman. He was a traveling underwear salesman. He spent all week in the car touring the Midwest. And apparently he'd made a bunch of money in the 1920s, and he lost everything in the [1929] Crash. So, he was closed off in a fairly . . . I think, I know, he was not a very happy man. I think he was probably a fairly bitter man. And my dad's mother, whom I knew best of all, she was wonderful. Her name was Clara, and we named our daughter after her. My third daughter. She was from the town of Hrubieszów and came over here and didn't speak very good English. Her husband left her, and she raised two kids. Wonderful woman.

ISAACS: Who was your father?

MAMET: He was a labor lawyer. A great champion of labor. And he grew up poor. I think he bluffed his way into Northwestern Law School. I think he went to junior college, and I think he falsified his credentials. He graduated, and he was editor of the *Law Review*. And he worked in a one-man shop—he had a couple of assistants later on—for labor unions.

ISAACS: Did he have the gift of oratory or persuasion?

MAMET: Oh, sure. That's what he did. He was a great, great negotiator.

ISAACS: Did you hear him plead?

MAMET: I never heard him plead, no. But I heard him expound on every topic under the sun.

ISAACS: He died not long ago?

MAMET: About five or six years ago, yeah.

ISAACS: And you buried him yourself, I gather?

MAMET: Yeah.

ISAACS: Tell me about that.

MAMET: The rabbi said, "They're burying your dad. You might want to think of doing it yourself. Just take a shovel from the grave-diggers and do it yourself." And so I was watching them bury my dad, and I went back and forth as we were on the road.

ISAACS: Everybody throws some earth on the coffin?

MAMET: That's right. It's symbolic.

ISAACS: Right.

MAMET: But the rabbi was saying I might find it of worth to do something more than symbolic. So I went back and forth thinking, "Oh, I'm going to make a fool of myself." And then thinking, "Well, it seems like a good idea. If I don't do it, I'll regret [not] having done it, so perhaps I should do it." So I did.

ISAACS: Why did the rabbi tell you it might help you to do that?

MAMET: Because, in the overused American phrase, it was participating in the process.

ISAACS: Who was your mother?

MAMET: She died about eleven years ago. She and my dad married, I think, during the war. She was a housewife. She was very, very smart and very beautiful. Later in life she got involved with teaching kids with speech defects. Worked very hard with that.

ISAACS: Your parents divorced, and she married a friend of your father's?

MAMET: That's right.

ISAACS: Was this a difficult experience for you and your sister?

MAMET: Yeah, somebody asked me that question. I was doing a whole bunch of press for a couple of movies coming up, and I said, "You'll have to ask me when I get over it." So, I don't think I can do better than that answer.

ISAACS: You're not over it yet?

MAMET: Well, I guess not.

ISAACS: But you're writing about it?

MAMET: Sure.

ISAACS: What was your stepfather like?

MAMET: I don't think I want to talk about it.

ISAACS: Your sister is a screenwriter.

MAMET: Yeah.

ISAACS: Were you close to her?

MAMET: Oh sure, I still am.

ISAACS: She came through, and you came through.

MAMET: Oh yeah, we're still here.

ISAACS: But these terrible experiences you had, did they color your whole early life?

MAMET: Well, I don't know that they were terrible experiences. I hope that the plays and the essays I've written are sufficiently interesting to stand on their own. And I perhaps delude myself that there's somewhat of a screen of a sufficient opacity between myself and my youth—whatever it may have been—to allow either myself and my audience to appreciate the work on its own without saying, "Oh, this must be true because . . ." I was interested to find that [Ernest] Hemingway just spent a couple weeks in war, in World War I. He left the Ambulance Corps and went up to the front to do something or other. He got a minor wound after a few days, and he was in a hospital, and that was it. But I guess it didn't take him a lot of war to "get the idea." And I think perhaps the same may be true of myself and my childhood.

ISAACS: There were good times in your childhood also?

MAMET: Sure.

ISAACS: Were you brought up as a Jew?

MAMET: Yes and no. I was brought up into what could be called the Episcopal Reform tradition. We were semi-observant as Jews. But my parents and their coterie and, perhaps, to a large extent a slice of their generation had really wanted to be Americans. They didn't want to not be Jews, but they wanted to be Americans. They were the kids of immigrants; they'd been very poor. They lived through the Depression. They lived through World War II and found out about the Holocaust. And through it all they wanted to succeed at what they'd been told it's possible to succeed at: being an American, being part of a large nondenominational community.

ISAACS: Can't Jews succeed in America and remain Jews?

MAMET: Of course. I mean, I think that their experience—both as a generation and as a mini-society—is very, very different than our experience today or than mine.

217

ISAACS: But you seem increasingly more aware of your Jewishness and pride of your Jewishness.

MAMET: Oh sure. Well, I think it's the nature of human beings to say, "I'm going to give my kids what I didn't have." In the case of my parents that was economic stability. In the case of myself it's community. And identity.

ISAACS: Do you do that in your family, as it were?

MAMET: I try.

ISAACS: Yes, but in *The Old Neighborhood* one of the men says to another that since he's married a non-Jewess, then perhaps the children aren't Jewish.

MAMET: Right. Well, that's one of the questions.

ISAACS: Do you usually tell your children they're Jewish?

MAMET: I don't have to. They are Jewish. They don't need anybody to tell them.

ISAACS: When did you begin to know that you would write?

MAMET: Oh, heck, I don't know. I always told stories, I always made up stories when I was a child. I think I started writing one day when I was around nineteen or twenty. I just sat down and started writing.

ISAACS: Plays?

MAMET: I started off writing plays, and I wrote essays.

ISAACS: You went to school in Vermont. What did you learn there?

MAMET: Well, I learned that Vermont is very, very beautiful. And I came to suspect that, as I later read in Mr. [Henry] Fielding—I thought he put it fairly succinctly—education is generally worthless, except in those cases when it can be said to be superfluous. You know, Thorstein Veblen wrote a very interesting book about higher education. He called it *Higher Education: A Study in Depravity.*

ISAACS: [*Laughing.*] What does that mean?

MAMET: That meant he thought that it was fairly much a shock, that it was a hazing process perpetrated on those with a little bit too much disposable income. And that's kind of been my experience. At least in the liberal arts department.

ISAACS: You were teaching acting, I think, at the same time you were first writing for the theater. So, you were always, from then on anyway, writing for performance.

MAMET: That's right.

ISAACS: Did other writers influence you at all?

MAMET: Oh, sure. I think prime among them was Harold Pinter.

You spoke of demotic language. That's what he was writing in all the *Revue Sketches* and *A Night Out* and *The Birthday Party*. And all of those plays dramatized things that I'd heard and seen and experienced. And they didn't appear to be a traditional dramatic expression. They were thrilling.

ISAACS: With pauses?

MAMET: Well, if you listen to it, a pause is part of the line.

ISAACS: So, the pause conveys meaning as well as the words convey meaning?

MAMET: Of course.

ISAACS: Is there a subtext? Is there something going on under the surface of your words?

MAMET: Well, I hope so. I mean, it seems to me bad drama to have everyone say what they think. Because in real life people never say what they think. They speak to gain something from the other person. Once in a while—

ISAACS: —language is performative.

MAMET: Perhaps. I would say perhaps it's closer to exhortative—manipulative—than performative. People always and only speak to get something from the other person. So *subtext* is a term I've never really understood. I almost think I know what it means, but I'm not sure.

ISAACS: It's always there, so you don't have to call it the subtext?

MAMET: I think that's perhaps what I think. Yeah.

ISAACS: In Chicago, when you were working there, there was the famous Second City Revue where sketches were performed. That obviously had an influence on the way in which you wrote in *Duck Variations* or—

MAMET: —Right.

ISAACS: What were the advantages and disadvantages of that sort of writing?

MAMET: Well, the—

ISAACS: Nothing would be longer than it actually needs to be, as it were.

MAMET: The scenes all seemed to be seven- or eight-minute sketches at Second City. In fact, I worked there as a kid as a busboy, and one of the groups that came over was from—the name just went out of my head—it wasn't Beyond the Fringe, but it was the other group [The Establishment] from the 1960s.

ISAACS: Right.

MAMET: Jeremy Geidt, one of the wonderful English actors, was in the group, an improvisatory touring theater group. And all of the sketches seemed to be a seven- or eight-minute sketch, perhaps not coincidentally, like the seven- or eight-minute blackouts of which television was made in those days, which were either dramatic or comedic blackouts. And you had a commercial, and you'd have another scene. And they made a great impression on me. Perhaps that was the human attention span. And you should make your point, then get on to another scene.

ISAACS: Can one construct an entire evening's play on that basis?

MAMET: Well, [Anton] Chekhov did. That's what those plays are.

ISAACS: What do you get from Chekhov?

MAMET: Well, Chekhov was a very good writer, and there are many things to be gotten from him. One of them is how screamingly funny minute interchanges are, which, I think, looking at his plays, he thought (when you read him talking about his plays) was the point of the whole exercise.

ISAACS: Do his characters communicate with each other or fail to communicate with each other?

MAMET: Well, I think that they did communicate with each other. You know, the Catholics say God always answers our prayers. Sometimes the answer is "no." So, the characters in Chekhov are communicating with each other, but most of the time the answer is "no."

ISAACS: Part of your subject matter seems to be men's relationships with men. Is that right?

MAMET: Yes, and part of it's men's relationships with women.

ISAACS: But less so.

MAMET: I don't know.

ISAACS: Is it harder for you to write parts for women than for men?

MAMET: No.

ISAACS: But I think you say somewhere that you have to work to find out what a woman has gone through or could be going through.

MAMET: I don't know. Did I say that?

ISAACS: I think so.

MAMET: Oh. Perhaps it was at the time.

ISAACS: But do men need the comfort of relationships with other men? And is that territory that you can stake out for them in what you write?

MAMET: Oh, I don't know. I mean, most of my last few plays have been about men and women. *Cryptogram, Oleanna, Speed-the-Plow,* and this new one, *The Old Neighborhood,* have been about men and women.

ISAACS: Must a writer write out of his or her experience?

MAMET: Well, I don't know. To be a writer, and especially to be a dramatist, is to be a sort of ur-psychotic or an ur-schizophrenic. One has, especially as a dramatist, two voices in one's mind all the time, and they both seem to make sense. And each one of them has an opposing view, or else it isn't drama.

So, the question is, what does experience mean? Is imagination experience? Is history experience? Or, you could even stretch the point past any useful elasticity and say insight is experience. I don't know. The point is, it should be true. And I think that a good writer, perhaps, is one who is not going to classify, not going to differentiate between, those three categories of thinking but one who just simply asks the question, "Is it true?"

ISAACS: When you write for the stage, you're in control. Can you be in control if you write for the movies or write for Hollywood, say?

MAMET: Well, somebody said, and it might have been Napoleon—it was one of those guys—who said, the whole trick is never give an order that can't be obeyed. So, when one writes for the stage, at least in this country, the very, very strong tradition is you get to be the king. You get to have it your way. Writing for movies, if one is directing, one gets to have it one's way, if you can get somebody—a sucker, for example—to give you the money to make that particular film.

ISAACS: When you write a screenplay for someone else to direct, do you, as it were, surrender it when someone else takes over?

MAMET: Oh, sure. There's no "as it were" about it. I mean, there you go.

ISAACS: But, when you direct yourself, you have fun?

MAMET: That's right. I have some fun writing for other people, too.

ISAACS: Does Hollywood aim high enough?

MAMET: Oh, golly, I don't know. It is what it is. And one of the things Hollywood is, is it's an extraordinarily predictable and blatant place. There's nothing that's hidden. Everything is exactly what it seems to be. I saw some pretty good movies last year.

ISAACS: *Speed-the-Plow* seems to suggest that it doesn't aim high enough.

MAMET: Well, I mean, one reason I wrote that is someone told me that; they told [Samuel Taylor] Coleridge he couldn't write a poem about an ass. Someone said you can't write a parody about Hollywood because it parodies itself. And it's true. But I wrote it, anyway.

ISAACS: You live, at least part of the time, in Vermont. What does that give you?

MAMET: It's extraordinarily beautiful. Nice people.

ISAACS: What do you do there?

MAMET: I write.

ISAACS: What do you do when you're not writing?

MAMET: When I'm not writing I try to spend some time in the woods, you know, with my family. Go cross-country skiing. I just came back from a hunting trip. I was up there hunting for two days.

ISAACS: What do you hunt?

MAMET: I hunt deer.

ISAACS: Do you shoot deer?

MAMET: No, but I should say that I feel a trifle craven admitting that I don't because it's my fault. I don't not shoot them because I think it's, it's wrong to shoot them. I don't shoot them because I'm not a great hunter.

ISAACS: . . . Do you go alone? How does it happen?

MAMET: What happens is it's a very different kind of hunting than you have in Britain. It's not driven game. You're out there, generally, by yourself. And in the case of this past weekend, in a pretty big wilderness all alone, in the middle of the wilderness, tracking a deer. That's the beauty of it. It's a great experience.

ISAACS: What does living in Vermont tell you about American democracy?

MAMET: I don't think it tells me anything about. . . . What are you suggesting?

ISAACS: Well, there's a piece you wrote that I read the other day about protesting a nuclear waste disposal proposal.

MAMET: Yeah. Well, one thing about Vermont is that it does still have the American tradition of small—of vociferous—local government.

ISAACS: And you like that?

MAMET: Oh, sure.

ISAACS: Are you part of that?

MAMET: No, I'm not. I'm not there enough of the time.

ISAACS: In writing about Jews recently, you've been saying that—or not so recently—but in your books and essays you've been arguing that they accept and shouldn't that there's not been a Jewish presidential candidate or vice presidential candidate, for example. What is it that concerns you there?

MAMET: Well, I think it's important for all kids to have heroes—Jewish kids no less than any other kind of kid. And so, as a Jew, I think it's important, especially as a dramatist, to help create those heroes. Or to tell our story, rather than to tell a story for export.

ISAACS: Are you religious?

MAMET: I think I'm, to a certain extent, religious, sure.

ISAACS: What does your religion mean to you?

MAMET: Well, I don't know if it's the kind of thing I want to talk about on television.

ISAACS: But you believe in God?

MAMET: Yeah, sure. Maybe I'm deluded, but I think everybody believes in God. But at the risk of sounding like a, what do you call those greeting cards, I think we call God by different names.

ISAACS: Do you meet him in the woods?

MAMET: Oh, I don't know. I don't want to get all gushy here.

ISAACS: Surely, having an ethnic identity and yet an American identity is precisely the American experience.

MAMET: Perhaps. I think that it probably is the American experience or the paradigmatic American experience. But, on the other hand, it's not the experience to which traditionally we have alluded. In America we've spoken for a lot of years about the melting pot. And I think that only recently have large aspects of the population come to recognize, or to avow, that perhaps that's neither the truth nor something that we should strive for.

ISAACS: That people should preserve their identities, not melt?

MAMET: Yes. I was brought up in the 1950s, when America as the melting pot with one-for-all and all-for-one was the stuff of every textbook and much of every day in the public schools. And it never was true. And I think that looking back what it meant was, on the part of the majority culture, everything will be okay if you'll be like me.

ISAACS: And it's a richer society if everyone is different in their own way?

MAMET: Well, I don't know if it's a richer society or not, but I think it's the truth. It's like the joke about the rabbit in moose stew, you know.

ISAACS: What's that?

MAMET: Well, it's in equal portions, one rabbit and one moose.

ISAACS: Could you have written what you've written if you'd been brought up in a narrower tradition?

MAMET: Heck, I don't know. It's very much a mystery to me.

ISAACS: But writing is about exploring the world, isn't it?

MAMET: I don't know what writing is about, except that I think some people's affections that way tend, and some people's don't. And I think that most of the attempts, on the part of academics, in any case, to make sense of what it is that people wrote, what it might or might not mean, are incomprehensible to me. As a reader of that psychobiography or interpretation and also as a writer, I don't recognize any of the stuff that's written about how and why people write.

ISAACS: You've said somewhere that in the United States violence triumphs over love. What did you mean by that?

MAMET: Well, I think if you look at our national mythology, it's a mythology of violence. Let me, perhaps, to push a point over the cliff again, perhaps violence is love. That's the end of so many American stories: the notably peaceful man is driven to the point where he must take revenge or must act to set things right through being violent.

ISAACS: Would you tell your children that that was wrong?

MAMET: Well, it is wrong. But the question, I think, dramatically is, "What does it signify?" Because it's really, as a national myth, an exhortation to bear arms. It's the attempt to discharge, if you will, uncathected energies. It's an attempt to balance one's real experience of life with what one is told, an attempt to do away with the anger that is caused by repression. That's what that violent myth means, the Western of the shoot-'em-up. It's not an invitation to go out and kill people. It's an attempt to try and do away with intolerable, unresolved perception.

ISAACS: As in *Shane* or *Bad Day at Black Rock?*

MAMET: Exactly.

ISAACS: What still makes you angry?

MAMET: Computers and especially computers on a telephone. I hate more than anything else in the world when a computer voice on the telephone says, "Thank you," because I'm not quite sure how one should respond. One obviously isn't supposed to say, "You're welcome." But, on the other hand, "Curse God and die, you son of a microchip" doesn't seem to be . . . there's still no one listening to that, either.

ISAACS: What's your greatest happiness?

MAMET: Well, I'm always pretty happy in the woods. I love writing. I love being with my family, with my friends. Working.

ISAACS: What do you fear?

MAMET: What do I fear? That's a really good question. What do I fear? Gosh. [*Pause.*] I have remembered, but I'm not going to tell you.

ISAACS: What do you still hope to achieve?

MAMET: Well, I'd kind of have to get a deer someday. Either one goes into the woods and it's a great experience and one comes out having not gotten a deer and says, "It doesn't make any difference. What a wonderful time. I wouldn't have traded those days for anything." But then I got up this morning and Rose, who lives down the road, said he'd shot this eight-point, 175-pound buck right across the road from my house, and how he was going to get it mounted and put it on a big board. And his head turned a little to the side. And I must admit I became envious.

ISAACS: How would you like us to remember you?

MAMET: Oh, I don't know. I don't know that it really makes any difference. My rabbi's a very smart guy. His name is Larry Kushner, and he said anybody's who's interested in making last requests has missed the whole point of being dead. So, I think that's true.

Games Mamet Plays

Robert Denerstein

Robert Denerstein, film critic for the *Denver Rocky Mountain News,* sat down with Mamet in early January 1998 in Park City, Utah, to discuss Mamet's new movie, *The Spanish Prisoner,* which won rave reviews at the annual Sundance Film Festival. At the festival to promote his film Mamet, uncharacteristically relaxed, met with numerous film critics. In this conversation with Denerstein he speaks at some length about "a spectrum of dramatic fascination with the hidden," melodrama, and the genre of the light romantic thriller.

David Mamet was nestled in the corner of a sofa in the hallway of the Yarrow Hotel in Park City, Utah. He'd traveled to January's Sundance Film Festival with his new movie, *The Spanish Prisoner,* and was spending a morning chatting with journalists.

With his close-cropped hair and penetrating eyes, Mamet has the look of an owl on the watch for prey. Appearances, however, can be deceiving. The playwright, author of landmark American works such as *American Buffalo* and *Glengarry Glen Ross,* speaks softly, sprinkling his conversation with references to such luminaries as Thorstein Veblen and Voltaire.

Based on his movies, you expect an interview with Mamet to be tricky, a series of tactical evasions. But, as Mamet discusses the writer's craft, he speaks with the kind of clarity that probably makes him a great teacher, an activity he occasionally pursues.

The Spanish Prisoner, which opens in Denver on Friday, demon-

From "Mamet on the Games Mamet Plays," *Denver Rocky Mountain News,* April 12, 1998, sec. D, 6. Copyright © 1998 Rocky Mountain News. Reprinted by permission.

strates Mamet's prowess. The movie deals with a con game set in the corporate world. Mamet accomplished a similar dramatic feat in 1987's *House of Games* but now extends his reach into the world of big money. A company stands to make billions thanks to a process discovered by one of its employees, an earnest researcher played by Campbell Scott.

"There's a spectrum of dramatic fascination with the hidden," Mamet said, explaining his interest in games. "That's what drama's about. Fairy tales are about the hidden. Things shift shapes. The stepmother turns out to be wicked. The woodsman turns out to be good. The beggar turns out to be king. The theme plays itself out all along the scale of drama."

The fifty-year-old Mamet knows drama helps us to confront our fears, to leap into treacherous waters with the playwright holding the life preserver.

"Melodrama enables us to work out our emotions, to undergo thrill without threat, to experience vicarious danger with security," he said. "Another aspect of melodrama is the thriller, where, again, things are not what they seem."

The Spanish Prisoner, which also stars Steve Martin and Mamet's [second] wife, Rebecca Pidgeon, may remind you of the kind of thriller Hollywood turned out during the 1930s and 1940s. The resemblance is not accidental.

"*House of Games* is a classic film noir, which is made up of a mixture of violence and irony," Mamet said. "To me *Spanish Prisoner* falls into the tradition of the light romantic thriller. The form of the light thriller, as far as I can tell, was created by Hitchcock.

"The form is fairly straightforward. There's the guy on the run. There's the girl who helps him. There are powerful people whose friends turn out to be the bad guys. There's the denouement in an extraordinarily improbable place. There's the deus ex machina, in which help comes from a place where there's no possible help, and everything's made right in the last twenty seconds."

The genre requires a hero with intelligence and innocence—in other words, Scott.

"I saw him first in *Longtime Companion*. I called him up and said: 'What a great performance. Let's work together.' A couple of projects on stage and film never quite came together. This project came up, and I sent it to him. In addition to being a superb actor, he's smack dab in the tradition of that Hitchcockian narrow-collar man, a courtly gentlemen. Robert Donat. Bob Cummings. Cary Grant."

Martin, a surprising casting choice, plays the mysterious Jimmy Dell, a wealthy New Yorker who encourages Scott to pursue a beef with his employers.

"I saw him onstage when he did [*Waiting for*] *Godot* with Robin Williams," Mamet said. "He's a superb actor. We knew each other a little through Ricky Jay" (a sleight-of-hand artist who also appears in Mamet's movie).

The corporate environment offers an abundance of possibilities for intrigue.

"Thorstein Veblen, my hero, said that behavior at the top of the food chain and behavior at the bottom of the food chain is exactly the same," Mamet said. "The lumpenproletariat and the masters of industry are the same rapacious critters. My experience has been that that's true."

Yet money has an undeniable allure.

"Edith Wharton wrote a book about some impecunious aristos who had fallen on hard times," he said. "They were living in the palaces of friends. She spoke about the 'demoralizing simplicity' of great wealth. That's a brilliant phrase. Being around great wealth seems easy. Everything seems to be clear and clean. What a thing to strive for."

Next up for Mamet, a new version of *The Winslow Boy,* a Terence Rattigan play that was made into a movie in 1950. He's also working on a new novel.

"I just had a novel panned by the *New York Times* (*The Old Religion,* a story based on the 1914 trial of Leo Frank). I'm writing another one and hope that they'll pan it next year," he said.

"You want to be panned?"

"I don't want to, but I think it's inevitable. My wife said, 'They look at it, and they say, he's going to write and direct movies and write plays and he's also going to write novels. That's not fair.' And she said, 'You know they're right.'"

At some point Mamet would like to make a movie based on the folktales of Jewish writer Isaac Luria.

"It starts out with these two ex-fighter pilots in Korea—I actually knew one of these guys—who go to work for the Haganah in Europe stealing planes and flying them to Israel just before the declaration of statehood," he said. "They take along an old guy who's dying, a survivor of the camps. They're on this fourteen-hour flight, and he starts telling them stories about life in the shtetl. It's based on the stories of Luria."

Mamet was relaxed in Park City, not his usual film festival condition.

"I went to Cannes with *Homicide* (1991). I was scared to death. It's the aesthetic equivalent of a colonoscopy," he said. "It's probably good for you, but on the whole you'd rather give it a pass."

But then show business isn't for the faint of heart.

"Show business is a tough racket, but then what isn't?" Mamet said, sounding very much like one of his characters. "It's like the cops say, 'You gotta get out there and eat that greasy sandwich.'"

Mamet with Manners

Renée Graham

Renée Graham met with Mamet in Boston in late spring 1999 to discuss two new projects, his period film entitled *The Winslow Boy* and a forthcoming three-person play, *Boston Marriage*, uncharacteristically featuring no male characters. In this conversation, rich in literary allusions, Mamet discusses his admiration for Terrence Rattigan's play on which his screenplay is based and *Winslow Boy*'s examination of power politics, racial hatred, and a family's devotion to the cause of right that led to their protracted legal battle with the British Admiralty. Moreover, he speaks about his attraction to the Edwardian rhythms and virtues that inform his film and play in startlingly different ways.

On a recent morning, David Mamet sipped his coffee, quoted the last stanza of a Rudyard Kipling ode to honor and heroism, and, in speaking about his latest film, *The Winslow Boy*, extolled such Edwardian virtues as "gentility, honor, and accountability." It seemed an incongruous moment: Such qualities are rare in the rakes and rogues who usually inhabit Mamet's films and plays, including the Pulitzer Prize–winning *Glengarry Glen Ross*. In a career spanning three decades as an actor, playwright, screenwriter, and director, Mamet is best known for creating characters propelled by back-alley morals and cutthroat ethics. In his (often) profane world of (mostly) men behaving badly, there is little black or white; usually there is an all-too-realistic ambiguity where any means necessary can be employed to reach a de-

From "Mamet with Manners," *The Boston Globe*, May 2, 1999, sec. N, 1, 17. Interview conducted by Renée Graham. Copyright © The Boston Globe 1999. Reprinted with courtesy of The Boston Globe.

sired end—such as concocting a fake war to divert attention from a presidential sex scandal in *Wag the Dog,* which Mamet co-wrote. So it is odd to hear Mamet speak of such Merchant-Ivory refinement in discussing one of his own films—almost as odd as it is to hear the notoriously media-reticent Mamet speak at all. But such is the nature of his latest film, a project Mamet has held dear for two decades, which even he considers "a departure from some of my other work."

That's an understatement. Set in England in 1912, *The Winslow Boy* is the story of a teenage Naval College cadet who's kicked out of school after he is accused of stealing a five-shilling postal order and forging the signature of the rightful owner. His family, convinced of the boy's innocence, risks everything to correct what they perceive as an egregious injustice. The film (which opens Friday) stars Sir Nigel Hawthorne, Jeremy Northam, Rebecca Pidgeon, Gemma Jones, and Guy Edwards.

And in what could be seen as another move away from the box in which some have attempted to place his work, Mamet—who has been criticized for a dearth of female characters—will premiere his latest play, the all-female *Boston Marriage,* at the American Repertory Theatre in Cambridge next month.

The Winslow Boy is based on a real-life British incident involving George Archer-Shee, a 13-year-old cadet booted from the Naval College in 1908 for theft and forgery. Though little known stateside, in England it became a subject of heated debate from the halls of Parliament to the local pub. In 1946, the story was turned into a four-act play, *The Winslow Boy,* by Terence Rattigan, who later adapted it into a 1950 film starring Robert Donat, Margaret Leighton, and Cedric Hardwicke.

Mamet first saw the film as a youngster in his native Chicago, and discovered the play about 20 years ago.

"When I saw the play, I thought, 'I'd like to direct that someday,'" he said, during an interview at the Four Seasons Hotel. "Eventually, I got a chance to."

While writing some revisions for an off-Broadway production of J. B. Priestly's 1934 play, *The Dangerous Corner,* Mamet again became "enthused" with the "genteel, Edwardian cadences" of Rattigan's play.

"With this work specifically, there was the precision of it which I found just marvelously inviting, restful, and challenging," Mamet said. "It's a very Apollonian piece, as opposed to low comedy or low drama. It's very much a drama of manners, and the manners themselves are essential. It's a movie about Edwardian virtues: gentility, honor, and accountability."

This is Mamet's first outing directing material he didn't write. Mamet made few changes to the 50-year-old script written by Rattigan and Anatole de Grunwald, maintaining that Rattigan is "the architect—I'm just the decorator.

"This is magnificent material," he continued. "It just doesn't get better than this material. Some of the scenes are just stunningly written."

What has continually drawn Mamet to this story is the theme of fighting for what one believes is right. To exonerate Ronnie, the Winslows—father Arthur (Hawthorne), mother Grace (Jones), sister Catherine (Pidgeon), and eldest son Dickie (Matthew Pidgeon)—hire hotshot barrister Sir Robert Morton (Northam). But in trying to prevent Ronnie's expulsion, they must challenge the authority and judgment of the Admiralty and the Crown.

It is a stance that comes with sacrifice. Their finances dwindle; Arthur's health deteriorates; Catherine, already an outspoken suffragette in the early feminist movement, is pressured by her status-conscious fiancé to drop the whole thing or he'll break off their engagement. These issues of heroism and sacrifice intrigue Mamet.

"If you look at the people who stood up to right a great personal cause—whether it's Emile Zola, Dr. King, Rosa Parks, Margarethe Cammermeyer, or St. Joan," Mamet said, "you say, 'My God, I hope and I pray if I'm put in that position I would be able to be strong' because the blandishments, the things which will cause resignation, are many."

In *The Winslow Boy,* Mamet finds his most heroic characters, although there are noble souls in some of his past work. Think of Kevin Costner's downright, upright Eliot Ness in Brian DePalma's film version of *The Untouchables,* which Mamet wrote, or Don Ameche's good-hearted Gino, the simple Italian shoemaker who will not lie, but still convinces a mob boss that he is *il capo di capo* in *Things Change,* which Mamet directed and co-wrote.

But there is an unassailable goodness to many of the people in *The Winslow Boy,* Mamet said.

"The brilliance of Rattigan's story is we see the heroism happen before our eyes. We aren't told, 'This is John Wayne, this is D'Artagnan,'" he said, referring to the famed swashbuckler of Alexandre Dumas's *The Three Musketeers.*

"We see from the very beginning a happy, contented middle-class family which has profited so much from their time and position in society, and is rightfully enjoying it," Mamet said. "Bit by bit they lose everything, but in return, they get to tell the truth."

Truth pulses in the center of all Mamet works, even if that truth concerns the flawed lives of men and women, unwilling or incapable of doing the right thing. But the greatest Mamet truth of all is this: He follows no path but his own.

With the frame of a middleweight, Mamet is 51, but looks a decade younger. His brown hair is close-cropped, and all that betrays his age is a beard with more salt than pepper. Dressed in a black shirt buttoned to the neck, and fatigue-green pants, Mamet is charming but intense. He is not a man for idle conversation, and one best pay attention or risk being left behind. The conversation can move from boxing to Kipling (an author he reveres) to his tendency to gain weight on movie sets, courtesy of those blasted treat-filled catering trucks.

He is audaciously bright, and when he talks in his deep, quiet voice, there is nary a snippet of the hard-edged language he has written for dozens of plays and films. He has written such films as *The Verdict, Hoffa, House of Games,* and last year's twisty thriller, *The Spanish Prisoner.* As playwright, he has penned *American Buffalo, Oleanna,* and *The Cryptogram.*

What has always distinguished Mamet's work is his ear for dialogue. His words are rhythmic and alive, written with a consciousness of how they will sound when spoken aloud. There are conversations between characters—the stop-and-start banter between Ed Harris and Alan Arkin as desperate real estate salesmen in *Glengarry Glen Ross* comes to mind—as fresh and unexpected as two jazzmen jamming.

Equally unexpected is Mamet's new willingness to talk to the media. In *The Winslow Boy,* there's a line written by Rattigan that could easily have come from Mamet. When Arthur Winslow wonders what to say to a newsman lurking about for a comment, Sir Robert says, "I hardly think it matters, sir; whatever you say will have very little bearing on what they write."

Mamet usually lets his work speak for itself, but a talk with *The Winslow Boy* star Hawthorne made him reconsider his feelings.

"I'm very proud of the film, very happy with the film," he said. "I was talking with Sir Nigel, as a matter of fact, and I said (talking to the media) is a bunch of bourgeois, isn't it? And he said, 'Absolutely not. If you have something you're proud of, and you'd like people to see it, help them sell the product.' He said, 'In what business do you not have to drive your chickens to market?'"

Mamet's next "chicken to market" is *Boston Marriage,* which has its world premiere at the ART [American Repertory Theatre] June 4. The play stars Rebecca Pidgeon (not only a cast member of *The Winslow Boy* but Mamet's wife and frequent collaborator), Felicity Huffman (of ABC's "Sports Night"), and Mary McCann.

Coined in 19th-century New England, the slang term "Boston marriage" often referred to a lesbian couple living together, although it could also mean two women in a living arrangement independent of men. Mamet describes the work as "a comedy of manners about two ladies of fashion at the turn of the century, and their maid."

ART has premiered a number of Mamet plays, including *The Cryptogram, Oleanna,* and *The Old Neighborhood;* it's an arrangement that suits the playwright, who lives in Newton with Pidgeon and their children. For years, Mamet lived on Dwight Street in Boston's South End, which he still regards fondly. He considers Shawmut Avenue "the most beautiful street in the United States"; he mounted his first professional play at the Boston Center for the Arts; and he could be spotted browsing at the annual Cyclorama flea market and antiques show.

He left the South End only reluctantly, and only when he could no longer abide a problem that has vexed many a Bostonian: parking.

"It was difficult with the kids because there was very little shopping and no parking. On Dwight Street, there's no room. You have to double-park your car in the middle of the street, then try to get your kid, and then your groceries, into the house," he said with an exasperated laugh. "It was very challenging."

Works by Mamet

Camel. Created 1969. © 1990.

Mackinac. Created 1975. © 1990.

Marranos. Unpublished. 1975.

American Buffalo. New York: Grove Press, 1977. Originally published in 1977 by Grove Press in a limited book club edition.

A Life in the Theatre. New York: Samuel French, 1978. New York: Grove Press, 1978.

Sexual Perversity in Chicago and The Duck Variations. New York: Grove Press, 1978.

The Water Engine and Mr. Happiness: Two Plays. New York: Grove Press, 1978.

Lone Canoe, or the Explorer. Unpublished. © 1979.

Reunion and Dark Pony. New York: Grove Press, 1979.

The Sanctity of Marriage. New York: Samuel French, 1982.

Squirrels. New York: Samuel French, 1982.

Glengarry Glen Ross. New York: Grove Press, 1984. Originally published in 1983 by Grove Press in a limited book club edition.

Goldberg Street: Short Plays and Monologues. New York: Grove Press, 1985. Includes *Goldberg Street, Cross Patch, The Spanish Prisoner, Two Conversations, Two Scenes, Yes But So What, Vermont Sketches: Conversations with the Spirit World, Pint's a Pound the World Around, Dowsing, Deer Dogs, In the Mall, Maple Sugaring, Morris and Joe, The Dog, Film Crew, Four* A.M., *The Power Outage, Food, Columbus Avenue, Steve McQueen, Yes, The Blue Hour: City Sketches, A Sermon, Shoeshine, Litko: A Dramatic Monologue, In Old Vermont,* and *All Men Are Whores: An Inquiry.*

The Shawl and Prairie du Chien. New York: Grove Press, 1985.

Three Children's Plays. New York: Grove Press, 1986. Includes *The Poet and the Rent, The Frog Prince,* and *The Revenge of the Space Pandas, or Binky Rudich and the Two-Speed Clock.*

Writing in Restaurants. New York: Viking Books, 1986. London: Faber and Faber, 1988.

House of Games. New York: Grove Press, 1987.

Three Jewish Plays. New York: Samuel French, 1987. Includes *The Disappearance of the Jews* (©1982, 1987), *Goldberg Street* (©1985), and *The Luftmensch* (©1984, 1987).

The Woods, Lakeboat, Edmond: Three Plays. New York: Grove Press, 1987.

Speed-the-Plow. New York: Grove Weidenfeld Press, 1988. London: Methuen Drama, 1996. Originally published in 1987 by Grove Press in a limited book club edition.

Some Freaks. New York: Viking Penguin, 1989.

Things Change. With Shel Silverstein. New York: Grove Press, 1988. London: Methuen Drama, 1989.

Five Television Plays. New York: Grove Weidenfeld Press, 1990. Includes *A Waitress in Yellowstone or Always Tell the Truth, Bradford, The Museum of Science and Industry Story, A Wasted Weekend,* and *We Will Take You There.*

The Hero Pony. New York: Grove Weidenfeld Press, 1990.

We're No Angels. New York: Grove Weidenfeld Press, 1990.

Bobby Gould in Hell. In *Oh Hell.* New York: Samuel French, 1991.

A Life with No Joy in It. Antaeus 66 (Spring 1991): 291–96.

On Directing Film. New York: Viking Press, 1991.

The Cabin: Reminiscence and Diversions. New York: Turtle Bay Books, 1992.

Homicide. New York: Grove Weidenfeld Press, 1992.

Oleanna. New York: Pantheon Books, 1992.

No One Will Be Immune and Other Plays and Pieces. New York: Dramatists Play Service, 1994. Includes *Almost Done* (monologue), *Monologue* (monologue), *Two Enthusiasts* (scene), *Sunday Afternoon* (scene), *The Joke Code* (scene), *A Scene–Australia, Fish* (scene), *A Perfect Mermaid* (scene), *Dodge* (scene), *L.A. Sketches, A Life with No Joy in It, Joseph Dintenfass,* and *No One Will Be Immune.*

Plays One. London: Methuen, 1994. Includes *Duck Variations, Sexual Perversity in Chicago, Squirrels, American Buffalo, The Water Engine,* and *Mr. Happiness.*

Plays Two: Reunion, Dark Pony, A Life in the Theatre, The Woods, Lakeboat, Edmond. London: Methuen, 1994.

The Village. Boston: Little, Brown, 1994.

A Whore's Profession: Notes and Essays. London and Boston: Faber and Faber, 1994.

The Cryptogram. New York: Dramatists Play Service, 1995. New York: Vintage Books, 1995.

An Interview. In *Death Defying Acts: 3 One-Act Comedies.* New York: Samuel French, 1995. Includes *Central Park West* (Woody Allen), *An Interview* (David Mamet), and *Hotline* (Elaine May).

Make-Believe Town: Essays and Reminiscences. Boston: Little, Brown, 1996.

The Old Neighborhood: Three Plays. New York: Vintage Books, 1998. London: Methuen Drama, 1998. Includes *Disappearance of the Jews, Jolly,* and *Deny.*

The Old Religion. New York: Free Press, 1997.

True and False: Heresy and Common Sense for the Actor. New York: Pantheon Books, 1997.

Three Uses of the Knife: On the Structure and Purpose of Drama. The Columbia Lectures on American Culture. New York: Pantheon, 1997. New York: Columbia University Press, 1998.

The Chinaman: Poems. New York: Overlook Press, 1999.

Jafsie and John Henry: Essays. New York: Free Press, 1999.

On Acting. New York: Vintage Press, 1999.

Short Plays and Sketches. New York: Random House / Time Books, 1999.

The Spanish Prisoner and *The Winslow Boy: Two Screenplays.* New York: Vintage Books, 1999.

Wilson: A Consideration of the Sources—Containing the Original Notes, Errata, Commentary, and the Preface to the Second Edition. London: Faber and Faber, 2000.

Adaptations

Red River. Translated and adapted by David Mamet from Pierre Laville's play *Le Fleuve Rouge.* Unpublished. © 1983.

The Cherry Orchard. Adapted by David Mamet from a literal translation by Peter Nelles of Anton Chekhov's play. New York: Samuel French, 1986. New York: Grove Press, 1987.

Vint. Adapted by David Mamet from Avrahm Yarmolinsky's translation of Anton Chekhov's story. *Orchards,* 15–24. New York: Broadway Play Publishing, 1987.

Uncle Vanya. Adapted by David Mamet from a literal translation by Vlada Chernomordik of Anton Chekhov's play. New York: Samuel French, 1988. New York: Grove Press, 1988.

The Three Sisters. Adaptation of Chekhov's play from a literal translation by Vlada Chernomordik. New York: Grove Weidenfeld Press, 1991. In *Motley Tales and a Play.* New York: Doubleday, 1998.

Books for Children

The Owl: A Story for Children. With Lindsay Crouse. Illustrated by Stephen Alcorn. New York: Kipling Press, 1987.

Warm and Cold. Illustrated by Donald Sultan. New York: Fawbush Editions and Solo Press, 1985. New York: Grove Press, 1988.

Passover. Illustrated by Michael McCurdy. New York: St. Martin's Press, 1995.

The Duck and the Goat. Illustrated by Maya Kennedy. New York: St. Martin's Press, 1996.

Nice Day and Scary Wolf. New York: St. Martin's Press, 1998.

Bar Mitzvah. Illustrated by Donald Sultan. Little, Brown, 1999.

Selected Short Prose

"The Bridge." *Granta* 16 (Summer 1985): 167–73.

"The Room." *Grand Street* 13, no. 4 (1995): 163–66.

"Soul Murder." *Granta* 55 (Autumn 1996): 73–76.

Filmography

The Postman Always Rings Twice. Directed by Bob Rafelson. With Jack Nicolson and Jessica Lange. Paramount, 1981.

The Verdict. Directed by Sidney Lumet. With Paul Newman, Charlotte Rampling, Jack Warden, and James Mason. Columbia Pictures, 1982.

The Untouchables. Directed by Brian De Palma. With Kevin Costner, Sean Connery, and Robert De Niro. Paramount, 1985.

House of Games. Based on a story by David Mamet and Jonathan Katz. Directed by David Mamet. With Joe Mantegna and Lindsay Crouse. Orion, 1987.

Things Change. Written with Shel Silverstein. Directed by David Mamet. With Joe Mantegna and Don Ameche. Columbia Pictures, 1988.

Ace in the Hole. Unpublished screenplay. © 1989.

We're No Angels. Directed by Neil Jordan. With Robert De Niro and Sean Penn. Paramount, 1989.

The Deer Slayer. Unpublished screenplay. © 1990.

Homicide. Screenplay by David Mamet. Directed by David Mamet. With Joe Mantegna and William H. Macy. Cinehaus / Bison, 1990.

Russian Poland. Unpublished screenplay. © 1991.

Glengarry Glen Ross. Directed by James Foley. With Al Pacino, Jack Lemmon, and Alec Baldwin. New Line Cinema, 1992.

Hoffa. Directed by Danny De Vito. With Jack Nicolson, Danny DeVito, and Armand Assante. Twentieth Century Fox, 1992.

The Water Engine. Directed by Steven Schachter. With Charles Durning, Patti Lupone, and William H. Macy. Amblin Television, 1992.

A Life in the Theatre. Directed by Gregory Mosher. With Matthew Broderick and Jack Lemmon. TNT, 1993.

Rising Sun. Screenplay by Michael Backes, Philip Kaufman, and David Mamet [uncredited]. Directed by Philip Kaufman. With Sean Connery, Wesley Snipes, and Harvey Keitel. Twentieth Century Fox, 1993.

Oleanna. Directed by David Mamet. With William H. Macy and Debra Eisenstadt. Samuel Goldwyn, 1994.

Texan. Directed by Treat Williams. With Charles Durning, William H. Macy, and Treat Williams. Chanticleer Films, 1994.

Vanya on 42nd Street. From screenplay based on David Mamet's adaptation of Anton Chekhov's *Uncle Vanya.* Directed by Louis Malle. With Wallace Shawn, Julianne Moore, and Larry Pine. Sony Pictures Classics, 1994.

Lolita. Unpublished screenplay. © 1995.

American Buffalo. Directed by Michael Corrente. With Dustin Hoffman, Dennis Franz, and Sean Nelson. Capitol Films, 1996.

The Edge. Original screenplay [*Bookworm*] by David Mamet. Directed by Lee Tamahori. With Anthony Hopkins, Alec Baldwin, and Elle Macpherson. Twentieth Century Fox, 1997.

The Spanish Prisoner. Screenplay by David Mamet. Directed by David Mamet. With Campbell Scott, Rebecca Pidgeon, Steve Martin, and Ben Gazzara. Sweetland Films, 1997.

Wag the Dog. Screenplay by Hilary Henkin and David Mamet. Directed by Barry Levinson. With Dustin Hoffman, Robert DeNiro, and Anne Heche. Tribeca / New Line Cinema, 1997.

Dr. Jekyll / Mr. Hyde. Unpublished screenplay. 1998.

Ronin. Screenplay by J. D. Zeik [story] and Richard Weisz [David Mamet]. Directed by John Frankenheimer. With Robert DeNiro, Jean Reno, and Stellan Skarsgärd. MGM, 1998.

Lansky. Directed by John McNaughton, Dennis Eisenberg, and David Mamet. With Richard Dreyfus, Eric Roberts, and Anthony LaPaglia. HBO, 1999.

The Winslow Boy. Directed by David Mamet. With Nigel Hawthorne, Gemma Jones, Jeremy Northam, and Rebecca Pidgeon. Winslow Partners / Sony Pictures Classics, 1999.

State and Main. Screenplay by David Mamet. Directed by David Mamet. With Alec Baldwin, Patti Lupone, Charles Durning, Sara Jessica Parker, and William H. Macy. New Line Cinema, 2000.

Index